RIDGEWALKS
in the
Canadian Rockies

Mike Potter

LUMINOUS
COMPOSITIONS

IMPORTANT SAFETY NOTE: Those who venture ridgewalking must be prepared for risks and must know how to evaluate them in order to proceed safely. See p. 14, "Ridgewalking Safety."

RIDGEWALKS
in the
Canadian Rockies

Mike Potter

Published by
Luminous Compositions
P.O. Box 909
Turner Valley, Alberta
Canada T0L 2A0

e-mail: luminous@telusplanet.net

Canadian Cataloguing in Publication Data

Potter, Mike, 1954-
  Ridgewalks in the Canadian Rockies

Includes bibliographical references and index.
ISBN 0-9694438-8-9

  1. Hiking—Rocky Mountains, Canadian (B.C. and Alta.)—Guidebooks.
2. Trails—Rocky Mountains, Canadian (B.C. and Alta.)—Guidebooks. I. Title.

GV199.44.C22R64 2001   917.1104′4   C2001-900040-5

Printed and bound in Canada by
Friesens, Altona, Manitoba R0G 0B0

Front cover photo: Ridgewalker John Blum on Ridge West of Helen Lake (Ridgewalk 112); Dolomite Peak on back cover is from same photograph.

Title pages photo: Ridgewalker on ridge south of Burstall Pass (Ridgewalk 83); Mt. Sir Douglas in distance.

Contents page photo: Mt. Wilcox North Peak (Ridgewalk 119) from descent of Tangle Ridge; Mt. Athabasca on right.

Acknowledgements (p. 10) photo: Mt. Wilcox North Peak (Ridgewalk 119) from descent of Tangle Ridge; Mt. Athabasca (centre) and Mt. Andromeda (right).

Photo p. 16: North to "Hector South" and Mt. Hector on Ridgewalk 106.

Contents

Characteristic limber pines on Whaleback Ridge [#10].

The author on high point of "Lantern—Lineham Ridge" [#30]; peaks of Highwood Range in distance.

Scene on "Long Prairie Ridge" [#39].

Highwood Ridge [#73] (left) and Grizzly Ridge [#74] (right) with "Paradise Valley" between; in distance are Mt. Lipsett [#34] and Odlum Ridge [#35] above south end of Highwood Ridge.

The author on high point of Parker Ridge [#115]; Cirrus Mountain on centre skyline.

West from approach to Tangle Ridge [#120]; Mt. Alberta on centre skyline.

Pinnacle on Ridges Beyond Kindersley Summit [#133]; subpeak at gr 721166 in centre mid-distance.

Snow formation on Whaleback Mountain [#139]; Mont des Poilus (centre) and Mt. Collie (right).

Alberta, who gave generously of pre-press advice.

Jim Beckel of Friesens' Calgary office gave help on questions regarding printing, as did Brad Schmidt of Technical Support at Friesens' Altona, Manitoba, plant.

Rob Cobban of Iconic Microsystems, Calgary, kept the show going with computer expertise and equipment.

Donna Nelson and Doug Shaw of Gem Trek Publishing, Cochrane, Alberta, gave assistance with maps and cartographic information.

John Blum of Woodruff & Blum Booksellers, Lake Louise, shared his knowledge of book retailing and also checked out quite a few of the ridges with the author.

This book is dedicated to Bodil, who knows what went into it...

Preface

Ridgewalks hold great appeal because of the views they offer: it's like being on a summit all day. There are changing vistas throughout a ridgewalk—it's not only the views from the top of a peak that are the reward.

Imagination and curiosity led me to explore ridgewalking, and these are qualities that will still come into play for others even with the descriptions I am providing in this book. It is my wish that people will enjoy their own style in doing these ridgewalks, and that they will discover variations and new routes.

Ridgewalking often holds challenges. While some ridgewalks are short and easy, many demand most of a day. Most ridgewalks call for skills in off-trail travel and routefinding. Further, because so many ridgewalks require cross-country navigation, there is no one 'right' way to do them. While the general approach is clear, the specifics can vary and so the sense of adventure is retained.

The first of the ridgewalks in this book that I ever did was to "Little Temple" near Lake Louise (see p.190). That was in 1987, having already spent several seasons in the Rockies. At first, in the natural pattern of a newcomer to the mountains, my focus was on established trails. But as my apprenticeship progressed, I began to enjoy checking out journeys that took me off the beaten track.

Of course, there were false starts and episodes of backtracking. However, patience and perseverance usually revealed a way to at least closely follow what looked from mapreading or reconnaissance to be a feasible line. By the summer of 1998, having just completed a book on fire lookout hikes, I began to concentrate on ridgewalks as a fun way to get to know new areas.

There were many possibilities, indeed they seemed almost endless, but by fall, 2000, I had completed most of the ridgewalks I had identified. I've compiled information based on those trips into this book, in the hope that it will inspire an appreciation of this intriguing way of experiencing the Rockies.

Mike Potter

Ridgewalkers on Akamina Ridge [#129]; peaks of Waterton Lakes National Park in distance.

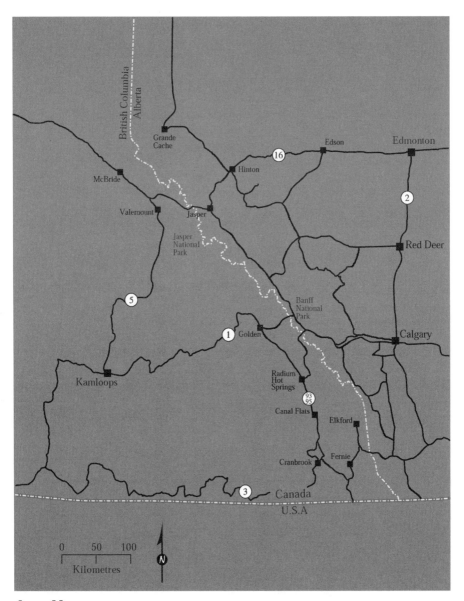

Area Map

Introduction

Ridgewalking is an enjoyable and often challenging way to experience the landscape.

Ridgewalking requires well-developed skills in routefinding since there is usually no trail to follow. Ridgewalking also demands experience in travel over rough ground, and in many cases calls for tackling steep sections 'hands-on.' Although the general term is ridgewalking, this is not usually a hands-in-the-pockets pursuit.

The attractions of ridgewalking include scenic vistas from open ridgecrests, and direct contact with wild country. Ain't no paved trails or handrails on these trips! There are also lots of opportunities to see wild flora and fauna (precautions are necessary with regard to the latter).

For those with the requisite background, ridgewalking in the Rockies is a very rewarding pursuit.

Presentation

Ridgewalks in the Canadian Rockies presents information on 141 trips. These are all journeys that can be done in one day, though some of them represent a very long day. There is the option to set up an overnight base at a backcountry campground to do some of them, but this book sticks to ridgewalks that can be done in one push travelling light.

The scope for ridgewalking in the Rockies is extensive. This book describes routes that are within protected areas, where the quality of the wilderness experience is typically higher than elsewhere. The area of coverage extends from Waterton Lakes National Park north to Jasper National Park in Alberta, and in British Columbia from Akamina—Kishenina Provincial Park north to Yoho National Park.

The names of the ridgewalks are those in accepted usage or relating to the orientation of the ridge in connection with features such as a mountain or adjacent drainages. If the name is an unofficial one first used by the author, it is given in quotation marks (e.g., "High Noon Hills").

The descriptions are organized into seven geographic sections, presented in the order of south to north, first for Alberta and then for B.C. The premise here is that this is roughly the sequence in which they open up for travel after winter's snows.

The information given begins with a listing of six criteria:

— Distance: This is the total trip distance, in kilometres (rounded off to the nearest kilometre). There are three types of trips: loop, linear—in which the route finishes away from the trailhead, and out-and-back—in which the trip returns back along the approach route. {There is often a loop for part of an out-and-back trip.}

— The type of route, i.e., whether trail or off-trail, or both. A time estimate for the entire trip is also given here, in the four categories of: up to 4 hr, 4—8 hr, 8—12 hr, and over 12 hr. **N.B.** The time given is for actual hiking, breaks not included.

— Elevation gain: Given in metres and feet (to the nearest five in each unit), this is the difference between the elevation at the trailhead and that at the high point; the cumulative elevation gain may be greater. Where exact elevations are not available, an approximate figure is obtained by extrapolation between contour intervals.

— Maximum elevation: Again, in metres and feet (rounded off as above).

— Map(s): This gives the relevant map(s) for the trip, either the excellent publications of Gem Trek (Tel. (403) 932-4208; www.gemtrek.com) or the government's NTS (National Topographic Series) 1:50,000 scale sheets. The proper maps must be taken on ridgewalks; those provided at the end of this book are for visual reference only and are not all at the same scale.

— Trailhead: How to get to the start of the ridgewalk. Distances are given in kilometres, as well as in miles for those whose vehicle's odometer is non-metric.

The main body of each description gives general directions for the route. **N.B.** It is not the philosophy of this book to take the reader by the hand, so a laborious synopsis of junctions is not provided. It is the responsibility of users to conduct their own navigation using the information and maps provided, in conjunction with their own full-size maps and with examination of features on the ground.

Six figure grid references (e.g., gr 012789) are often used to give the location of points referred to in the text. If not familiar with these, consult the map {right margin of NTS sheets} and/or get instruction. **N.B.** Grid refernces given in the text are for older maps using the NAD 27 system; newer maps using the NAD 83 system have slightly different grid references for the same location.

The main description typically gives details such as features in view, other ridgewalks in sight, wildflowers and wildlife that can be seen along the way, and background on the origin of placenames.

Ridgewalking Safety

Ridgewalking can be a hazardous activity. It usually involves off-trail travel, which requires well-developed skills in routefinding and mapreading. Many of the ridgewalks described in this book have sections where both hands and feet must be used to negotiate steep terrain.

Those who venture ridgewalking must be prepared for risks and must know how to evaluate them in order to proceed safely.

Among the hazards that may be encountered while ridgewalking are: loose scree, precariously-balanced rocks and boulders, rockfall, cliffbands, canyons, steep

Pinnacles on the Molar Pass to North Molar Pass ridgewalk [#107].

snow slopes, cornices (overhanging wind-created snow deposits that can collapse if walked upon), avalanches (yes, even while hiking; spontaneous cornice collapse can be one cause), river fords, sudden weather changes, lightning (especially while out in the open on a high ridge), dense vegetation while bushwhacking, and wildlife including bears. Bear spray is worth considering; bear awareness is essential.

Dehydration is a potential concern while ridgewalking since there are usually no water sources once on a ridge; wind can exacerbate this possibility. Take lots of fluids to start with. Any backcountry water should be filtered and/or treated.

The inherent hazards mentioned illustrate the necessity of having the proper equipment while ridgewalking. Particularly important are good boots, and clothing for wind and rain. It can be cold up high on a ridge even in summer if the wind is blowing, and you can get wet and chilled very quickly out in the open if it starts raining or snowing. Mitts and headgear should be put in the pack as standard practise. An ice axe is necessary for travel on steep snow slopes—know how to use it to self-arrest in case of a slide.

Sunglasses and sunscreen are important especially when in the open at high elevations. Always carry a first aid kit: even if not needed personally, it might help someone else. Take emergency supplies such as a space blanket, extra layers, matches, a flashlight, and spare high-energy food. The trick is to be prepared and able to spend a night out if need be.

It's wise to leave word of your intentions with someone who will alert the authorities if you are overdue. Voluntary safety registrations are available in some jurisdictions; if used, make sure to sign in once out from the ridgewalk.

Ridgewalking Lightly

Consideration for the land and its inhabitants is part of any wilderness outing; care for the environment is very important while ridgewalking since much of travel is off-trail. The author chose not to include three ridgewalks that he researched for this book when it became apparent that describing them would lead to ecological damage. On one of the three, in Kananaskis Country, the author coincidentally met wildlife biologists Stephen Herrero and Mike Gibeau, who told him of the importance of that ridge as wildlife habitat and expressed their concerns about disturbance (it is occasionally visited by club trips). The other two ridgewalks not included here are from Yoho and Jasper national parks; again, the decision not to describe them came after discussions with park managers and environmentalists.

Take care while ridgewalking to avoid trampling vegetation; if travelling off-trail in a large party, disperse as much as possible rather than moving in single file, which concentrates the impact. Walk on rocks and bare earth where feasible. Avoid causing soil erosion.

Be conscious of the needs of wildlife, especially in the spring when most animals have their young. Respect any area closures put in place by park managers: they are for the benefit of wildlife, which after all is a major reason for setting aside protected areas. Choosing another ridgewalk is not difficult.

Don't litter. And take out litter to leave an area better than before.

Practise proper backcountry sanitation...giardia ain't fun.

The Descriptions

Section 1 Waterton Lakes National Park and Whaleback Area

Silhouettes on Whaleback Ridge.

1 Vimy Peak and Vimy Ridge

Map p. 249

Distance: 35 km out-and-back with loop

Trail/off-trail: 8—12 hr

Elevation gain: 1080 m (3540 ft)

Maximum elevation: 2379 m (7805 ft)

Maps: Parks Canada 1:50,000 Waterton Lakes National Park (1988) and NTS 1:50,000 Waterton Lakes 82 H/4

Trailhead: Small parking area on the north side of Chief Mountain Highway, 0.5 km (0.3 mi) southeast of its junction with Highway 5.

"Psst. Wanna see Crypt Lake without taking a boat? Wanna see it without squeezing through a tunnel? Have we got a ridgewalk for you!"

This outing starts with a 6.4 km level stroll on the Wishbone trail, which begins across the highway from the trailhead. It passes through aspen stands and meadows, with one creek crossing, to get to the junction for Vimy Peak and Vimy Ridge. This enjoyable stretch offers opportunities to see fauna and flora—the author identified almost 100 species of wildflowers on a late June day. Note that if returning this way, there are several Y-junctions with apparent game paths, so make note of these.

At the signed intersection, begin a steady climb. A feature of this section is a waterfall below the north aspect of the rock outcrop known as the Lions Head. The trail ascends through coniferous forest to break out into upper subalpine terrain with larches and open meadows. Snow lingers in this north-facing bowl into late summer.

A less well-defined trail heads up toward Vimy Peak, switchbacking across the east face before reaching the northeast ridge. An easy scramble leads to the summit, which reveals the townsite of Waterton Park over 1000 metres below. The full expanses of Middle and Lower Waterton lakes lie to the north, with many peaks all round.

Highlights from the top of Vimy Peak include Chief Mountain and Mt. Cleveland in Glacier National Park, Mt. Blakiston (the highest point in Waterton Lakes National Park), and of course Crypt Lake as promised (it may still be partly covered with ice depending on the time of year). The trail into and out of the renowned tunnel can be seen, as well as high Crypt Falls immediately below the lake. Lower on Hell-Roaring Creek are Burnt Rock Falls, so-named for the hard dolomite that the water plunges over into a basin eroded from softer rock.

Among the other ridgewalks in view in this area of enticing ridges are Ruby Ridge (#2), Avion Ridge (#4), Galwey Massif North Peak (#7), Bellevue Hill (#3), and Lakeview Ridge (#6).

To venture along Vimy Ridge, head south from the peak, turning the two outcrops on the east side if wished. A dip and a swoop, with a drop to the north, lead

18

Vimy Ridge, and south to Crypt Lake and Mt. Cleveland (Glacier National Park) in the distance on the right.

to the bump at gr 921346. As can be seen from Vimy Peak, from a saddle of sorts on the knoll to the northeast there is an isolated set of switchbacks on the northwest aspect of the open slope. This can be used to exit now, or if want to explore further, bear southeastward along the ridge to the high point at gr 929328. This bit involves balancing along the upthrust edges of a syncline, which can be seen when looking back.

From this high point (roughly equal in elevation to Vimy Peak), Akamina Ridge (#129) can be discerned. Also visible is the apparently straightforward route to a yet higher feature at gr 940321, crowned with a cairn. However, with a thunderstorm approaching, the author did not continue there—and unless Vimy Peak were skipped and one proceeded directly to the ridge, it would make for a long day especially if going back via the Wishbone trail.

There is the option, described by park staff, of descending to the Crypt Lake trail. If contemplating this, talk with the wardens and make sure the boat is running to get across Upper Waterton Lake. In 2000, the departure times from Crypt Landing were 4 p.m. and 5:30 p.m.; call (403) 859-2362 to confirm. Additionally, remember that the ferry goes to the townsite...a fair distance from the Wishbone trail if a car shuttle has not been set up. [A bus service operates that may be able to arrange a drop off at the Waterton River bridge, about 1 km from the trailhead.]

As mentioned above, there are lots of wildflowers on this trip; the ones on the ridge proper that stand out are: sky pilot (the author found one albino clump), spotted saxifrage, alpine spring beauty, and moss campion. Bighorn sheep, marmots, and pikas live in the high country seen on this trip.

The name Vimy for the peak and ridge comes from the famous World War I battle of Vimy Ridge in France.

2 Ruby Ridge

Map p. 249

Distance: 9 km linear

Trail/off-trail: 4—8 hr

Elevation gain: 850 m (2790 ft)

Maximum elevation: 2415 m (7920 ft)

Maps: Parks Canada 1:50,000 Waterton Lakes National Park (1988), and NTS 1:50,000 Sage Creek 82 G/1 and Waterton Lakes 82 H/4

Trailhead: Park at the Lineham trailhead, 9.0 km (5.6 mi) along the Akamina Parkway from its start at Highway 5.

This interesting ridge is named because of the bright red colour of its rock. Hike about 1.5 km up the Lineham Creek trail, along which grows lots of beargrass: the tall white flowers an icon of the southern Rockies. Other species of note include Mariposa lily, both silver-leaved and silky scorpionweeds, kittentails, moss campion, double bladder pod, spring beauty, and Jacob's ladder.

At the level stretch at the high point, before the trail starts to drop back down toward the creek, head up north over open ground. A band of purple scree taxes the energy at and above treelimit. The angle eases near the top of the southwestern peak of Ruby Ridge. This is slightly higher than the northeast peak, and lies at the east end of a ridge connecting to the summit of Mt. Blakiston. The waterfall from the Lineham Lakes, gushing through a cleft in Lineham Cliff, is an impressive sight, especially early in the summer when the snowmelt is on. A bonus is the sight of tiny Ruby Lake in a basin below Mt. Blakiston: an area favoured by grizzly bears. Mt. Lineham's daunting east ridge belies the easy west ridge.

Connecting to the northeast peak entails some scrambling down small cliffbands to the saddle, after which the going is straightforward. A phalanx of subalpine larches reaches just to the saddle from the west. The northeast end of the ridge is the "ruby-est," and presents a rounded profile. Ripple patterns on rocks testify to the sedimentary geology of the range. From here the full extent of Cameron Lake is in view, with the north face of Mt. Custer in Glacier National Park sweeping up from its south end. The route of Akamina Ridge (#129) is evident too. Part of the Avion Ridge route (#4) can be spied to the northwest.

Also from this point is a view southeast down Cameron Creek to the town campground and part of Upper Waterton Lake. Bellevue Hill (#3) lies to the northeast, to the right of Mt. Galwey (#7).

Descent is to the east, then down the southeast ridge from where the bridge across Blakiston Creek to Crandell campground comes into view. Crandell Lake soon appears too. The route looks more difficult upon looking back up from partway down,

North from Ruby Ridge with Mt. Dungarvan (left) and the Galwey Massif [#7].

but that's often the case! Don't count your chickens yet, however, since at the bottom a major cliffband forces a traverse right to hit the drainage from between the two peaks just above the road. This spot is 1.6 km from the trailhead.

South from Lakeview Ridge [#6] to Bellevue Hill [#3]; Vimy Peak [#1] rises above its east end, with Mt. Cleveland in Glacier National Park on centre skyline.

3 Bellevue Hill

Map p. 250
Photo p. 21

Distance: 11 km loop

Off-trail/trail: 4—8 hr

Elevation gain: 765 m (2510 ft)

Maximum elevation: 2110 m (6920 ft)

Maps: Parks Canada 1:50,000 Waterton Lakes National Park (1988) and NTS 1:50,000 Waterton Lakes 82 H/4

Trailhead: Pull-off on the north side of the Red Rock Parkway, 3.0 km (1.9 mi) from its start at Highway 5.

This ridgewalk lives up to its name, which is French for "beautiful view." Bellevue Hill can, like most places in Waterton, be very windy. Doing this route in the direction described makes for a steep haul up but has the benefit of going down (rather than pushing up) through thick vegetation at the north end.

From the trailhead, walk west along the Red Rock Parkway (watch for traffic on this narrow road) for about 1 km, past a small pull-off on its south side. Once past the cliffs at the south end of Bellevue Hill, point north and shift into climbing gear. It's a stiff grunt up the ridge, but—as promised—the views steadily unfold.

And there are myriad wildflowers, including double bladder pod, whose bright yellow helps to enliven what may otherwise seem like interminable scree. Other species of note include rock jasmine, silver rockcress, kittentails, wild blue flax, forget-me-not, and that harbinger of the alpine, moss campion. Clark's nutcrackers and Townsend's solitaires are typical avian inhabitants of the area. Black bears frequent the vicinity, so make noise where appropriate.

A small knoll after almost 500 metres of gain provides a respite before the gentler angle to the southeast subpeak. From here, dip to the west and up again, then veer north on the amble to the high point. The sheer tower of Mt. Galwey is a mere 2 km to the west; other landmarks in view include Mt. Crandell and Mt. Blakiston. To the southeast is Lower Waterton Lake, with beyond Vimy Peak (#1) and Sofa Mountain. Chief Mountain is in sight near the end of this outing.

Descent is to the northeast over several undulations prior to plunging down north toward Galwey Brook. Intersect the trail into Horseshoe Basin in the meadow at the high point before it drops west to the brook, and turn east on a somewhat over-grown path. At the bottom of the hill, near an old corral, turn south at a signed junction on the trail that parallels Bellevue Hill in the vast meadows to its east.

This trail gives an excellent appreciation of the abrupt transition from prairies to mountains that is Waterton's distinguishing characteristic, and leads right back to the trailhead in some 3 km, completing the loop.

4 Avion Ridge and Beyond

Map p. 251

Distance: 28 km and-and-back with loop

Trail/off-trail: 8—12 hr

Elevation gain: 1165 m (3820 ft)

Maximum elevation: 2655 m (8710 ft)

Maps: Parks Canada 1:50,000 Waterton Lakes National Park (1988) and NTS 1:50,000 Sage Creek 82 G/1

Trailhead: Parking area at the end of the 15.0 km (9.3 mi) long Red Rock Parkway, which branches off Highway 5 on the north side of Blakiston (Pass) Creek.

Though the approach is long, this ridgewalk is deservedly well-known for its panoramic vistas.

From the trailhead, go west up the valley of Bauerman Creek on the wide road that leads past the Goat Lake junction at 4.3 km and to the Snowshoe campground in just over 8 km. Here turn right onto the narrower trail that reaches forested Castle River Divide in about 3 km, having passed the spur into Lost Lake roughly two-thirds of the way along.

Leave the established trail at the saddle to go east along the (cont. p. 24)

The author and view north from the high point on Avion Ridge.

(Cont. from p. 23) cleared national park boundary. After some 1.5 km, break into the open at the northwest end of horseshoe-shaped Avion Ridge, whose cliffs at this spot drop off precipitously. Now veer southeast—in places on a beaten path—to follow the ridge, gaining its high point at gr 104487.

There are fine views, particularly intriguing due to the famed green and red colouration of the argillite rock of the region. To the south over Bauerman Creek are Mt. Bauerman, Lost Mountain, and Anderson Peak (all three are visited on Ridgewalk 5). Further to the southeast are Mt. Blakiston, the highest peak in Waterton Lakes National Park, and in the distance Chief Mountain. The Castle River runs to the north from just below the ridge; there are clearcuts in its valley.

The book **Place Names of Alberta, Volume I: Mountains, Mountain Parks and Foothills** states that the name of the ridge derives from a shape resembling that of an aircraft ("avion" being French for airplane). This seems obscure; in any case, the author found another connection in the shape of the rare wildflower sky pilot *(Polemonium viscosum)*, whose purple flowers grace the alpine scree in season.

Many other species of flora can be seen on this outing; especially rewarding are Mariposa lily, bluebead lily, silver-leaved scorpionweed, tiarella (foam flower), puccoon, Oregon grape, bronze bells, creeping beardtongue, kittentails, alpine spring beauty, moss campion, and the distinctive beargrass. White-tailed deer may be sighted in forested areas, and mountain goats at higher elevations. Subalpine larches grow at treelimit. Clark's nutcrackers, those bold birds, are denizens of the high country.

From the high point, stick to the ridge as it descends and curves to the north. After a dip, either keep to the trail that traverses below the ridge on its west side, or clamber up to the crest (some scree, which even if it's a pretty purple is still tiring). Both options culminate in the saddle above Goat Lake at gr 112504.

If the day is advanced, or energy is depleted, descend to Goat Lake and the trail that leads down to the valley and thus out via the road taken at the start. If inclined for more wandering, climb up to Newman Peak [gr 115509], which gives fine views into Yarrow Creek. A further extension is possible by dropping slightly and then climbing to the knoll at gr 127511, which is over 2650 metres in elevation.

Outstanding in the panorama from this point is the long series of purple ridges to the north, very inviting yet not included in this book as they are not (at present at least) in a protected area. To descend, backtrack to the southwest and then drop onto a slope leading to a narrow gully that represents a weakness in the cliffband below. **N.B.** Take care in routefinding in this section. Join the trail above Goat Lake and head back to the start.

Whatever version of the described route is taken, this outing makes for a very rewarding ridgewalk.

5 Mt. Bauerman to Anderson Peak

Map p. 251

Distance: 26 km loop

Trail/off-trail: 8—12 hr

Elevation gain: 1210 m (3970 ft)

Maximum elevation: 2698 m (8850 ft)

Maps: Parks Canada 1:50,000 Waterton Lakes National Park (1988) and NTS 1:50,000 Sage Creek 82 G/1

Trailhead: Park at Red Rock Canyon at the end of Red Rock Parkway.

This excellent circuit for the energetic—it takes in four summits—was described to the author by Waterton warden Edwin Knox, and its calibre confirmed by accomplished scrambler Roberto Pavesio. With these recommendations, the "looks like it could be interesting" musings became "gotta check it out!"

The approach to the ridgewalk proper is via the established trail up Bauerman Creek. It takes roughly three hours to hike to the unnamed saddle above Twin Lakes [gr 079455]. Now head off-trail up to the east, at first through open forest, then soon above treelimit on grassy slopes. The long gradual ridge leads to a false summit in a half hour or so from the pass; the top of Mt. Bauerman is 10 minutes further on.

This first and lowest of the four peaks of the day can be a good (cont. p. 26)

Anderson Peak (left) and Lost Mountain from below the summit of the unnamed peak.

(Cont. from p. 25) spot for lunch, though being in Waterton the wind will likely be blowing. To continue the ridgewalk, drop easterly into a saddle...en route admiring the rugged northeast face of Mt. Bauerman. Animal paths appear here-and-there; the author saw two mountain goats on this stretch (they were being buzzed by two golden eagles, but the goats were adults and the eagles immatures, so it wasn't much more than an irritation to the mammals, whose young are preyed upon by the full-grown birds). The ridge narrows and has trees along its crest, but a way can be found easily. Above the dip and again in the open, veer northerly and pass a small cairn with stick shortly before an unnamed summit [gr 115458]. Now it's time to get Lost: the mountain of that name, that is. The ridge running southeast is dramatic but goes readily, albeit with several brief detours on the descent to the dip (these dekes to the right are necessary to avoid rock outcrops).

The final section to the summit of Lost Mountain is on angular rocks that mostly make for nice scrambling but watch for loose ones. The cairn on the top is built of these block-like pieces, distinct from the scree that characterizes most of this outing. A staircase-like section of ridge leads northeast down to a saddle, following which is a slog up scree to Anderson Peak. At 2698 metres in elevation, this is the third-highest point in Waterton Lakes National Park (after Mt. Blakiston and Mt. Lineham).

The most spectacular part of the view is of the sheer north cliffs of the sub-peak to the east, but many landmarks can be identified—including Chief Mountain to the southeast. Other ridgewalks in sight include Avion Ridge and Beyond (#4), the top of the Galwey Massif North Peak (#7), Bellevue Hill (#3), and Akamina Ridge and the ridge to its west (#129 and #130).

Descent can be made straight south, at first on mostly easy, quick scree, with one short rockband to negotiate. Lower down this south-facing basin is grassy (appealing to bighorn sheep), while lower still the going becomes a little more difficult due to shintangle aspens. A final stint of bushwhacking near the drainage, which sports nice cascades, leads to the trail on the north side of Blakiston Creek.

An hour's amble down this pleasant valley, which has its own red rocks and features attractive Blakiston Falls, completes this perfect loop with superb scenic satisfactions.

Mount Bauerman and Bauerman Creek are named after Hilary Bauerman (1835-1909), geologist for the commission that surveyed the Canada/U.S. boundary from the Pacific Ocean to the Rocky Mountains. Lost Mountain lost out in the original names sweepstakes and is stuck with a generic moniker. Anderson Peak owes its name to Lt. Samuel Anderson of the Royal Engineers, Secretary to the same outfit as Bauerman and Chief Astronomer of the second commission, which worked from Lake of the Woods to the Rockies.

6 Lakeview Ridge

Map p. 250
Photo p. 28

Distance: 16 km loop

Trail/off-trail: 4—8 hr

Elevation gain: 570 m (1870 ft)

Maximum elevation: 1930 m (6330 ft)

Maps: Parks Canada 1:50,000 Waterton Lakes National Park (1988) and NTS 1:50,000 Waterton Lakes 82 H/4

Trailhead: Turn east off Highway 6 for the buffalo paddock in Waterton Lakes National Park, go downhill past the viewpoint and keep straight where the bison viewing loop starts to the left. Park clear of the turning area at the gate at the end of this road.

This enjoyable circuit visits a seldom-seen part of this gem of a park and lives up to the promise of its name.

From the gate at the start, it's easy to take a shortcut straight along the fence rather than looping left around a couple of ponds on the old road. Hit the road, turn right, then in short order turn left. Follow the track past an old corral, with signs indicating the way into Horseshoe Basin.

Climb west up the gradual hillside through intermittent meadows bedecked with wildflowers, then drop gently to Galwey Brook. Now cross the brook (maybe having to remove boots to keep dry feet) and change direction to head north up one of its tributaries. After wandering along some 2 km on the level, take a series of long switchbacks to a saddle where the trail drops to Oil Basin.

For this ridgewalk, however, forsake the beaten path and climb east to the high point of the day. Mt. Galwey (#7) rises to the southwest, while at least Lower Waterton Lake is visible to the southeast from this spot.

It is feasible to head southerly from here, but ahead is revealed a classic route (albeit with some thickets of dead and stunted trees, but adversity builds character, right?). First go northeast down to a saddle, then up to a second knoll before angling east and then south along an undulating ridge to a third, prow-like knoll. The latter bit has a cliffy eastern aspect. Middle Waterton Lake is now in sight, reinforcing the ridge name. Sofa Mountain reclines to the southeast.

Bears (both black and possibly grizzly), wolves, moose, elk, white-tailed deer, and bighorn sheep {plus attendant wood ticks} are among the wildlife that may be seen, or at least recognized via sign, in this rich habitat.

To finish off the day, descend south to the base of the ridge before veering southeast through meadows above Galwey Brook to a track along the park boundary. Take this south back to the start.

Lakeview Ridge [#6] from the approach.

Northeast from the north ridge of the north peak of the Galwey Massif; Lakeview Ridge [#6] on the right.

7 Galwey Massif North Peak

Map p. 250

Distance: 22 km out-and-back

Trail/off-trail: 8—12 hr

Elevation gain: 1065 m (3495 ft)

Maximum elevation: 2425 m (7955 ft)

Maps: Parks Canada 1:50,000 Waterton Lakes National Park (1988) and NTS 1:50,000 Waterton Lakes 82 H/4

Trailhead: As for Ridgewalk 6, Lakeview Ridge.

A massif is "a mountainous mass with several summits, but recognizably of a piece," as defined in **World Mountaineering** (general editor Audrey Salkeld, Raincoast Books, Vancouver, B.C., 1998). The Galwey Massif may be small as they go, but it fits the bill; this ridgewalk leads to the peak at the north end of the massif: the highest point on the 2.5 km long summit ridge.

Take the same trail as for Lakeview Ridge (#6), leading to the unnamed saddle between Horseshoe and Oil basins. From the pass, head first west and then southwest over the undulating ridge, at times on snippets of sheep trail. There is a some scrambling en route to the top [gr 852474].

From this north peak of the Galwey massif, the vista includes Bellevue Hill (#3), Chief Mountain in the distance to the southeast, numerous peaks in Montana's Glacier National Park, Ruby Ridge (#2), and Mt. Blakiston. Part of Avion Ridge (#4) is visible to the west.

A saddle to the northwest connects toward Mt. Dunvargan; the route presents steep terrain, unknown to the author. The Galwey Massif summit ridge leading to the south peak is definitely technical.

Rock formations on the east face of the massif are reminiscent of those in Bryce Canyon National Park, Utah, in terms of shape, colour, and lighting.

Golden eagles frequent this peak, including one seen right at the summit cairn. Seeming incongruous on such an outing, the bawling of cattle can usually be heard from below.

To descend, either retrace the approach, or perhaps shorten the distance by taking one of two spurs running down to the east.

The name Galwey comes from an officer in the Royal Engineers who was on the British contingent of the International Boundary Commission that demarcated the 45th parallel from Lake of the Woods to the Rockies in the years 1872 to 1876.

8 Cloudy Ridge

Map p. 249

Distance: 20 km out-and-back

Trail/off-trail: 8—12 hr

Elevation gain: 1030 m (3380 ft)

Maximum elevation: 2515 m (8250 ft)

Maps: Parks Canada 1:50,000 Waterton Lakes National Park (1988) and NTS 1:50,000 Waterton Lakes 82 H/4

Trailhead: Go west on Spread Eagle Road from Highway 6, 30.8 km (19.1 mi) south of the three flags and sign on the west side of the highway at the south end of Pincher Creek or approx. 14 km (9 mi) north of the junction of Highways 5 and 6 at the spur road to Waterton Park townsite. At the T-junction 8.4 km (5.2 mi) from the highway, turn south on Yarrow Creek Road and drive for 1.3 km (0.8 mi), passing the gate for Cloudy Ridge Ranch where the main road turns east after 900 metres (0.6 mi) and continuing another 400 metres (0.2 mi) on a rough track to a parking area.

Cloudy Ridge rises in the seldom-visited northern portion of Waterton Lakes National Park; the route involves bushwhacking, but makes a worthwhile journey.

From the trailhead, the simplest and most direct approach is to head south on the obvious wide swath. This undulates a bit and has a few damp spots, but is preferable to trying to follow Yarrow Creek. Ford Yarrow Creek to the well site access road near the signs for the park boundary. Follow the road for about 600 metres to where it bends west and several red-and-white flare stacks come into view. [N.B. The noise of this operation can be heard on most of this outing.] On the south side of the bend look for a barbed wire gate in the fence and a post with a small sign that flips to show 'O' or 'I,' presumably Out or In with regard to anyone at the warden cabin. A grassy vehicle track leads to the small cabin, from which the footpath leads away in an easterly direction. There is some stinging nettle on the sides of the trail.

The trail leads to the base of Cloudy Ridge in appoximately 1.5 km, shortly after joining what appears to be a more heavily travelled trail (note for return). A faint path leads off from the defined trail through the meadow in the desired direction. However, this soon disappears and there ensues a bushwhack through forest and/or sidehill gouging. Rather than expend all that effort for at most 100 metres of elevation gain, the recommendation is to continue on the established trail for 1 km or so. Once beneath the distinct open

A distant view of the north aspect of Cloudy Ridge.

knoll, strike up the slope—don't bother going for the top, rather aim for the north shoulder and then swing around to the saddle at gr 843524.

Now on the ridge proper, there remains a spate of trees to negotiate (some of which can be avoided below the crest in the open on the east side). Finally above the trees, reach a small cairn that is quite old as it has orange lichens growing on it. The route ahead appears to have a few doubtful bits but they all go, either by veering right and then cutting back or by being tackled head on.

The final bit is up a gully of purplish argillite, followed by some scrambling to reach the large (over 1.5 metre tall) cairn of flat rocks that represents the high point of this ridgewalk. {Although there is higher ground to the southwest, going any further gets into much more demanding terrain with cliffs, steep slopes, and crumbly ledges.)

The 'summit' gives rewarding views as it is. North past the Shell gas plant can be seen Pincher Creek and the Porcupine Hills beyond, while to the east is Lakeview Ridge (#6). The start of the ridgewalk up the north peak of the Galwey Massif (#7) is visible, though Mt. Dungarvan blocks the peak (as it does Sofa Mountain, Vimy Peak (#1), and Chief Mountain).

Mt. Cleveland, highest point in Glacier National Park, is visible above the rounded top of Mt. Crandell, while to the south Ruby Ridge (#2) is recognizable beneath a subpeak of Mt. Blakiston (summit not in view). To the west, Newman Peak [reached in the extension of Avion Ridge (#4)] rises south of the unnamed peak at the west end of long Spionkop Ridge running north of Yarrow Creek. The landmark of Castle Rock, with its cleft summit block, stands out to the northwest.

It may look tempting to descend to the north and then along the arm to the northeast, or at least to drop off Cloudy Ridge from near treelimit to the drainage on the park boundary. But take it from experience (a thrash involving alder-bashing, bushwhacking, sidehill-gouging, fallen-log-tripping, and fallen-log-hopping, with stinging-nettle-meeting to top it off), the best bet is to reverse the route up.

Cloudy Ridge was named, according to **Place Names of Alberta** (Aphrodite Karamitsanis, University of Calgary Press, 1991), "for its distinctive shape." Just try to pick a day when it isn't cloudy to go up!

A tenacious limber pine on "Bob Ridge" [#9]; Whaleback Ridge [#10] to the east.

9 Little Whaleback Ridge

Map p. 252
Photo p. 31

Distance: 18 km loop

Trail/off-trail: 4—8 hr

Elevation gain: 405 m (1330 ft)

Maximum elevation: 1775 m (5820 ft)

Map: 1:50,000 NTS Maycroft 82 G/16 [100 ft contour interval with 50 ft supplementary contours on east half of 1970 edition]

Trailhead: Turn west off Highway 22 just north of the Oldman River bridge and keep right at the junction just beyond (left leads down to a picnic area). Travel on the main road for 13.5 km (8.4 mi), parking on the other side of the gate at the end of the gravel road just beyond Bobs Creek Ranch.

This loop taking in three different ridges in the new (1999) Bob Creek Wildland Provincial Park makes for a full day; there is the option to do portions only of the route described.

Cross Bob Creek at the start, possibly on a makeshift log footbridge, and head up the valley on a wide track. Keep straight at the intersection with the Beaverdam Creek trail to the right, and continue another 200 metres or so to get north of a branch of Bob Creek. Leave the road here (gr 974306), heading west to cross the creek and gain the southeast end of Little Whaleback Ridge.

Reach the southernmost knoll (gr 959318) and, before heading north along the ridge, stop to savour the views. The valley of Camp Creek is immediately below to the west, with the Livingstone fire lookout (visited on Ridgewalk 11) further in that direction. Distinctively-shaped Chief Mountain is the most distant of the landmarks to the south and southeast.

The undulating ridge runs almost due north, with many of the signature limber pines of the Whaleback area. If desired, it is possible to drop off the ridge east to Bob Creek at gr 958345. Otherwise, continue along the crest to gr 954375, at which point a wide track descends east. (This junction is just 100 metres north of a wide track dropping to the west.)

Follow the track steeply down, past a shed and corral on the left, to the portal for the wide meadows at the head of Bob Creek. Either take the track down the valley, or head southeast across the meadows to approx. gr 976366, which is at the bottom of an open slope leading onto the northeast end of the untracked ridge herein called "Bob Ridge." {This unofficial name has a double significance, in that the ridge lies above Bob Creek, while the name also honours Bob Blaxley—whose **The Whaleback: A Walking Guide** (Rocky Mountain Books, 1997) played a major role in creating awareness of the area and its ecological importance.}

After the grassy ramp ends, climb right up through trees to the crest of "Bob Ridge." Continue south over the high point and down to a branch of Bob Creek. Hit another track here, which again can be followed down the valley, or—if still up for some glorious ridgewalking—head for Beaverdam Creek Ridge.

Pick up the obvious track leading up the northwest ridge from gr 977337, and take it up to a fence. Where the track dips down, hop the fence and veer left, passing just below the high point. Now head southwest and south down the ridge to gr 980321, at which point two options present themselves. Dropping west leads to a dip reached by quad track, then up to the southwest arm, which can be followed down. Keeping to the left on the steadily descending southeast arm reveals classic limber pines, a fitting finale to a full but rewarding day.

The last bit is on track down Beaverdam Creek past the Forest Reserve boundary sign to the track in Bob Creek valley just a few hundred metres above the trailhead.

Foraging Clark's nutcracker photographed on Whaleback Ridge [#10].

10 Whaleback Ridge

Map p. 253
Photos p. 6, p. 17, and p. 33

Distance: 27 km loop

Trail/off-trail: 8—12 hr

Elevation gain: 415 m (1360 ft)

Maximum elevation: 1740 m (5705 ft)

Map: NTS 1:50,000 Maycroft 82 G/16 [100 ft contour interval with 50 ft supplementary contours on east half of 1970 edition]

Trailhead: Small parking area before gate, on west side of Highway 22, 4.2 km (2.6 mi) south of the junction with Highway 520.

Whaleback Ridge was the subject of controversy regarding preservation of its rare and mostly undisturbed montane (low elevation) landscape. 1999 saw the establishment of Bob Creek Wildland Provincial Park and Black Creek Heritage Rangeland, two contiguous protected areas.

Access to Whaleback Ridge from Highway 22 is over leased land in the Heritage Rangeland; permission must be obtained in advance by calling (403) 625-2348. {The author was told in 1999 that one must keep calling until successful in speaking to someone at this number; reply would not be made to messages left on the answering machine.}

Head west up the draw from the trailhead on old road. About 2 km later, gain the south shoulder of Black Mountain. Descend about 100 metres and veer southwest on another track, which goes more-or-less south. Pass under the powerline and continue on a course essentially parallel to it. Go through a gate and through an aspen grove that has a small galvanized shed for salt blocks off to the right.

Break out into open grassland again for a while; later the track bends southwest and runs beside a fence. Among the options to gain the ridge, the author chose to leave the valley here. Climb the fence about 100 metres beyond where the track joined it and head west up the mostly open slope, aiming for the crest at gr 007330. Scar-like bits of old eroded vehicle tracks can be followed some of the way.

Some gnarled limber pines with dramatic profiles eke out an existence along this section. The crest of the ridge, just north of and above a saddle with a fence corner, gives fine views west. Included in the panorama are Little Whaleback Ridge, "Bob Ridge," and Beaverdam Creek Ridge, which can all be visited on Ridgewalk 9. Further to the west is "Livingstone Lookout Ridge," another ridgewalk destination (#11).

The route of this outing is generally along the fenceline to the north, although the angle of the strata and the proliferation of trees often prevents travel on the spine of the ridge. There is usually a cleared gap parallel to the fence. Dips in the ridge hold ephemeral ponds. After about 2 km, the ridge jogs east; rather than going to the top at gr 002350, it is preferable to angle down northeast from the dip just before it {thus avoiding some very thick young Douglas-firs} into a saddle.

A section of ridge separate from the main ridge runs for about 700 metres (more limber pines and another salt block 'shed') before the route goes west. Don't, however, climb to the knoll at gr 001358; rather, drop north and pick up a track that stays below the ridge to its east. This leads to a junction (another salt block holder) where the track descends to the east: this can be taken out, but the full outing keeps on.

Climb northwest up a gully to reach the ridgecrest again, and resume the northerly course. A sign marks the erstwhile boundary of an ecological reserve; the old road here can be taken down to the east. Otherwise push on north; it is just as well to stick close to the fence (more trees now). Shortly after crossing a cutline, take the descent route on an old road to the east starting at a green ecological reserve sign on a fence [gr 997406]. The going is vague at first, travelling through overgrowth including thimbleberry and possibly stinging nettle, but it becomes better defined lower down.

Keep right at the wider track reached soon after crossing under the powerline once in the valley again, and take this back to the south shoulder of Black Mountain and so out. As reinforcement that this is grasslands habitat, a September visit will require picking many seeds out of socks at the end of the day!

Option: If time and energy permit, the author recommends traversing Black Mountain, which to be truthful has more meadow sections than Whaleback Ridge. The best spot to gain the base of the north ridge is from the dugout at gr 015403. Simply head east and then south along the open crest (well-defined path at first). A fenceline appears near the summit and can be followed to a gate. The fence disappears east for a while: keep south until rejoin it along the now more heavily treed ridge of Black Mountain back to the approach road.

South along "Livingstone Lookout Ridge" [#11]; Oldman River below to west.

11 "Livingstone Lookout Ridge"

Map p. 252
Photo p. 35

Distance: 19 km linear

Trail/off-trail: 8—12 hr

Elevation gain: 710 m (2330 ft)

Maximum elevation: 2172 m (7125 ft)

Map: NTS 1:50,000 Maycroft 82 G/16

Trailhead: Park off the Forestry Trunk Road (Highway 940) on its east side, opposite the road up the north side of the Oldman River Valley, 45 km (28 mi) north of Coleman or 60 km (37 mi) south of Highwood Junction.

This ridgewalk on the western boundary of the new (1999) Bob Creek Wildland Provincial Park gives excellent views as well as boasting an historical element.

Given that the temporary bridges across the Oldman River connected with logging operations described in the author's **Fire Lookout Hikes in the Canadian Rockies** (Luminous Compositions, 1998) are gone, approach is now via a ford of the Livingstone River to the north.

From the trailhead, go east (a high-clearance vehicle can likely negotiate the first kilometre or so) and then drop southeast to a ford of the Livingstone above its confluence with the Oldman. Caution: Although normally straightforward, this is hazardous in high water. Now head south through open terrain to a junction some 2 km beyond the ford, at which point turn east to begin the climb onto the ridge.

Recent bulldozing soon comes to an end where join the older access road. Pass a gate 800 metres from the intersection and climb steadily to work above a prominent rock outcrop. The route then bends south to a saddle [gr 898332] before switchbacking up to the west to reach the crest of the ridge.

Just a short distance south along the ridge stands the Livingstone fire lookout [gr 896324], which as expected grants a sweeping panorama over the area. The Oldman River lies below to the west, while further off in that direction are peaks of the continental divide including Tornado Mountain and Gould Dome. The signature profile of Crowsnest Mountain appears to the southwest.

Chief Mountain and other peaks in the International Peace Park (Waterton Lakes {Canada} plus Glacier {United States} national parks) lie to the southeast, as well as sheer Castle Rock. South of The Gap through which flows the Oldman, the continuation of the Livingstone Range features Thunder Mountain. Off to the north is Hailstone Butte, site of another ridgewalk (#14). And of course to the east are the rolling Little Whaleback (#9) and Whaleback (#10) ridges.

The fire lookout is staffed early in the season; the observer later moves over to the Sugarloaf lookout to the west, which is the highest active lookout in Canada. Wildlife along the ridge includes pikas, golden-mantled ground squirrels, least chipmunks, and occasional bighorn sheep. Among the bird species are blue grouse and Clark's nutcracker.

A variety of wildflowers grow in the alpine habitat of the ridge, such as Jacob's ladder, rock jasmine, valerian, white mountain avens, forget-me-not, roseroot, alpine cinquefoil, spotted saxifrage, alpine milkvetch, and alumroot.

The ridgewalk continues to the south, now off-trail. After 3.5 km, reach the site of the original Livingstone fire lookout [gr 896291], which was established in the late 1920s or early 1930s. The 12-foot-square cabin is now gone, although the foundations remain, along with various debris. Amazingly, as of 1996, nearby there still stood several of the poles used to bring the telephone line to the lookout.

To exit off the ridge, go south toward The Gap on a sketchy trail, descending about 1.2 km to a saddle [gr 893277]. Here drop to the west on fairly well defined switchbacks. Once down through a series of rockbands, the trail (ambiguous in places) descends through the forest in a northwesterly direction. It hits the level of the Oldman River approx. 1.2 km from the saddle, opposite a corral.

The best bet, provided the ford is feasible, is to cross here to Highway 940. Otherwise, head north along the east side of the valley, sometimes on old roads. Eventually (in about 6 km) arrive at the junction leading up to the lookout that was taken earlier in the day, then go out via the wade of the Livingstone.

The range and the river were named after the famous African explorer David Livingstone by Capt. Blakiston of the 1857-1860 Palliser Expedition.

North from the high point of Chaffen Ridge [#12]; Horseshoe Ridge on the right.

12 Horseshoe Ridge and Chaffen Ridge

Map p. 254
Photo p. 37

Distance: 30 km linear

Trail/off-trail: 8—12 hr

Elevation gain: 610 m (2000 ft)

Maximum elevation: 2225 m (7298 ft)

Map: NTS 1:50,000 Langford Creek 82 J/1

Trailhead: Go east from Highway 940 (Forestry Trunk Road), 11.2 km (6.9 mi) south of the junction with Highway 532, on an old road with muddy sections. Park on the west side of the Livingstone River as close as safely possible to the ford to the east side, which is several hundred metres northeast of the turn-off from the highway.

Horseshoe Ridge and Chaffen Ridge rise in the northwestern corner of the recently established Bob Creek Wildland Provincial Park; these two remote ridges are well worth a visit.

The start of this outing is—appropriately—up Ridge Creek, which no self-respecting ridgewalk guidebook author could pass up on, eh? Ford the Livingstone River from the trailhead and pick up an old road that runs south a short distance before veering east to follow up the valley on the north side of Ridge Creek.

Keep right at a Y-junction after about 2 km (a cutblock lies opposite on the south side of the creek): this more direct option rejoins the main track on the other side of the meadow. Keep straight, not right, at the next junction. Go through a barbed wire fence at the narrows (approx. gr 875503). After a further 1.5 km or so, do not go north up the more open valley but keep east (a track will be seen going up the initial slope).

On the final approach to the saddle [gr 904525] between Ridge and Riley creeks, don't veer north on the better-defined trail but keep straight through the forest. The sudden cliffband at the saddle grants expansive views east over lush grassy foothills. The trail heads southeast, dipping slightly before gaining open meadows. The path gets vague here, but the way is clear: gain the ridge, go south, take a jog west, then go south again to the eastern outlier of Horseshoe Ridge [gr 905508]. {There is a wide cutline that leads up to the ridge from before the saddle but it is just a straight swath and taking it would preclude the first dramatic view with cliff.} After the first meadow, much of this section is rocky underfoot. (And, to keep truth-in-advertising, it's only on the stretch from the saddle that entry is made into the protected area.)

An interesting feature shortly before reaching the outlier is the presence of several ephemeral ponds on the crest of the ridge; less appealing is the evidence of logging in the basin of Owl Creek below to the east. It's a short stroll to the slightly higher western 'summits' of Horseshoe Ridge. To stay within the park as much as possible, the described route descends southeast from the eastern outlier. A good trail leads down to the south notch of the saddle between Deep and Hunter creeks [gr 923493] (there is a cairn in the north notch).

It appears feasible to head down Deep Creek here, but if the day is still young and energy levels are high, a well-defined trail leads temptingly onto Chaffen Ridge. Climb south up the steady grade for a little over 1 km, crossing a barbed wire fence, then bend westerly along the crest of the ridge. The trail, which in 2000 had been recently travelled by dirt bikers and was liberally marked with pink flagging tape, leads along (at times below) undulating Chaffen Ridge, taking various bearings to south and southwest.

The wildflowers to be found on this outing include lots of both silky lupine and Parry's townsendia with its large purple blossoms. Spotted saxifrage, white mountain avens, rock jasmine, dwarf larkspur, wild blue flax, creeping beardtongue, Jacob's ladder, glacier lily, golden fleabane, and forget-me-not also occur on the ridges.

Bob Creek Wildland Provincial Park is left at gr 903456, just above a forested dip, but it's recommended to continue another kilometre or so to the high point. Crowsnest Mountain is the prominent landmark to the southwest, but even its imposing profile is eclipsed by the spectacular shape of the peaks to the west. These are known unofficially as The Elevators, in keeping with their sheer sides—like the grain elevators that once proliferated on the prairies. Another intriguing view is of an isolated castle-like rock formation on Whaleback Ridge to the east.

Even if it's hazy, the silhouettes of Chief Mountain, Mt. Cleveland, and Castle Mountain should be visible off to the southeast and south. With binoculars the Waterton Lakes National Park ridgewalks on the north peak of the Galwey Massif (#7) and on Cloudy Ridge (#8) can be recognized [maybe Vimy Peak and Vimy Ridge (#1) too]. Closer at hand to the south is the "Livingstone Lookout Ridge" (#11), while to the north are Hailstone Butte (#14) and Mt. Burke, which both also sport fire lookouts (the latter no longer in service), and the broad level top of Plateau Mountain.

The well-defined trail continues past the high point, possibly connecting with the trail in White Creek, but unless up for some exploring and unless a car shuttle has been set up, it's best to descend west from just southwest of the high point. There is open ground at first, but even once in the trees the going is easy, with only some low alders in places. After about 500 metres of westerly travel, head in a beeline north on the obvious ridge. The descent is gradual until the end, where a plunge of almost two hundred metres vertical leads to Deep Creek.

Exit west via Deep Creek, and via is the right word: there are quite a few crossings on cow trails until join a road up on the north terrace. This leads down to another ford of the Livingstone and connection with the Forestry Trunk Road about 2 km south of the trailhead.

The name of Horseshoe Ridge is descriptive. The name of Chaffen Ridge comes from a family who homesteaded near the area in 1905 and whose spelling was actually Chaffin.

Section 2 Southern Kananaskis Country

The high point of Indian Graves Ridge.

13 Indian Graves Ridge

Map p. 255

Distance: 9 km loop

Trail: up to 4 hr

Elevation gain: 225 m (740 ft)

Maximum elevation: 1690 m (5545 ft)

Maps: NTS 1:50,000 Langford Creek 82 J/1 and Stimson Creek 82 J/8

Trailhead: Park off Highway 532 (Johnson Creek Trail) east of the Willow Creek bridge (on either north or south side of the road), approx. 3.7 km (2.3 mi) west of the Kananaskis Country entrance sign. **N.B.** Although not closed over winter, Highway 532 gets little winter maintenance (essentially none west of Indian Graves).

This short ridgewalk makes for a good early season excursion thanks to its low elevation and its situation in the foothills.

A short stint up the Willow Creek trail (old road) gets things underway, then veer right up through a few trembling aspen trees to the open slopes at the south end of the ridge. The steep rocky rib can be circumvented on the right, or tackled straight on with some quasi-technical scrambling.

Soon up on the level section of the ridge, the views are impressive given the minimum of effort expended. Rolling ridges stretch off in all directions, with loftier peaks rising on the horizon to the west. The landmarks in sight include Hailstone Butte (#14), part of Plateau Mountain, Sentinel Peak, and Mt. Burke with the old Cameron fire lookout on its summit.

Continuing north (following a fence and crossing other fences where required), the trail descends back into trees. Overgrown in places, it eventually cuts northwest down to a saddle. The track gets muddy and rutted as climbing up through forest on the other side, but sticking to it sees arrival at a former wellsite.

Return from here can be made most directly by way of the road in the draw to the southeast. Another possibility is to exit via a trail that at first ascends south to a high point before bailing off to the west in the drainage of a tributary of Willow Creek. In either case, once on the Willow Creek road, head southeast back to the trailhead.

An optional extension to this rather brief outing can be made into the Willow Creek Hills, although much of the way is in trees. Go north from the wellsite on a trail near a fence: it's best to stick close to the fence even though it leaves the ridgecrest. Veer west into a dip [gr 865720], then climb to the high point. Descend north to the saddle at gr 856735, where the established trail from the valley of Hay Creek to the east carries on west (albeit vague at first). Once down by Willow Creek, follow the old road south out to the trailhead.

14 Hailstone Butte

Map p. 253

Distance: 4 km loop

Trail/off-trail: up to 4 hr

Elevation gain: 335 m (1100 ft)

Maximum elevation: 2364 m (7755 ft)

Map: NTS 1:50,000 Langford Creek 82 J/1

Trailhead: "Teardrop Lake," the unofficial name for the small body of water just west of the high point on Highway 532 (Johnson Creek Trail), approx. 4 km (2.5 mi) east of the junction with the Forestry Trunk Road (Highway 940). The east end of Highway 532 is some 29 km (18 mi) south of Longview on Highway 22. **N.B.** Although not closed over winter, Highway 532 gets little winter maintenance (essentially none west of Indian Graves).

The high point on Hailstone Butte sports a fire lookout cabin, a good indication of the fine view obtained from the top on this short ridgewalk.

The route leads up the draw northwest from the trailhead. The faint path fades out on grassy slopes less than a kilometre from the trailhead. Although a more direct line toward the lookout can be taken through the cliffband above, an approach that avoids some backtracking is to keep north to the saddle at the head of the draw.

An airy traverse across the scree slope above Skene Canyon leads to a series of rock steps up to the left (west), which connects with the ridge close to the lookout. [Please respect this as a personal residence as well as a workplace, and do not disturb the fire observer on duty.]

If it is clear, Chief Mountain near Waterton Lakes National Park is visible to the south, and Crowsnest Mountain to the southwest. Immediately to the west is the broad summit of Plateau Mountain, which was an ice-free refugium during the last major glaciations. To the east are foothills (with the Chain Lakes Reservoir visible) and prairie; Calgary's city skyline can also be discerned.

Many wildflowers grow on Hailstone Butte, including alpine forget-me-not, roseroot, umbrella plant, sawwort, mountain sorrel, bladder locoweed, moss gentian, alumroot, valerian, alpine milkvetch, silky lupine, alpine bistort, creeping beardtongue, spotted saxifrage, and moss campion.

Wildlife that occurs in the area includes deer, elk, moose, bighorn sheep, marmots, pikas, and golden-mantled ground squirrels.

An enticing and easy loop is possible by roaming south over gentle terrain to the south end of the butte [gr 815636]. Here there is patterned ground: circular arrangements of rocks brought up by churning of the soil due to frosts. It is a simple matter to drop more-or-less due east right back to the trailhead.

The author looking to the south end of Hailstone Butte from near the fire lookout.

The author on Unnamed Ridge [#15], looking south to Pasque Mountain [#16] on the right.

15 Unnamed Ridge

Map p. 254
Photo p. 43

Distance: 9 km linear

Off-trail: 4—8 hr

Elevation gain: 490 m (1605 ft)

Maximum elevation: 2395 m (7855 ft)

Maps: NTS 1:50,000 Fording River 82 J/2 and Mount Head 82 J/7

Trailhead: Small parking area on the south side of Highway 940 (Forestry Trunk Road), 10 km (6 mi) south of the Cataract Creek bridge and 1.2 km (0.7 mi) west of Wilkinson Summit. **N.B.** Highway 940 is closed between Cataract Creek campground and Wilkinson Summit from December 1st to April 30th.

This walk along what is unofficially called Unnamed Ridge is rescued from its anonymity by great views. (The name apparently arose so as to not get into conflict with the Geographic Names Board by applying a more descriptive handle.)

As is often the case, even though some maps may show the ridge in green—suggesting it is forested—parts of the crest are open, allowing for fine vistas. These materialize shortly after the start, when (after the steep haul up onto the south end of the ridge) Pasque Mountain (#16) comes into sight.

Some routefinding is called for: in general, bear northeast near the beginning and climb until intersecting the ridge, with meadows below to the east. (There are some thick stands of young lodgepole pine in this dry habitat; also animal paths and cutlines to be crossed and/or followed as their direction warrants.)

The panorama improves as rise gradually toward the high point at gr 735658, with peaks to the west beyond intervening valleys, and the large flat expanse of Plateau Mountain to the east. Hoary marmots and pikas live up here, as do wildflowers including shooting star, stonecrop, spotted saxifrage, rock jasmine, golden fleabane, creeping beardtongue, white mountain avens, and forget-me-not.

There are a few subalpine larches north of the summit, among which can be found such bird species as Clark's nutcracker and blue grouse. Rather than being a purist and continuing the last kilometre or so to the north, the author elected to use a cutline that dropped off to the west from about gr 729704. There is one detour to skirt a cliffband.

This hits Wilkinson Creek at the confluence with a tributary: either cross here and continue west on the cutline to Highway 940, or proceed upstream a ways before crossing. (It's not worth sticking to the east bank until reach the bridge at gr 715687 just to avoid a ford.)

16 Pasque Mountain

Map p. 255

Distance: 15 km linear

Trail/off-trail: 4—8 hr

Elevation gain: 700 m (2295 ft)

Maximum elevation: 2544 m (8343 ft)

Map: NTS 1:50,000 Fording River 82 J/2

Trailhead: Park at the entrance to a gated logging road on the west side of Highway 940 (Forestry Trunk Road), 8.5 km (5.3 mi) south of the Cataract Creek bridge. **N.B.** Highway 940 is closed between Cataract Creek campground and Wilkinson Summit from December 1st to April 30th.

An old road gives good access to this superb ridgewalk in the southern end of Kananaskis Country.

It can be a bit confusing getting onto the spur that leads to the north ridge of Pasque Mountain. From the gate, take the logging road that crosses Wilkinson Creek, then turn right and go over another bridge. Don't go uphill on a travelled road marked with bronze diamonds; rather, keep left on a rehabilitated road.

The going can be marshy as passing above the drainage to its (cont. p. 46)

The author looking north from Pasque Mountain.

(Cont. from p. 45) northwest. Cut south to cross the creek and soon after look for an inconspicuous opening that reveals an old road crossing another branch of the creek. Take the switchbacks up to the north end of the spur [gr 716632], then rise along it before veering southwest on more zig-zags. Break out of the trees (including larches) and into meadows to reach the north ridge at gr 709616. Now the way is clear: just face south and go!

There is a high point about 500 metres before the true summit of Pasque Mountain at gr 716587. Besides a plethora of cutblocks, the view includes a skyline to the west that presents a line of dramatic grey peaks. The panorama extends from Crowsnest Mountain in the southwest to Mist Mountain in the northwest. Other ridgewalks in view include Raspberry Ridge (#17), Unnamed Ridge (#15), Hailstone Butte (#14), even Bull Creek Hills (#21) off to the north.

The ridgewalk continues by heading east, down to the saddle at gr 725592, then over a small bump to the knoll at gr 737594. Another saddle lies ahead prior to the final rise to the summit of the unnamed ridge east of and parallel to Pasque Mountain. The route continues northwesterly, with a steep dropoff at the end. A stretch of trees leads down to a tributary of Wilkinson Creek, which can be followed quite easily to Highway 940. (Several trails may be crossed but this is the most direct way out.)

The spot where hit the road happens to be near the trailhead for Unnamed Ridge (#15); it is some 2 km from the start of this outing.

The author on the south part of Raspberry Ridge; Unnamed Ridge [#15] on the left (below Plateau Mountain) and Pasque Mountain [#16] in the centre.

17 Raspberry Ridge

Map p. 256

Distance: 10 km linear

Trail/off-trail: 4—8 hr

Elevation gain: 645 m (2115 ft)

Maximum elevation: 2350 m (7710 ft)

Map: NTS 1:50,000 Mount Head 82 J/7

Trailhead: Unmarked, gated road to the west off Highway 940 (Forestry Trunk Road), 1.7 km (1.1 mi) north of the entrance to Cataract Creek campground and 11.4 km (7.1 mi) south of the three-way junction of Highways 40, 940, and 541 at Highwood Junction.

Although there is an established trail to the top of Raspberry Ridge, this route represents an alternative that traverses the ridge.

From the trailhead, go past the gate and stick to the main road up Cataract Creek for about 1.5 km. Then keep on the north side of the creek on a smaller road (used as a snowmobile track in winter) that roughly parallels the bigger one. This leads to the base of the southern end of Raspberry Ridge, which is gained by pushing up through a band of trees onto steep grassy slopes. The ridgecrest sports trees and rocky ribs, turning grassier and more open near where the old road to the fire lookout on the summit cuts through to the west side from the meadows on the east. The road can be followed, or the ridge proper kept to for the final kilometre or so to the top.

Many species of wildflowers thrive on the ridge, including rock jasmine, saw-wort, white mountain avens, creeping beardtongue, forget-me-not, spotted saxifrage, stonecrop, Jacob's ladder, silky scorpionweed, and umbrella plant. Small mammals that live in this habitat include least chipmunk, Columbian ground squirrel, golden-mantled ground squirrel, and pika. Northern harriers prey on these rodents; other birds to be found on the ridge include Clark's nutcrackers and dark-eyed juncos.

A highlight of the view from the fire lookout is the revelation of Crowsnest Mountain far off to the south. In closer proximity are the peaks of the High Rock Range on the continental divide to the west, with the gap of Fording River Pass breaking the wall north of west. The Calgary skyline is visible to the northeast, Mt. Burke (with the abandoned Cameron fire lookout) lies to the east, and Plateau Mountain to the southeast.

Descend to Etherington Creek via a series of rolls on the mostly open ridge, which bends to the northwest. The last stretch is through forest, with fallen trees, alders, and shrubs; happily, they are easier to go down through than to push up through. In order to reach the road on the north side, a ford of the creek may be necessary or rockhopping might suffice. Turn right out to the campground near Highway 940.

The author on Hells Ridge; forested Junction Hill [#26] in left centre and Mt. Head on the right.

Cairn on "Baril—Fitzsimmons Ridge" [#20]; Mist Mountain in distance, with in front Odlum Ridge [#35] to left and Nameless Ridge [#33] to right.

18 Hells Ridge North End

Map p. 257

Distance: 8 km linear

Trail/off-trail: 4—8 hr

Elevation gain: 305 m (1000 ft)

Maximum elevation: 1930 m (6330 ft)

Map: NTS 1:50,000 Mount Head 82 J/7

Trailhead: Small parking area on the east side of Highway 940 (Forestry Trunk Road), just north of the Etherington Creek bridge and the entrance to Etherington Creek campground about 6 km (3.7 mi) south of Highwood Junction.

The unusual name of this ridge comes from the trouble that ranchers had in retrieving cattle off it; for walkers, however, it is actually quite heavenly.

Once on the old road on the east side of Etherington Creek, pick a spot and head up to the right: the author went for 25 minutes before leaving the trail and hit the ridgecrest at about gr 694812 after ascending a grassy draw. This high point on the route is almost exactly at the end of the open ridge; to the south, trees grow on top.

Views are expansive, including west up Baril Creek to the gap of Fording River Pass, on either side of which continental divide peaks fill the horizon. In the mid-distance are the ridgewalks that run from Cataract Creek to Carnarvon Creek (#17, #19, #20, and #27), and to the northwest is Junction Hill (#26)—a continuation of Hells Ridge north of the Highwood River. To the northeast are the Bull Creek Hills (#21), while to the east can be discerned the north end of the north ridge of Mt. Burke and "Zephyr Ridge" (#22 and #23).

Hells Ridge is a dry habitat {Perhaps the name has a double meaning?} and thus a good place to sight blue grouse. Pikas have colonized rock slide areas such as below the cliff on the west side near the summit. Wildflowers that thrive here include silver-leaved scorpionweed, spotted saxifrage, and stonecrop.

It is very pleasant to amble north along the ridge with its grassy crest. The descent at the north end requires a bit more attention on granite-like rocks with black lichens growing on them. At the bottom, turn left and parallel the Highwood River past a small cabin to a ford of Etherington Creek, above which is Highway 940.

19 "Etherington—Baril Ridge"

Map p. 257

Distance: 8 km linear

Trail/off-trail: 4—8 hr

Elevation gain: 480 m (1575 ft)

Maximum elevation: 2120 m (6955 ft)

Map: NTS 1:50,000 Mount Head 82 J/7

Trailhead: Etherington Creek campground entrance off Highway 940 (Forestry Trunk Road) about 6 km (3.7 mi) south of Highwood Junction.

Although the least appealing of the four ridgewalks between Raspberry Ridge and the Strawberry Hills (delicious sounding names eh?), this link in the series still has its rewards.

Things start off well with the quick approach up Etherington Creek to the narrows. The old road is even on the north side of valley thanks to a bridge, so there is no need for a ford. A drift fence makes a suitable indicator for the turn up right off the road onto the ridge.

Either zigzag up grassy slopes or take to the rock rib (woodrat sign) for a touch of scrambling. Both lodgepole pine and limber pine grow on the ridge, together in places. Generally, though, the terrain is open, with good views west (albeit with logging cutblocks).

There are several cairns at the high point; the extensive vistas are suggested by the ability to spot the arch on Mt. Tyrwhitt over 35 km away. Stay up on top and enjoy the panorama for as long as possible, because the rest of this is not a lot of fun.

Disappointingly, the trees rise high on the north side of the ridge, so almost the entire descent is through forest. It wouldn't be so bad if it stayed fairly open as at first, but the cover becomes dense stands. These small lodgepole pines sprouted up after a 1930s fire, which has also left many fallen trees. As can be gathered, pushing through and clambering over this stuff doesn't make for easy travel.

Thus a sigh of relief is in order when the old road on the south side of Baril Creek is suddenly stumbled upon. Turn right and take it out to Highway 940, probably resolved not to do this route again.

20 "Baril—Fitzsimmons Ridge"

Map p. 257
Photo p. 48

Distance: 10 km linear

Trail/off-trail: 4—8 hr

Elevation gain: 555 m (1820 ft)

Maximum elevation: 2140 m (7020 ft)

Map: NTS 1:50,000 Mount Head 82 J/7

Trailhead: Small parking area on the west side of Highway 940 (Forestry Trunk Road), 3.3 km (2.0 mi) south of Highwood Junction.

This ridge near Highwood Junction is mostly forested on its eastern side but entices with a grassy crest revealing superb sweeps of scenery.

Start up the old road south of Baril Creek, then turn right off it opposite the open slopes leading up to the summit [gr 654809]. The point to head down to a ford of the creek comes just after a spur to the right rejoins the main road. It's a bush bash, but only takes five minutes down. Once crossed to the other side, the forest is not as thick and doesn't last long.

The south-facing slopes are steep; if so inclined, a prominent rib makes for nice scrambling on orange rock embedded with small pebbles. Limber pines with their shapely silhouettes fringe the ridge above the rib, and provide shade if it's a hot day.

In an unusual touch, fireweed surrounds the small cairn at the top of the ridge. Views here encompass a long line of peaks on the continental divide, plus a collection of other ridgewalks: Junction Hill (#26), Hells Ridge North End (#18), and Strawberry Hills (#27) are the most prominent. Energetic ridgewalkers can link this route with the last of those three.

Animal paths run along the ridge as head north, and lower down near Fitzsimmons Creek many of them parallel the creek on its south side. A ford and a scrabble up the bank lead to the old road to the north of Fitzsimmons Creek, which leads to Highway 40. A ford of the Highwood awaits at the finish, after crossing the flats through a broad swath that hits the river just below the farthest downstream picnic table at the Fitzsimmons trailhead.

21 Bull Creek Hills

Map p. 256

Distance: 10 km linear via Pack Trail Coulee

Trail/off-trail: 4—8 hr

Elevation Gain: 720 m (2360 ft)

Maximum elevation: 2175 m (7135 ft)

Map: NTS 1:50,000 Mount Head 82 J/7

Trailhead: For options 1, 2, and 3, the Sentinel trailhead 4.0 km (2.5 mi) west of the Kananaskis Country entrance sign on Highway 541, and 5.4 km (3.3 mi) east of Highwood Junction; for option 4, park off the highway on the south side 2.9 km (1.8 mi) west of the Kananaskis Country entrance.

The Bull Creek Hills make for a good early season ridgewalk. These were the stomping grounds of R.M. Patterson, author of the classic **The Buffalo Head** and former proprietor of the ranch of the same name.

First on the agenda is getting to Grass Pass, which can be accomplished in a variety of ways. The options include

(1) the trail up Pack Trail Coulee,

(2) by means of an interesting variation on the ridge to the west (which offers a bit of scrambling and a scenic route along a ridgecrest dotted with Douglas-fir and limber pine),

(3) the ridge east of Pack Trail Coulee, and

(4) via open slopes west of Fir Creek (gained from the highway 100 metres east of the trailhead) and the upper part of the ridge east of Pack Trail Coulee. This option leads past a leaning Douglas-fir; this and option 3 pass the famous Boundary Pine described by Patterson.

From Grass Pass, take the track leading northeast up the gradual slopes. (If options 3 or 4 are taken, Grass Pass can be bypassed to head directly north onto the Bull Creek Hills.) The track peters out at the first knoll, from which drop slightly heading north, then veer northeast once more to gain the crest at about gr 724886, between the two westernmost of a cluster of three bumps. A highlight of this section is the presence of kittentails...no, not young cats, but the rare wildflower. Other species in bloom include forget-me-not, dwarf larkspur, spotted saxifrage, silver rockcress, silver-leaved scorpionweed, Jacob's ladder, moss phlox, Parry's townsendia, white mountain avens, stonecrop, and balsamroot.

Go east over the two tops in that direction, descend northeast into an open saddle, then climb to the high point of the outing at gr 733886 (survey marker). The fine vistas include west to Mt. Head and other peaks of the Highwood Range, north over the valley of Flat (Trap) Creek and beyond, and south in a bird's eye view over

The famous Boundary Pine in the Bull Creek Hills.

several neighbouring ridgewalks.

Descent can be made to the south into the headwaters of Marston Creek, or—to prolong the enjoyable part—keep on the ridge to the east until it comes to an end, then wander southeast down open slopes. This area is replete with wild colour, including that of silky scorpionweed, fairy bells, leather-leaved saxifrage, yellow paintbrush, yellow locoweed, low larkspur, puccoon, and the uncommon smooth blue beardtongue.

Intersect a road north of Marston Creek that leads east, but leave it (goes onto private land) to cross the creek. Climb south through forest, possibly near the Kananaskis Country boundary fence, to gain the ridge, then drop to the highway near the entrance flags.

Another option in this area, especially attractive early in the season before the higher elevations of the Bull Creek Hills are accessible, is to ramble on "Fir—Marston Ridge" between the creeks of those names. One way of approaching this outing is to head north to the ridge from the entrance flags at the end of the Bull Creek Hills trip, then go west. A rockband beyond the knoll at gr 743867 can be negotiated via a gap.

The route continues just below the ridgecrest, which is treed, to the high point (cairn of brown rocks) at gr 735868. From here a ridge runs north to gr 727885 in the Bull Creek Hills: yet another possibility for exploration. The intial bit is treed; the way becomes more open after crossing a cutline. There is a fine view of evidence of geological processes in the form of a syncline adjacent to an anticline—rock folds that are respectively cupped and arched.

The descent from "Fir—Marston Ridge" is south, at first over rocky terrain, with thick trees too, but then over easy ground. Reach the highway some 2 km west of the start.

22 Mt. Burke North End of North Ridge

Map p. 259

Distance: 19 km loop

Trail/off-trail: 8—12 hr

Elevation gain: 845 m (2770 ft)

Maximum elevation: 2300 m (7545 ft)

Map: NTS 1:50,000 Mount Head 82 J/7

Trailhead: Sentinel day-use area south off Highway 541, 4.0 km (2.5 mi) west of the Kananaskis Country entrance sign and 5.4 km (3.3 mi) east of Highwood Junction.

Even though this route offers eight kilometres of ridgewalking, that represents just over half of the total length of the north ridge of Mt. Burke. Nevertheless, this outing constitutes a challenging excursion.

The adventure begins right off the bat with a ford of the Highwood River, at most times a straightforward proposition but not to be underestimated in times of high water. Once across the river, head east at first, then cut back southwest into a large meadow {site of Native ceremonies; respect any cultural objects}. The north end of this ridge has two arms, either of which will serve as approach {both arms have more Native sites}.

The author ended up on the western arm, the true end of the ridge, after cutting up from the meadow and striking a clear corridor partway up. Once on the ridge the going is easy, at first through trees, then—after a little more than a kilometre—in open areas comprised mainly of bearberry cover. Views soon unveil to the west: low Mt. Mann (#24), Hells Ridge (#18), and glimpses of peaks on the continental divide.

An hour or so after starting, the route ahead hoves into sight. It undulates over rounded tops before changing character to rocky terrain that requires more attention to the route. From the vantage point of this ridge can be seen a cutline running right down through Painted Canyon: a case of "the sacred and the profane" given the Native rock art in the canyon.

An interesting literary reference to this area, describing the rock art and this ridge, is in R.M. Patterson's book **The Buffalo Head**. Patterson describes his 1936 visit to Painted Canyon and tells of getting up onto the ridge, where he obtained sobering confirmation of the huge size of a forest fire moving in from the west. (Interestingly, Patterson refers to the ridge as part of the Lookout Range, alluding to the now-abandoned fire lookout cabin on the summit of Mt. Burke.)

Patterson also later used this ridge to get a view of the upper portion of Cataract Creek, whose meadows eventually come into sight. The most difficult section of this ridgewalk occurs after the penultimate bump at gr 744776: to progress to the high

54

North along the north end of the north ridge of Mt. Burke from the high point, showing the crux. Other ridgewalks in view, from right to left: "Zephyr Ridge" [#23], Bull Creek Hills [#21], Gunnery Mountain [#25], Mt. Mann [#24], Junction Hill [#26], and Hells Ridge North End [#18].

point at gr 747774, descend a short distance to the south. Then pick up a steep scree gully to the right, hugging the base of the rockband past a small cave until beyond the rockband below. Now cut back to the left and contour into the saddle before the final rise.

The high point of this ridgewalk grants excellent views to the west, including of Baril Peak and Mt. Armstrong. In the mid-distance is Raspberry Ridge (#17), site of a modern fire lookout. To the northwest below Mist Mountain can be discerned Odlum Ridge (#35), and to the north are the Bull Creek Hills (#21).

Descent is made to the east to a grassy saddle where a trail leads north down into a basin at the head of a small creek (the first water since starting). Next go over a low ridge west of a round knoll before connecting with the Zephyr Creek trail just below Zephyr/Bear Pass. Head down the valley, with its demarcation of evergreen forest on the west slopes below the ridge just walked and dry open heights to the east. Be sure to check out Painted Canyon if time permits.

An optional connection links this ridgewalk with "Zephyr Ridge" (#23), doing the latter in the opposite direction of the description.

23 "Zephyr Ridge"

Map p. 259

Distance: 19 km loop

Trail/off-trail: 8—12 hr

Elevation gain: 745 m (2445 ft)

Maximum elevation: 2200 m (7215 ft)

Map: NTS 1:50,000 Mount Head 82 J/7

Trailhead: Sentinel day-use area south off Highway 541, 4.0 km (2.5 mi) west of the Kananaskis Country entrance sign and 5.4 km (3.3 mi) east of Highwood Junction.

This winding ridge east of Zephyr Creek passes above Painted Canyon, site of intriguing Native rock art.

After fording the Highwood River (caution in high water), go east on a track until the junction with an old road heading southwest, then head directly up the north end of this ridge. [An option is to continue about 400 metres east and then turn north up a more open slope.] The going is clear and at a steady incline for the first kilometre, before tapering to a gentler grade leading to the high point at gr 736824. There are impressive views down into the valley of Zephyr Creek with intervening slabs.

From the high point, turn east on an undulating ridge where grassy patches alternate with treed sections. Head for gr 747825, where you may come upon some pink flagging tape tied around a rock. {It is possible to do a shorter variation from here by going northeast to gr 752831, then either going down to the northwest or heading further northeast past a saddle and then going down northwest.}.

To continue on "Zephyr Ridge," go south, then southeast, then south again along the mostly open ridgecrest. The goal is the rounded knoll at gr 756807, whose gentle appearance belies the fact that it is the highest point on this outing. Scattered subalpine larches dot the eastern aspect just below the top, on a divide between Miller Creek and Bear Creek. Views to the south include Hailstone Butte (#14), site of a modern fire lookout, and Mt. Burke with the abandoned lookout from the 1920s.

From the knoll, venture southwest (often in trees, with some alders) toward gr 746796, rejoining the continuation of the original ridge south of the gap of Painted Canyon. Once on this crest, which has slabs to the west, traverse south over another top before descending to Zephyr/Bear Pass.

Return via the Zephyr Creek trail, detouring up Painted Canyon if there is enough time. An optional extension can be made by combining this ridgewalk with the north end of the north ridge of Mt. Burke (#22). This makes for a long day!

North from "Zephyr Ridge" north of Painted Canyon, including Bull Creek Hills [#21].

East from Mt. Mann [#24]; Bull Creek Hills [#21] on left and Highwood River on right.

57

24 Mt. Mann

Map p. 259
Photo p. 57

Distance: 8 km linear

Trail/off-trail: up to 4 hr

Elevation gain: 450 m (1475 ft)

Maximum elevation: 1905 m (6250 ft)

Map: NTS 1:50,000 Mount Head 82 J/7

Trailhead: Sentinel day-use area south off Highway 541, 4.0 km (2.5 mi) west of the Kananaskis Country entrance sign and 5.4 km (3.3 mi) east of Highwood Junction.

Mt. Mann, a low peak near Highwood Junction, makes for an interesting short outing that can be done a number of different ways. The necessary fords of the Highwood River are best done at times of low water, in early spring or later in the season, not at times of high flow.

Once safely across the river, head south up Cataract Creek on an old road. At the top of the first hill, reached after about five minutes, the first option presents itself: taking the east ridge direct to the summit. This is steep and straightforward except for the scrambling and routefinding called for to get through the obvious cliffband, which requires experience and a willingness to scout around a bit.

If not comfortable with this more adventurous approach, the other choice is to keep south past the lower falls on the creek. After about 2 km, turn west from the confluence at gr 714819, up an inconspicuous side drainage. [A reference point is the forested knoll at gr 719798 that can be seen from the main trail but which is not passed beneath.] Staying on the north side of the drainage, preferably on game trails, go about 400 metres before turning north up meadows with occasional trees. Later the forest is thicker but a trail—used by horse travellers—has become apparent and winds about to eventually reach the top.

The open meadow facing east from near the summit grants a fine panorama. Among the ridgewalks in view are Bull Creek Hills (#21), "Zephyr Ridge" (#23), and Mt. Burke North End of North Ridge (#22). Glimpses to the west earlier included sight of Hells Ridge (#18), "Baril—Fitzsimmons Ridge" (#20), Strawberry Hills (#27), Bishop Ridge (#29), and Junction Hill (#26).

Descent from Mt. Mann can be by reversing either of the two approaches, or by one of two other possibilities. The first is to the southeast, at first skirting below the initial cliffband, then dropping steeply through young aspens and veering right above the overhanging lower cliffband until where easy treed slopes lead down to the Cataract Creek trail. The fourth option, and perhaps the most recommended (though not the most scenic due to thick trees) is to head northwest from the top. A small knoll is encountered not far down: go over it and keep on the same course. Traverse left above a rockband until reach a gap with fallen trees. Near the bottom of the slope, a higher cliffband forces one to the left...go with the flow and continue all the way down to the Highwood River. {The entire way down is through forest with a luxuriant mossy floor.}

It's simplest to cross here and walk back along the highway, though a stint of bushwhacking will connect with a usually dry stream channel (can be seen from above) that leads back east to opposite the start.

Mt. Mann is an unofficial name that may have to do with an early logger.

Down southwest ridge of Gunnery Mountain [#25] to the Highwood River.

South from Junction Hill [#26]; (l to r) Mt. Burke, Plateau Mountain, and Hells Ridge [#18].

25 Gunnery Mountain

Map p. 256
Photo p. 59

Distance: 5 km loop

Off-trail/trail: up to 4 hr

Elevation gain: 600 m (1970 ft)

Maximum elevation: 2080 m (6820 ft)

Map: NTS 1:50,000 Mount Head 82 J/7

Trailhead: Park off Highway 541 on the south side (narrow shoulder), 0.2 km (0.1 mi) west of a cattleguard and 1.0 km (0.6 mi) west of the Eyrie Gap turnoff. {This spot is 6.5 km (4.0 mi) west of the Kananaskis Country entrance sign on Highway 541, and 2.9 km (1.8 mi) east of Highwood Junction.} [More spacious parking can be found at a widening on the south side of the highway, 0.5 km (0.3 mi) west of this spot.]

This route leaves right from the highway to go up the southwest ridge of Gunnery Mountain, a name that is connected with roadbuilding. Billy Gunnery was an early 20th Century foreman with the Lineham Lumber Company, which pushed through a tote road known as Gunnery Grade that passes under this feature.

Cross a derelict barbed wire fence shortly after the start, and proceed along the obvious line. Some scrambling will come into play on steep rocky sections after initial meadows. Many and varied are the wildflowers that grow here, among them wild blue flax, nodding onion, alumroot, purple geranium, puccoon, stonecrop, roseroot, silver-leaved scorpionweed, white mountain avens, spotted saxifrage, and the tiny rock jasmine.

The top of Gunnery Mountain grants good views, including of many nearby ridgewalks: Bull Creek Hills (#21), "Zephyr Ridge" (#23), Mt. Burke North End of North Ridge (#22), Hells Ridge (#18), Raspberry Ridge and the three ridges north of it (#17, #19, #20, and #27), and Junction Hill (#26).

To make a loop trip, descend north—through trees at first, then more open— to the notch at gr 701865. N.B. Bear diggings here! Join a trail and follow it west until it becomes indistinct on grassy slopes of a rib. Pick it up again down in the trees, where it soon leads into and crosses a rocky drainage. It contours, then fades, at which point simply head down, keeping to the terrace.

There is an animal path on the west side of the drainage for a while, then where the creek sides get steep it's best to switch to the more open east side. Eventually come out right at the trailhead.

26 Junction Hill

Map p. 256
Photo p. 59

Distance: 6 km linear

Trail/off-trail: up to 4 hr

Elevation gain: 710 m (2330 ft)

Maximum elevation: 2230 m (7315 ft)

Map: NTS 1:50,000 Mount Head 82 J/7

Trailhead: Park off the road at Highwood Junction (the junction of Highways 541, 40, and 940), 9.4 km (5.8 mi) west of the Kananaskis Country entrance sign on Highway 541 and 38.4 km (23.8 mi) south of Highwood Pass on Highway 40.

This ridgewalk is another of the good early season choices, and can be done before the Highway 40 gate at Highwood House opens for the summer on June 15th. If done in April or May, lots of bright prairie crocus flowers will offer their greeting.

To get started, simply head northwest across open slopes past an animal exclosure. Eventually intersect the old exploration road and turn right to climb through trees (welcome shade on a hot day) around a knoll to the saddle at gr 6588848. [Another approach is to take to the ridge to the west.]

From the saddle, head north over a bump and then commence a climb of almost 400 metres elevation gain. Shortly before reaching the summit of Junction Hill, a dropoff to the north appears suddenly: turn right for the top. This vantage point grants a 360-degree view, including many other ridgewalks and the landmark of Mist Mountain off to the northwest.

It's hard to say how often it might happen, but the author had an immature golden eagle take off from just below the summit when he arrived one May 1st: it was apparently on the renowned migration north. Clark's nutcrackers, blue grouse, Townsend's solitaire, and northern flicker (a species of woodpecker) are among other birds that can be observed on this outing. Another, somewhat less appealing, form of life in the vicinity comes in the shape of ticks, drawn by the bighorn sheep that frequent the area.

The most interesting descent is via the southeast ridge, with rocky outcrops below to the west. At the very bottom, just above the highway, veer right and scoot down a steep gully to avoid sheer construction rockcuts. A saunter of less than a kilometre accomplishes the return to the beginning of this trip.

This route can easily be done in the opposite direction.

27 Strawberry Hills

Map p. 258

Distance: 13 km linear

Trail/off-trail: 4—8 hr

Elevation gain: 440 m (1445 ft)

Maximum elevation: 1965 m (6445 ft)

Map: NTS 1:50,000 Mount Head 82 J/7

Trailhead: Fitzsimmons Creek day-use area on Highway 40, 2.8 km (1.7 mi) west of Highwood Junction and 35.6 km (22.1 mi) south of Highwood Pass. **N.B.** Highway 40 between Highwood Junction and the Kananaskis Lakes spur road is closed Dec. 1st—June 15th.

This is the northernmost of the series of four ridgewalks that has its southern end at Raspberry Ridge. The Strawberry Hills feature large open high meadows with fine views.

Once across the Highwood River from the trailhead, pick up the trail southwest over the flats toward the forested valley of Fitzsimmons Creek. Take the old road along the north side of the creek to below the high point situated at gr 625835.

Turn right to ascend the ridge, which after a short distance through forest opens into grassy slopes festooned with wildflowers such as wild blue flax, silky lupine, common harebell, northern bedstraw, and kinnikinnik. The shrub wolf willow, with its distinctive odour, and limber pines, with their characteristic windswept profile, also grow in this dry south-facing habitat.

At the first high point, a well-defined trail suddenly materializes that proves to be that of horse parties coming up from Strawberry Creek. The trail drops west into a dip and climbs up to a second bump, then descends northwest into the headwaters of the creek. (Be aware that bears frequent the willow meadows in this vicinity.)

This makes an excellent approach to the higher northern portion of the Strawberry Hills, up to whose summit the route now lies. The top, as expected, has superb views of peaks on the continental divide, especially those close at hand including Mt. Armstrong, Mt. MacLaren, Mt. Strachan, and Mt. Muir. The first three names have a World War I connection, while the fourth honours Scottish-born Alexander Muir (1830-1906), who wrote the words and music of "The Maple Leaf Forever" in the year of Canadian confederation.

The summit also grants a view of the feature north of McPhail Creek that author R.M. Patterson christened the Hill of Flowers. Additionally, there are views of such other routes described in this book as Odlum Ridge (#35), Nameless Ridge (#33), "Lantern—Lineham Ridge" (#30), and Cat Creek Hills (#28).

The north end of the northwest ridge stays clear most of the way down, with

The author in the northern Strawberry Hills, looking north over a panorama including Bishop Ridge [#29] in centre beyond the Hill of Flowers, and Odlum Ridge [#35] and Nameless Ridge [#33] beneath Mist Mountain on the right.

a final treed section before Carnarvon Creek. The author ran across some pieces of flagging tape, blazed trees, and cut branches, but they didn't seem to lead anywhere, so head right to the creek, alert to some steep rocky sections just above the water that may have to be skirted.

A short ford and a scurry up the bank connect with the old road above Carnarvon Creek. Turn right and follow it out to Highway 40, with two fords (of McPhail Creek and the Highwood River) thrown in on the way.

If desirous of continuing the linked routes from Raspberry Ridge north as purely as possible, veer north off the Fitzsimmons Creek trail where Ridgewalk 20 hits it and head for the knoll at gr 634837. Then head westerly to connect with the ridgewalk described above at the first high point.

Least chipmunk on cairn in Cat Creek Hills [#28].

28 Cat Creek Hills

Map p. 258
Photo p. 63

Distance: 9 km loop

Trail/off-trail: 4—8 hr

Elevation gain: 555 m (1820 ft)

Maximum elevation: 2140 m (7020 ft)

Map: NTS 1:50,000 Mount Head 82 J/7

Trailhead: Cat Creek day-use area on Highway 40, 5.7 km (3.5 mi) west of Highwood Junction and 32.7 km (20.3 mi) south of Highwood Pass. **N.B.** Highway 40 between Highwood Junction and the Kananaskis Lakes spur road is closed Dec. 1st—June 15th.

This loop in the Cat Creek Hills is worth doing anytime between June 15th and November 30th when the stretch of Highway 40 leading past the trailhead is open. (If keen when the gate is down, the extra 6 km each way from Highwood Junction can be covered on foot or by bicycle.)

From the far end of the parking area, start off on the interpretive trail that soon crosses the highway and meanders along with intriguing stops. The route to the hills crosses the creek (ford required) where an older highway once ran; however, before taking off this way, it's recommended to make the short detour to the lower falls.

Back at the ford, pick up the old highway on the other side, then almost immediately switch left to another old road. Right away, to avoid a long zigzag, take a well-defined path up to the left. Turn left again where rejoin the old road, and continue around the curve before taking another shortcut up to the left. This connects with yet another old road, which keep on as it descends to the forks of Cat Creek.

Before the confluence, go right to travel above the east branch of Cat Creek. This old mining track {alders thriving} climbs gently to the ridge, where veer left. Now on a trail, climb toward the summit of the Cat Creek Hills [gr 653874]. The top of Junction Hill (#26) is just over a kilometre to the southeast, and the Strawberry Hills (#27) rise across the Highwood Valley to the southwest. Mist Mountain stands out to the northwest.

The panoply of wildflowers along this excursion includes northern bedstraw, sticky purple geranium, wild bergamot (horsemint), yellow columbine, pearly everlasting, stonecrop, spotted saxifrage, alumroot, and wild gaillardia (brown-eyed Susan).

Complete the loop by descending the southwest ridge, which features a couple of bumps along the way. At the bottom, either follow the old road parallel to Highway 40 back to the shortcuts and out, or continue straight down to the highway.

29 Bishop Ridge

Distance: 17 km out-and-back with loop

Trail/off-trail: 8—12 hr

Elevation gain: 870 m (2855 ft)

Maximum elevation: 2545 m (8350 ft)

Map: NTS 1:50,000 Mount Head 82 J/7

Trailhead: Park on the shoulder of Highway 40, 1.3 km (0.8 mi) north of Lineham Creek day-use area {which is 12.2 km (7.6 mi) west of Highwood Junction}, and 24.9 km (15.4 mi) south of Highwood Pass. **N.B.** Highway 40 between Highwood Junction and the Kananaskis Lakes spur road is closed Dec. 1st—June 15th.

This ridgewalk lies close to the divide, providing superb views north and south along the line of serrated limestone peaks.

To start, drop down to the Highwood and ford the river: a straightforward crossing at most times. Head northwest along a level old road to Loomis Creek, and look for a two-log footbridge just upstream from the previous crossing. Once on the far side, veer left uphill on a shortcut to the old road that goes up the valley of Loomis Creek.

The first two fords in the narrows can be avoided by staying on the north bank for 100 metres (beware of bears), and a well-defined bypass farther along skirts a wet section. But it is worse to try to bushwhack again to avoid the next two fords...far better to keep to the established track. Shortly after the second of this pair (cont. p. 66)

The high point of Bishop Ridge; Mist Mountain in centre and Mt. Lipsett [#34], Highwood Ridge [#73], and Grizzly Ridge [#74] to left.

(Cont. from p. 65) of fords, leave the valley of Loomis Creek by turning left at a junction. After a final ford, another old road heads southwest up Bishop Creek.

There is quite a bit of alder across the trail along this section, although as of 1999 some had recently been cleared. Breaking out of forest, the road curves round to traverse across open slopes below an outlier of Bishop Ridge. Across the valley to the southeast from here is the first view of the Hill of the Flowers [gr 535895], so-named by pioneer R.M. Patterson.

Pass below a saddle and continue straight at a junction farther on, working to the very head of the valley of Bishop Creek. This lies in the alpine zone, with the steep east face of Mt. Bishop rising high above. The road makes a switchback to run a short distance back east, but it should be left and a faint bulldozed track followed to the base of a gully that lies behind a rocky rib.

Now completely off-trail, hike steeply up the gully to reach the saddle at gr 513899. From here, climb northeast along the ridge, with some scrambling required at a rocky fin running across the grain of the land. The high point of Bishop Ridge [gr 516906] reveals a panorama of sharp grey peaks, the most prominent being Mt. Loomis to the northwest and Mt. McPhail to the south—known to Patterson as Pyramid Mountain, for obvious reasons. Many ridgewalks in the vicinity can also be scoped out or fondly recalled.

The most direct return is by way of the east ridge (which sports a number of unusual freestanding pinnacles) to a saddle [gr 522909]. Head down the gully on a faint path back to the road and then out to the start.

The name of the ridge, mountain, and creek are in honour of WWI pilot William A. ("Billy") Bishop, who was awarded the Victoria Cross among other medals.

Northwest from "Lantern—Lineham Ridge," with (l to r) Mist Mountain and peaks of the Misty Range, Nameless Ridge [#33], "Picklejar Hills" [#31], Mist Ridge [#32], and the Highwood Range.

30 "Lantern—Lineham Ridge"

Map p. 259
Photo p. 6

Distance: 13 km linear

Trail/off-trail: 4—8 hr

Elevation gain: 970 m (3180 ft)

Maximum elevation: 2700 m (8855 ft)

Maps: NTS 1:50,000 Mount Rae 82 J/10 and Mount Head 82 J/7

Trailhead: Lantern Creek day-use area off Highway 40, 17.4 km (10.8 mi) west of Highwood Junction and 21.0 km (13.0 mi) south of Highwood Pass. **N.B.** Highway 40 between Highwood Junction and the Kananaskis Lakes spur road is closed Dec. 1st—June 15th.

This outing involves exposed scrambling, so is best tackled by those experienced and comfortable in such maneuvers. The alternative is to do the latter portion in the opposite direction to that described, and backtrack for the return.

Take the Lantern Creek trail toward Picklejar Lakes, soon getting views of the objective ridge. Do not descend north from the saddle near the lakes [gr 567983]; rather, turn up the ridge to the east. 'Up' is the operative word here, for—as examination of the contour lines on a topo shows—the way ahead is steep and along a sharply-defined crest.

A beaten path leads up a draw between rocky outcrops, topping out on a grassy section. Ahead a slab appears to perch right on the crest, but going up through a chimney-like gap above a slight dip reveals a grassy bench to the north behind the sharp edge. This delivers one to a small flat area with another rocky bit following, which the author elected to bypass in a draw below on the north side.

Another more level bit leads to the crux of the route: a sharp rocky rib whose negotiation involves hand-over-handing on the upper edge while finding footholds on the slab. It's a short stint, perhaps 25 m long, but it may well feel longer and falling is not an option. To be succinct, this is venturing into what many would regard as roping-up ground: decide accordingly.

To maintain interest, the ridge beyond the crux remains intricate, with several mini-gendarmes and lots of small peaks-and-dips where the rock strata is tilted vertically. The ridge then veers southeast on easier ground, though there is a false summit to keep up the sense of adventure on this outing.

From the unnamed high point [gr 583978] there is a window of sight to the northeast that takes in some foothills and even the Calgary skyline. A distinctive landmark to the west is Mt. Joffre with a pronounced anticline on its east face. Of course, there are a good number of other ridgewalks in view, including "Picklejar Hills" (#31), Mist Ridge (#32), Nameless Ridge (#33), Odlum Ridge (#35), and others (cont. p. 68)

(Cont. from p. 67) to the south culminating in Raspberry Ridge (#17).

To complete the loop on this outing, descend south over moderately difficult ground to the high point [gr 582972] of what Gillean Daffern calls Lineham Ridge in her **Kananaskis Country Trail Guide, Third Edition, Volume 2** (Rocky Mountain Books, 1997). From here there is a stretch of nice grass, then a section of rockier terrain before another grassy bit previous to dropping into the trees. There is one point where a jog left must be made to stay on the desired ridge; don't drop into the west branch of Lineham Creek. This portion of the outing (which can be done as a linear trip if tricky scrambling is not in the cards) gives nice views east into the series of cirques with sharp, narrow dividing ribs along the upper basin of Lineham Creek.

A faint trail develops prior to the thick forest and leads down the ridge, which makes an elegant curve as seen from above. The trail is well-defined for the most part, but curiously becomes vague near the bottom [gr 596925]. If the way is lost, the simplest thing is to head south and soon join the trail along Lineham Creek.

Two shallow fords lead to a climb quite high onto the true right bank so as to avoid a gorge. Then it's a cruise down to Highway 40.

Southeast from eastern "Picklejar Hill;" sharply defined "Lantern—Lineham Ridge" [#30] in sunshine left of centre.

31 "Picklejar Hills"

Map p. 260

Distance: 8 km loop

Trail/off-trail: up to 4 hr

Elevation gain: 690 m (2265 ft)

Maximum elevation: 2460 m (8070 ft)

Maps: Gem Trek 1:50,000 Bragg Creek and Elbow Falls, and NTS 1:50,000 Mount Rae 82 J/10

Trailhead: Picklejar Creek day-use area off Highway 40, 20.1 km (12.5 mi) west of Highwood Junction and 18.3 km (11.3 mi) south of Highwood Pass. **N.B.** Highway 40 between Highwood Junction and the Kananaskis Lakes spur road is closed Dec. 1st—June 15th.

This short circuit provides an interesting excursion close to Highway 40.

Head up the valley of Picklejar Creek on its east side, being sure to keep right very soon after the start: just after a left turn, leave what seems to be the main trail to cross a small watercourse in muddy ground. Thereafter the way is well-defined: keep to it until past the draw leading up to the saddle between the two "Picklejar Hills."

Immediately below the southeast ridge of the eastern peak, head up on open ground to the summit [gr 546004] via the steep slope, which has a rocky rib for the last bit. (One treed section can be skirted below to the west.)

About five minutes descent leads to the saddle between the two peaks, where an old road soon ends after climbing over from the northwest. Another ten minutes is all it takes to get to the top of the western peak [gr 542998]. This affords a nice view of Mist Ridge (#32); Odlum Ridge (#35) and Nameless Ridge (#33) can also be reconnoitered from here.

Descent is by means of the southeast ridge, which sports some subalpine larches, as well as other conifers. The outbound trail is joined a mere 750 metres or so from the parking area.

Picklejar Creek gets its name from the lakes at its head (instead of the other way round, as is usual), which were thus dubbed because the angling was so easy the fish could reputedly be caught in—Guess what?—a picklejar.

32 Mist Ridge

Map p. 260

Distance: 23 km loop

Trail/off-trail: 8—12 hr

Elevation gain: 745 m (2445 ft)

Maximum elevation: 2515 m (8250 ft)

Maps: Gem Trek 1:50,000 Bragg Creek and Elbow Falls, and NTS 1:50,000 Mount Rae 82 J/10

Trailhead: Mist Creek day-use area off Highway 40, 20.6 km (12.8 mi) west of Highwood Junction and 17.8 km (11.0 mi) south of Highwood Pass. **N.B.** Highway 40 between Highwood Junction and the Kananaskis Lakes spur road is closed Dec. 1st—June 15th.

This scenic ridgewalk is a long one, best done around the time of the summer solstice.

From the trailhead, cross Highway 40, take a quick right, then turn left onto the wide trail up the valley of Mist Creek. About a kilometre later, keep right at a Y-junction and climb into a side drainage. Keep straight where a branch of the multifarious exploration roads throughout Kananaskis Country heads right toward the "Picklejar Hills" (#31). Now, somewhat discouraging, there is a loss of elevation before the climb resumes in gradual zigzags. After passing horse corrals and travelling beneath a southeastern outlier, switchback up (passing some larches) toward the south end of Mist Ridge. This is gained by a stint of gentle meadow ascent after the old road ends.

Now the real fun begins! With spacious views to either side, and easy terrain that allows relaxed enjoyment of those views, head northwesterly. There is a considerable dip after the first kilometre-long level section, but it's not a tricky descent and the elevation lost is gradually regained (with a few undulations along the way).

While sauntering along this pleasant stretch, savour such wildflowers as rock jasmine, moss campion, silky scorpionweed, golden fleabane, wild blue flax, alpine bistort, three-flowered avens, spotted saxifrage, forget-me-not, Jacob's ladder, and white mountain avens. Mountain goats, bighorn sheep, pikas, and least chipmunks appreciate the variety of flora too.

The highest point on Mist Ridge is at its north end [gr 514059], which besides the superlative view of the Misty Range to the west, now allows a glimpse into the Sheep Valley to the north. The gentler west aspect of Gibraltar Mountain, which contrasts with its sheer east face, lies revealed above a grassy saddle to the east.

Rickerts Pass [gr 501064] is the low point before the ridge continues west to Storm Mountain, and is the the bailing-off spot for this outing. (The pass is reached by either going south around the knob at gr 506061, or—more directly—by a sidling tra-

North along Mist Ridge toward Rickerts Pass.

verse to its north.)

Pick up the trail that leads all the way down the valley of Mist Creek back to the start, a somewhat anticlimactic finish to a top-of-the-line ridgewalk.

Cast-off elk antler on Nameless Ridge [#33]; Mist Ridge [#32] to northeast.

33 Nameless Ridge

Map p. 260
Photo p. 71

Distance: 7 km linear

Trail/off-trail: up to 4 hr

Elevation gain: 615 m (2015 ft)

Maximum elevation: 2480 m (8135 ft)

Maps: Gem Trek 1:50,000 Bragg Creek and Elbow Falls, and NTS 1:50 000 Mount Rae 82 J/10

Trailhead: Grassy area on north side of Highway 40, 7.0 km (4.3 mi) southeast of the Mount Lipsett day-use area and 150 m (0.1 mi) west of where Highway 40 passes over the unnamed tributary of Storm Creek in the drainage between Mt. Lipsett and Mist Mountain {25.2 km (15.6 mi) west of Highwood Junction}. **N.B.** Highway 40 between Highwood Junction and the Kananaskis Lakes spur road is closed Dec. 1st—June 15th.

This short but sweet trip takes in what was formerly unofficially known as Eagle Ridge. Head north from the edge of the trailhead meadow; the entrance is marked with large boulders, a stump, a small cairn, and a survey marker post. At an old road, turn right and parallel Highway 40 for about 400 metres, crossing the creek from the drainage between Mt. Lipsett and Mist Mountain. Continue through overgrowing vegetation, then turn left at a cairn to climb on an initially vague trail.

Break out into the open after about 30 minutes, and continue up the draw on the west side of the creek. The trail fades out below the saddle at gr 498010. This dip gives the first views north into the valley of Mist Creek. Continue up to the right (east) through a series of low rockbands to the high point [gr 503010]. This culmination of the ridge allows particularly fine views for so little effort, including Mist Ridge (#32) to the northeast, "Picklejar Hills" (#31) and "Lantern—Lineham Ridge" (#30) to the east, and Odlum Ridge (#35) to the south. Mist Mountain looms to the northwest.

The open terrain of this outing is home to such wildflowers as prairie crocus, alpine forget-me-not, rock jasmine, white mountain avens, kittentails, shooting star, alpine buttercup, silver rockcress, bladder locoweed, valerian, silky scorpionweed, spotted saxifrage, Jacob's ladder, Parry's townsendia, blue beardtongue, umbrella plant, and moss campion. Feasting on the succulent forage are pikas and elk (a cast-off antler might be seen: any found should be left as small creatures gnaw on them for vital minerals). And, yes, even if the name has changed, eagles still do frequent the area.

Completion of the outing is via descent southeast along the ridge; subalpine larches reach up almost to the crest on the east side. Follow the ridge to its end via a steep final drop-off, or bail south to a tongue of meadow that connects more directly with the highway. If preferred, the old road can be taken west back to the start.

34 Mt. Lipsett

Map p. 257

Distance: 9 km linear

Trail/off-trail: 4—8 hr

Elevation gain: 705 m (2310 ft)

Maximum elevation: 2570 m (8430 ft)

Maps: Gem Trek 1:50,000 Bragg Creek and Elbow Falls, and NTS 1:50,000 Mount Rae 82 J/10

Trailhead: As for Ridgewalk 33, Nameless Ridge. **N.B.** Highway 40 between Highwood Junction and the Kananaskis Lakes spur road is closed Dec. 1st—June 15th.

Mt. Lipsett is a low peak that has a meandering approach, but once out in the open views are good and there is an interesting exit.

The start is the same as for Nameless Ridge (#33); however, instead of going right at the old highway, go left briefly and then right. The reclaimed road gradually climbs the forested southeast ridge of Mt. Lipsett. Eventually break out above the trees and leave the old road (which soon peters out in any case) to forge a more direct line north. An almost level area precedes the summit [gr 471014], situated just over a kilometre southwest of much higher Mist Mountain.

Despite being dwarfed by its neighbour, Mt. Lipsett does grant a bird's-eye view of the valley leading northwest to Highwood Pass. It also serves as a fine place from which to suss out such other ridgewalks as Highwood Ridge (#73), Grizzly Ridge (#74), and Odlum Ridge (#35). There are some subalpine larch trees near the top, and the alpine feel of the spot is enhanced by the presence of the bright pink flowers of moss campion. It's a straightforward matter to drop northwest to a saddle and gain the lower summit at gr 462017.

Descent can be made down the ridge due south from this point, hitting the highway just north of a small stream that originates at the saddle.

Southeast from Mt. Lipsett, including Odlum Ridge [#35] to left and Bishop Ridge [#29] in centre.

35 Odlum Ridge

Map p. 257

Distance: 8 km linear

Off-trail: 4—8 hr

Elevation gain: 640 m (2100 ft)

Maximum elevation: 2497 m (8190 ft)

Maps: Gem Trek 1:50,000 Bragg Creek and Elbow Falls [east peak not shown], and NTS 1:50,000 Mount Rae 82 J/10

Trailhead: Park off Highway 40, 5.8 km (3.6 mi) southeast of the Mt. Lipsett day-use area and 1.2 km (0.7 mi) west of the trailhead for Ridgewalks 33 and 34. **N.B.** Highway 40 between Highwood Junction and the Kananaskis Lakes spur road is closed Dec. 1st—June 15th.

Sure, there is an established trail up Odlum Creek that gives access to Odlum Ridge, but it's a long approach and still involves steep off-trail travel. If we're gonna go ridgewalking, we may as well go for the gusto, so the main description here is of a direct ascent up the northwest ridge of the west peak of Odlum Ridge.

From the startpoint, head south and soon descend to Storm Creek, which is easily forded (at least most of the year). [Avoid a steep, eroded cutbank, about 400 m long, which is on the north side of the creek.] Head south again, on the east side of a small drainage. Aim for the base of the northwest ridge of the west peak [approximate gr 490975]. The going is easy and open at first, then becomes steeper and shrubby.

However, soon strike the ridge, which has a nice grassy section near the base. Then a long stretch of rocky ground lies ahead before reaching the zone of subalpine larches. Later break out of the trees and hit grassy slopes for the final stretch to the west peak [gr 499968].

From the west peak, descend east to a saddle, then climb northeast to the central peak [gr 507971]. Interesting tilted rock outcrops plunge down to the north along this section. Continuing on the traverse, drop southeast to a second saddle, then gain elevation back as veer east up to the east peak [gr 521963]. Again, there are unusual rock formations along the way.

The views from this vantage point encompass many other ridgewalks, including Nameless Ridge (#33), Mist Ridge (#32), "Picklejar Hills" (#31), "Lantern—Lineham Ridge" (#30), Cat Creek Hills (#28), Junction Hill (#26), Strawberry Hills (#27), Raspberry Ridge (#17), Bishop Ridge (#29), Grizzly Ridge (#74), Highwood Ridge (#73), and Mt. Lipsett (#34). Of course, the surrounding peaks merit attention, prominent among them being Mist Mountain nearby to the north. Also in sight are many summits of the Elk Range on the continental divide to the west, including Mt. Odlum. The name, by the way, comes from a Canadian military leader in World War I.

The author on the east peak of Odlum Ridge, looking west to the central and west peaks and the Elk Range on the skyline.

There are lots of wildflowers on Odlum Ridge, among them red paintbrush, silver-leaved scorpionweed, stonecrop, valerian, spotted saxifrage, and wild strawberry. Raptors cruise the ridges, especially in autumn, and blue grouse frequent this terrain [the author came upon one sitting guru-like on the ridge of the central peak]. Packrat sign is evident in the saddle between the central and east peaks. An unusual observation was of a spider on the cairn of the central peak, coloured orange in apparent camouflage to match the orange lichens on the rocks.

Descent from the east peak is to the north, then northwest, into the drainage from the basin between the east and central peaks. Go north, crossing Storm Creek again to hit the highway about 3 km from the trailhead. (If time, weather, or inclination suggest a quick escape off the ridge, it appears feasible to drop north from either of the west or central peaks.)

Northern aspect of Storm Mountain and abruptly truncated northwest spur from Little Arethusa [#36].

75

36 Little Arethusa

Map p. 260
Photo p. 75

Distance: 4 km linear

Trail/off-trail: up to 4 hr

Elevation gain: 565 m (1855 ft)

Maximum elevation: 2730 m (8955 ft)

Maps: Gem Trek 1:50,000 Bragg Creek and Elbow Falls, and Kananaskis Lakes; and NTS 1:50,000 Mount Rae 82 J/10

Trailhead: Park on the east shoulder of Highway 40, 1.3 km (0.8 mi) south of the entrance to the parking area 0.4 km (0.2 mi) south of Highwood Pass. **N.B.** Highway 40 between Highwood Junction and the Kananaskis Lakes spur road is closed Dec. 1st—June 15th.

The south ridge of this subpeak of Mt. Arethusa makes for a short but steep excursion near Highwood Pass. Pick up an unofficial trail leading through trees south of the creek draining from Arethusa Cirque. (Note that deep snow may lie here well into July.) Rather than following the path to its end, after some 600 metres cross the creek and head north up a draw. This leads into the basin between Little Arethusa and Mt. Arethusa, so eventually climb up to the west to gain the bottom of the south ridge of Little Arethusa. There are quite a few subalpine larches in this area.

The ascent to the top of Little Arethusa is over typically steep Rockies scree with some bigger, more solid rocks and ribs to give better purchase. Near the false summit are some unusual overhanging rock fins. The slopes to the east become progressively steeper. The south aspect of Mt. Rae hoves into sight at the summit, while below to the west lies Highwood Pass. Above the pass is Highwood Ridge (#73), beyond which can be seen some of Grizzly Ridge (#74). On the horizon to the west is Mt. Joffre, sporting a huge arched anticline on its east face; to the northwest are some of the Royal Group, Mt. Sir Douglas, and even Mt. Ball far in the distance. Below and nearby is undulating Pocaterra Ridge (#72). The impressive northern aspect of Kananaskis Country's Storm Mountain rises close by to the southeast, featuring the abruptly truncated northwest spur. Further south are the gentler contours of Mt. Lipsett (#34).

Globeflower, western anemone, and western spring beauty grace the approach to Little Arethusa, while on the ridge are found bladder locoweed, a few roseroot, silver rockcress, moss campion, and lots of purple saxifrage. Bighorn sheep gambol about with abandon on this sort of vertical landscape.

Descent can be made by reversing the route, or—if confident on steep scree with small rockbands—it's possible to beeline directly down to Highwood Pass.

Mt. Arethusa's name comes from a British warship sunk in World War I, which was in turn named after a figure of Greek mythology.

Section 3 Central Kananaskis Country

Ridgewalker John Blum on the north end of the eastern "Entrance Ridge."

Turner Valley Tune-ups

The author has grouped the ridgewalks from #37 "Entrance Ridges" to #48 Volcano Ridge and Allsmoke Mountain (except for # 45 Bluerock Mountain) as the **Turner Valley Tune-ups**. This nickname originated because they are accessible from that town in the foothills near Kananaskis Country, and because most of them are short outings that make for good warm-ups for longer ridgewalks.

The author moved to Turner Valley from Banff in 1999, and has enjoyed numerous rambles on these ridges in his new 'backyard.' Most of these ridgewalks are off-trail trips but the terrain is easy: rolling hills with many open meadows and aspen stands. The hiking season is year-round in this area, with snowfalls that usually don't accumulate deeply or last long thanks to chinook winds. (**N.B.** Highway 546 west of the Sandy McNabb campground entrance is closed December 1st—May 14th.)

These ridgewalks green up early in spring, feature myriad wildflowers in summer, and display beautiful fall colours.

---

37 "Entrance Ridges"

Map p. 261
Photo p. 77

Distance: 8 km loop

Trail/off-trail: up to 4 hr

Elevation gain: 195 m (640 ft)

Maximum elevation: 1580 m (5180 ft)

Map: NTS 1:50,000 Turner Valley 82J/9 [contour interval 50 ft]

Trailhead: Park off the road on the north side of Highway 546, 15.5 km (9.6 mi) west of the four-way stop at the intersection of Highways 22 and 546 in Turner Valley. There is a grassy shoulder off the widening in the pavement. This is just inside the eastern boundary of Kananaskis Country, which is actually some 0.3 km (0.2 mi) east of the entrance sign.

"Entrance Ridges" are so-named because of their location near the entrance to Kananaskis Country on Highway 546.

Go north from the trailhead, possibly having to skirt west of a boggy area. Stay to the west of a fence; if the gate at the junction with a fence running west is closed, re-close it upon passing through. Descend steeply to a meadow, whose watercourse can be crossed via a culvert slightly west of the fenceline. A well-defined animal trail leads north, but soon forsake it in order to do this route in the direction described. (It can just as easily be done the other way round, but this approach gets higher sooner.) Go northwest up open grassy slopes to gain a gentler grade on the ridge;

views west to rugged peaks quickly appear.

Wildflowers such as prairie crocus, shooting star, three-flowered avens, golden bean, and wild strawberry adorn the ground early in the season. Later on, such species as western wood lily, both red and yellow paintbrush, heart-leaved arnica, low larkspur, northern bedstraw, death camas, lungwort, puccoon, forget-me-not, and yellow locoweed make their appearance.

Red-tailed hawks nest in the area. American kestrels and Townsend's solitaires also occur in the vicinity, and elk (or at least sign of them) can be found. This westernmost of the two ridges is more heavily vegetated yet still quite open, mostly being covered in trembling aspen. A faint trail follows its crest.

The high point of the day is at the northwest end of this arm [gr 782156]. Descend east to the saddle at gr 785157, where a salt lick for cattle can be seen. From the dip between the two ridges, it is a short climb (albeit through some thick young aspens) to the eastern ridge.

Before veering southeast to complete the loop, it is worth indulging curiosity to take the well-defined track to the northwest for a bit. The going is level for a while, then drops to an open stretch before going into the trees to reach a second meadow area. This gives views to the chain of four landmarks of Mt. Glasgow, Mt. Cornwall, Banded Peak, and Outlaw.

Otherwise, views west from this arm are blocked by its slightly higher neighbour to the west, but compensation comes in the more open going and sweeping vistas over classic foothills landscapes. The good going finishes before the true southeast end of the ridge when come to a fence that marks the demarcation with private property, so drop off south along the fence line.

There is a potentially wet section in the hollow before the southeast end of the first of these two ridges (coltsfoot blooms early here). This can be avoided by taking a sharp turn west at a "No Hunting or Trespassing" sign on the boundary fence at the base of the sideslope, to connect with a trail through trees. This leads back to the fence, where go up a slight rise to join the inbound route, which is followed out.

The wetlands to the east, although not in a protected area, still harbour a variety of wildlife, including common snipe. These chunky birds are easily recognized in flight by their long bills, but it is difficult to locate the males when they are doing their high "winnowing" courtship displays, in which those mysterious ventriloquistic sounds are made during swoops with the tail feathers held out and vibrated by the air.

38 "High Noon Hills"

Map p. 261

Distance: 5 km out-and-back

Off-trail: up to 4 hr

Elevation gain: 100 m (330 ft)

Maximum elevation: 1540 m (5050 ft)

Map: NTS 1:50,000 Turner Valley 82 J/9 [contour interval 50 ft]

Trailhead: Park off the road on the north or south side of Highway 546 near a device protected by wooden poles, 1.9 km (1.2 mi) west of the entrance sign to Kananaskis Country. (There is an ample parking area at the Sheep River ranger station, 1.1. km (0.7 mi) further west.)

These low hills make for an enjoyable ramble. The unofficial name comes from that of the ranch to the east of the Kananaskis Country boundary, which this ridgewalk reaches.

Go east a short distance from the trailhead to where the road embankment starts rising, then head southeast to a gate in the fence parallel to the highway. Soon reach a large meadow and skirt along its left edge. Curve right at the top of the open area to join a well-defined animal path that leads onto the ridgecrest.

Continue southeasterly, mostly through aspen groves, to the high point of the first hill at the tip of a grassy meadow [gr 785124]. A carpet of wildflowers covers this area in season, among them low larkspur, silky lupine, forget-me-not, wild carrot, golden bean, puccoon, and yellow violet. Other species that can be found on this jaunt include prairie crocus, shooting star, wild strawberry, fireweed, wild rose, meadow rue, heart-leaved arnica, northern bedstraw, lungwort, star-flowered Solomon's seal, purple geranium, early blue violet, three-flowered avens, yellow locoweed, blue-eyed grass, and paintbrush. Elk are common in the area; their winter gnawing can be seen on the bark of many aspens.

From the first hill, descend to the saddle at gr 790124, then climb to the high point of the day at gr 794125. This is just west of the summit of this second hill, which lies on the other side of the fence marking the boundary between Kananaskis Country and the High Noon Ranch. As the sign says, "No Trespassing." The view from the meadow at the top is expansive, taking in "Sandy McNabb Hills" (#40), Windy Point Ridge (#42), and Foran Grade Ridge (#41).

Return is by backtracking, by no means a bad thing.

Wildflowers on the western "High Noon Hill;" Highwood Range in distance.

West from "Long Prairie Ridge" [#39], including Bluerock Mountain [#45] left of centre, and Windy Point Ridge [#42] above Foran Grade Ridge [#41] in centre.

39 "Long Prairie Ridge"

Map p. 261
Photos p. 7 and p. 81

Distance: 5 km out-and-back (or loop)

Trail/off-trail: up to 4 hr

Elevation gain: 120 m (395 ft)

Maximum elevation: 1540 m (5050 ft)

Maps: Gem Trek 1:50,000 Bragg Creek and Elbow Falls, and NTS 1:50,000 Mount Rae 82 J/10

Trailhead: Park off Highway 546 near an exclosure 300 metres (0.2 mi) west of the entrance to the Sheep River ranger station, which is 3.0 km (1.9 mi) west of the Kananaskis Country boundary.

This route gets its unofficial name from Long Prairie Creek to the northeast, even though the drainage can't be easily seen from the ridge. There are, however, great views to the west from this level, open feature (most of which can't be seen from the road).

Head north from the trailhead, picking up a path to the east of the exclosure. Go through a gate after approx. 250 metres, and turn left on a wide trail (used for cross-country skiing when there's enough snow). This travels on a contour for about 700 metres before reaching a large meadow to the north. Veer up right here—there's a bit of trail below the trees. Keep angling up right to reach the ridgecrest: this course avoids an area of fallen trees, apparently blown down in a windstorm, that lies further south.

Now bend left to follow the remarkably level ridge running in a northwesterly direction; despite the green colouration on the topo maps, there are big meadows with views to the west. The panorama takes in rolling foothills, a horizon full of mountains, and nearer at hand such tempting options as Foran Grade Ridge (#41) and Windy Point Ridge (#42).

The ridge runs for over a kilometre, with a semblance of a path in many places. Partway along cross two trails, the first in a corridor of small aspens in a meadow, the second the wider Death Valley trail among aspens. (That trail's name comes from the fact that it drops into Death Valley Creek, itself so called following the demise of horses who gorged on lush grass.)

Wildflowers that thrive on this ridge include fireweed, wild strawberry, silky lupine, wild rose, blue-eyed grass, both white and purple geranium, puccoon, yarrow, shrubby cinquefoil, low larkspur, death camas, and western wood lily. Wild horses frequent this area, as well as black bears and mule deer.

Sticking to the gentle ridge on easy ground regardless of the lack of well-defined trails, keep above the valley for as long as possible. Moose Mountain comes into sight off to the north. Eventually the grassy slopes end. Either stay high by returning the same way, or take a cutline (which fortuitously appears just at this point) down to the left, soon hitting a trail. Turn left again on what can have muddy stretches.

On single track through the open bits, stay at the base of the ridge, ignoring a trail to the right (not actually connected to this one) that goes into the trees. This path soon heads into forest too, and after a vague section all of a sudden joins the wide cross-country ski trails again at a three-way junction.

Going left on the Death Valley Link leads most directly to the highway near the access road into Sandy McNabb campground, if desired (e.g. if a car shuttle is set up). Straight ahead a pleasant stroll along the Long Prairie Loop leads back to the start, the only possible fly-in-the-ointment being a five-way intersection where stumble upon [not literally, hopefully] the new barbed wire fence. Keep on the main track, which soon veers left into the open field where took off from the trail near the start. To get to the trailhead, keep to the track as it runs along the edge of the meadow to the right and winds through the trees on a level course, now on familiar ground.

Northwest from western "Sandy McNabb Hill" [#40]; Windy Point Ridge [#42] above Foran Grade Ridge [#41] in centre.

40 "Sandy McNabb Hills"

Map p. 261
Photo p. 83

Distance: 6 km out-and-back

Trail/off-trail: up to 4 hr

Elevation gain: 60 m (195 ft)

Maximum elevation: 1490 m (4885 ft)

Maps: NTS 1:50,000 Mount Rae 82 J/10 [contour interval 100 ft] and Turner Valley 82 J/9 [contour interval 50 ft]

Trailhead: Turn left into Sandy McNabb campground, 1.7 km (1.1 mi) west of the Sheep River ranger station, and turn left again immediately to park in the open area before the loop road of the equestrian campground.

These two hills above the Sheep River east of Sandy McNabb Campground hold their unofficial name in further commemoration of that pioneer conservationist. Alexander "Sandy" McNabb appreciated the wild qualities of the region, perhaps like places he had known in his native Scotland, and as a Turner Valley resident in the early 1900s frequented this area on fishing trips.

Starting from the trailhead signs on the south side of the parking area, go about 20 metres, then turn left. Some 75 metres further on, at a post numbered "31," keep straight; the main trail goes right. Keep straight until approximately 100 metres beyond a post with map and the number "37," and a nearby picnic table. Now go ahead where the main trail (arrows) turns left.

The way is vague at first but soon a well-defined trail leads up to the western hill, trees on the left and open meadows on the right. A sudden drop-off to the east marks the top, which grants views of Bluerock Mountain (#45), Windy Point Ridge (#42), and Foran Grade Ridge (#41).

A beaten path continues down beside an old fence, easily stepped over at the bottom of the initial grade. From this point on, navigation is cross-country but easy, up and down a series of dips and bumps. Pass a well-defined trail in the first saddle (and perhaps briefly step onto a cross-country ski trail) en route to the east hill.

A spot used for salt blocks is seen along the way, as well as an apparent hunting platform in a tree. Mule deer and elk use the vicinity. Wildflowers on this outing include puccoon, heart-leaved arnica, yellow locoweed, star-flowered Solomon's seal, dwarf larkspur, silky lupine, a wild mint, and lungwort in shady spots.

The clearest views east are from the south ridge of the small knoll with lodgepole pines at the southeast end of the east hill [gr 776110]. The "High Noon Hills" (#38) are visible, as well as the valley of the Sheep River and foothills terrain outside of Kananaskis Country.

Return by retracing your steps.

41 Foran Grade Ridge

Map p. 262

Distance: 7 km loop

Trail/off-trail: up to 4 hr

Elevation gain: 235 m (770 ft)

Maximum elevation: 1685 m (5525 ft)

Maps: Gem Trek 1:50,000 Bragg Creek and Elbow Falls, and NTS 1:50,000 Mount Rae 82 J/10

Trailhead: Parking area on the north side of Highway 546, 1.6 km (1.0 mi) west of the entrance to Sandy McNabb campground, at sign for Sheep River Wildlife Sanctuary. **N.B.** Highway 546 west of the Sandy McNabb campground entrance is closed December 1st—May 14th.

This is an easy loop with good views, making an excellent early season choice.

Pick up the trail just to the east of the parking area, and soon go through a gate, then into a large meadow. Shortly enter the trees (mostly aspen) and wind up to the ridge.

The first open view is to the west over the gorge of the Sheep River and up the valley, with such landmarks as Bluerock Mountain (#45), the east face of Gibraltar Mountain, Mist Mountain, and Junction Mountain. Windy Point Ridge (#42) is nearer at hand.

Shooting star, wild strawberry, and kinnikinnik can be seen along the ridge, while lower down on this outing grow wild gaillardia (brown-eyed Susan), three-flowered avens, early blue violet, and low larkspur. Blue grouse frequent the (cont. p. 86)

The author at the north end of Foran Grade Ridge, looking northwest.

(Cont. from p. 85) ridge; yellow-bellied sapsuckers (vocal in spring) and northern flickers—both woodpecker species—occur in the vicinity.

Continue northerly along the ridge, passing a short avenue of flat stones leading to a viewpoint, and eventually travel in forest with limited views west. Where the trail drops off the ridge to the west, it's worthwhile keeping to the crest and continuing north on a faint path to open meadows for fine views.

Either way, switchback down to the saddle and trail junction at gr 721149, and turn left to head down south to the highway. [Note that if the connection to Windy Point Ridge (#42) is attempted, it is stiff going up a steep grassy slope and that stinging nettle grows among the trees near the bottom.]

Once down to the highway, cross the road and take the trail parallel to the traffic but below it and with much better views into the Sheep River gorge. A section through meadow leads gently up to a signed junction mere metres from the start.

As an alternative approach to this ridgewalk, try doing it the other way round. Start at the parking area left off the highway, 1.7 km west of the trailhead described above, and pick up the trail in the grassy meadow ahead at the edge of the gorge of the Sheep River. Turn right and cross the road in 100 metres to pick up the Windy Point trail, which leads up the draw to the saddle. Turn right on the Foran Grade Ridge trail, zigzagging up to the ridgeline (once there, taking the detour to the left is recommended).

Take the trail southward from the high point, and to finish this shorter but more scenic option, stay south on the ridge where the trail crosses over to descend to the east. Soon break into meadows, with an area of cleared trees, and reach the true end of the ridge. Descend to the highway and cross to the trail above the Sheep River to return to the beginning.

West from first high point of Windy Point Ridge.

42 Windy Point Ridge

Map p. 262

Distance: 9 km linear

Off-trail: 4—8 hr

Elevation gain: 285 m (935 ft)

Maximum elevation: 1750 m (5740 ft)

Maps: Gem Trek 1:50,000 Bragg Creek and Elbow Falls, and NTS 1:50,000 Mount Rae 82 J/10

Trailhead: Parking area on the south side of Highway 546, 4.5 km (2.8 mi) west of the entrance to Sandy McNabb campground. **N.B.** Highway 546 west of the Sandy McNabb campground entrance is closed December 1st—May 14th.

This easily accessible ridge has attractive open meadows at its south end; although the going becomes more forested farther on, it's still an enjoyable ramble.

At the start, there is a new (2000) gate through the barbed wire fence. Ahead lies a steep haul up grassy slopes. The grind is mitigated by excellent views right away and by a plenitude of wildflowers. These include prairie crocus, shooting star, yellow locoweed, golden bean, puccoon, early blue violet, silver-leaved scorpionweed, yellow draba, kinnikinnik, and wild strawberry. Shrubby species include juniper and wolf willow.

Bighorn sheep wander about nonchalantly, and lots of their droppings lie on the ground. Evidence of bushy-tailed woodrats is visible on the precipitous rocks of the cliffband.

The ridge tapers up to a grassy top, then there is a short level section (embroidered with trembling aspen on the left) before a high point. The slightly higher 'summit' hides in the trees a little farther on, with a defined trail leading to it. Continuing northwest entails a slight descent, in quite open terrain, to a bump at gr 713152.

An open slope drops southwest from this knoll, but the main ridge runs on northward. A well-used game trail stays on the crest among trees, with scat of predators and prey. Before the high point around gr 712158, descent can be made east on mostly open ground (one fence in the meadow) to connect with the Windy Point trail. It in turn leads up the valley of a branch of Death Valley Creek to the saddle at the junction with the north end of the Foran Grade Ridge trail. Head down to the highway, or perhaps take in Foran Grade Ridge too (#41).

The main route continues northerly from the high point, then drops west to a saddle. A short climb west leads to a section of open ridge with views west. Keep north over undulations to a wide cutline [gr 704169]. Descend to the southwest (steep at first, wet areas later) to intersect the Missinglink trail at gr 688164, where turn south out to the highway in about 3 km.

43 Green Mountain

Map p. 261

Distance: 9 km out-and-back with loop

Trail/off-trail: 4—8 hr

Elevation gain: 395 m (1295 ft)

Maximum elevation: 1845 m (6050 ft)

Maps: Gem Trek 1:50,000 Bragg Creek and Elbow Falls, and NTS 1:50,000 Mount Rae 82 J/10

Trailhead: Park off Highway 546 at the Gorge Creek bridge in the pronounced dip 500 metres (0.3 mi) west of the junction with Gorge Creek Trail (gravel road). [Don't block access to the facilities on the northeast side.] **N.B.** Highway 546 west of the Sandy McNabb campground entrance is closed December 1st—May 14th.

This description gives the most direct approach to Green Mountain: a route that entails a ford of the Sheep River, which could be hazardous.

Drop to the river and cross to the south bank, a straightforward maneuver except in high water. Go south through fairly open terrain to pick up an old logging road climbing up to the west. This leads to a terrace above the river, where the road turns south, goes through a gate, and shortly arrives at a large meadow with views of Green Mountain. Keep south to intersect the Sheep Trail, used mainly by equestrian parties. Take this south to Dyson Falls, ignoring orange diamonds and keeping straight on the shortcut just before, then go east to cross the creek. Climb up past the intersection with the Junction fire lookout trail and climb gradually.

Before the trail descends, leave the established path and cut up to the north. If a bit of a dip is encountered, head up right until it tapers off. There are steep open slopes and unusual rock formations; the survey markers at the 'summit' are in a treed area. A partial traverse of Green Mountain can be made by heading northwest from the top, through trees at first but later in the open. The terrain tends to direct the traveller to the northwest, above a cliffband; staying on a course for the north ridge may be an option. The final descent is over rocky ground; pikas like the country, though ankles may not.

At the bottom, where the going becomes more level near Dyson Creek, pick up the wide cutline (overgrown in places) that runs southwest back to the inbound route.

Rock formations on Green Mountain; Bluerock Mountain [#45] on right skyline.

Bluerock Mountain [#45] from northernmost "Indian Oils Hill" [#44].

44 "Indian Oils Hills"

Map p. 261
Photo p. 89

Distance: 6 km loop

Off-trail: up to 4 hr

Elevation gain: 390 m (1280 ft)

Maximum elevation: 1935 m (6345 ft)

Maps: Gem Trek 1:50,000 Bragg Creek and Elbow Falls, and NTS 1:50,000 Mount Rae 82 J/10

Trailhead: Indian Oils parking area off Highway 546, 5.0 km (3.1 mi) from the junction with Gorge Creek Trail {road}. **N.B.** Highway 546 west of the Sandy McNabb campground entrance is closed December 1st—May 14th.

This route makes for an interesting circuit, albeit with some bushwhacking. The first part of the outing leads to a hillock with good views.

Simply cross the road from the trailhead and get on the east side of a small drainage, then traverse up right through mixed aspens and conifers to a grassy slope. Either stay on this slope for a while and then angle up right to the ridge, or—for a more adventurous option—gain the rocky rib.

This could be named "Packrat Rib" as there is abundant evidence of those rodents. Note that unless prepared for rather steep quasi-technical climbing, it's best to avoid the lower sections of this rib. Higher up there's easier scrambling, where it's possible to enjoy ferns and sage.

Either way, reach gentler ground on the ridge and continue up, with limber pines dotting the ridge. Golden bean (also called buffalo bean), a yellow member of the pea family, blooms on the ridge in spring. Stonecrop occurs near the top.

The summit of the hillock is open and affords a 360-degree vista. Revealed to the northwest are the peaks of Threepoint and Bluerock mountains, the latter of which is traversed on Ridgewalk 45. More to the north, rounded Mt. Ware stands out and Surveyor Ridge can be discerned (both visited on Ridgewalk 47). Almost due north and farther off is the south end of Volcano Ridge (#48), then to the northeast is Missinglink Mountain (#46). To the south is Junction Mountain, with the Junction fire lookout on its northeast ridge.

A short trip can be made by returning from here, but it's possible to continue on to make a loop. It should be feasible to drop west to a saddle with a small lake (according to the map), then go up to intersect the Indian Oils trail. But the going looks heavy through thick coniferous forest, and although the distance is greater, the ridge to the north is open and features animal paths. Taking it leads down to the small meadow at gr 622113, from which head west taking faint animal paths. Gain elevation to intersect the established Indian Oils trail about 1.5 km east of the saddle at gr 612104 {rest bench and hitching post}.

From here it's an easy ascent northwest to the knoll at gr 611106, which represents the high point of this outing. It offers views mainly to the west, though from the northern edge of the open area there are glimpses of Mt. Rose and Threepoint Mountain. Back at the saddle, the trail can serve as an exit. However, if in an exploratory frame of mind, keep southeasterly and soon come to the edge of a cliffband. Follow along the level top of this feature until it drops off.

Skirt left to avoid the steep section, then from the bottom of the meadow head down through forest, aiming left to cross a small creek and pick up the final knoll at gr 622101. Where the level top of this ends, veer right to hit open meadow, which follow down and around to the east before making the final steep descent to the highway near the start.

Cave with icicles on traverse of Bluerock Mountain [#45].

45 Bluerock Mountain

Map p. 263
Photo p. 91

Distance: 22 km out-and-back with loop

Trail/off-trail: 8—12 hr

Elevation gain: 1210 m (3970 ft)

Maximum elevation: 2810 m (9215 ft)

Maps: Gem Trek 1:50,000 Bragg Creek and Elbow Falls, and NTS 1:50,000 Mount Rae 82 J/10

Trailhead: Turn north off Highway 546 at the entrance to the Bluerock equestrian campground, which is 1.0 km (0.6 mi) west of the entrance to the Bluerock campground. Keep straight at the 3-way intersection after 200 metres (0.1 mi), then after just 20 metres turn left into a parking area. **N.B.** Highway 546 west of the Sandy McNabb campground entrance is closed December 1st—May 14th.

This ain't one of the "Turner Valley Tune-up's" (see p. 78); rather, it's an alpine ridgewalk with sections of difficult scrambling—best left until quite a few other ridgewalks are under the belt.

Take the trail that starts on an old logging road on the south side of Bluerock Creek. After about 2 km, drop abruptly to cross the creek. Work northwest up the slopes above the creek, reaching a small rest bench in meadows at the high point of the trail in a further 3.5 km or so. The elevation gain to this spot is already over 500 m, but there's that and more to go!

The ridgewalk proper leaves the trail to push north on increasingly rocky ground. Gain a level stretch after reaching a subpeak, but before proceeding have a look ahead to the crux to decide whether to attempt it or not. To avoid the major cliffband that blocks the ridge, suffer some sidehill-gouging to the left on loose stuff to reach the base of a gully that provides the key to this traverse.

Note that this is tricky terrain, challenging enough that downclimbing would be dicey. Take care, and back off if that's the wise move. Wet sections due to melting snow may present particular hazards.

If get to the top of this gully, the rest of the traverse is quite straightforward. A surprise along the way is a small cave, which could have icicles inside. Along this ridgewalk, it might feel as if on a remote expedition, then the incongruous sound of bawling cattle will carry up from below to the east: welcome to multiple-use country...

The summit of Bluerock Mountain gives extensive vistas, including of numerous other ridgewalks. Among them are Missinglink Mountain Southwest Ridge (#46), Windy Point Ridge (#42), Foran Grade Ridge (#41), "Long Prairie Ridge" (#39), "High Noon Hills" (#38), "Sandy McNabb Hills" (#40), and Green Mountain (#43). There is a register at top, in a small piece of PVC pipe.

There is a descent route into the northwest headwaters of Gorge Creek, however going that way would make for a very long day. The option is to go due north down to the notch at gr 550155, and then bail east. The proviso here is that this is back into steep scrambling again, with a leap of about two metres necessary to get through the last rockband onto easier terrain. This jump is onto potentially ankle-turning scree; it will help if there's snow to land on (as there may still be even in late July).

Take the drainage to the east, on a moraine-like crest at first and then meadows, to intersect the Gorge Creek trail. Turn south and go a little over 1 km to the junction with the Bluerock Creek trail. Turn southwest onto it and climb about 300 m over some 3.5 km to the high point reached earlier (much earlier) in the day. The rest of the way back is familiar, though by this stage it's not likely to pass in a blur.

The name of Bluerock Mountain is descriptive of its geology.

West-facing cliff on Missinglink Mountain Southwest Ridge [#46].

46 Missinglink Mountain Southwest Ridge

Map p. 261
Photo p. 93

Distance: 5 km loop

Road/off-trail: up to 4 hr

Elevation gain: 330 m (1080 ft)

Maximum elevation: 1830 m (6000 ft)

Maps: Gem Trek 1:50,000 Bragg Creek and Elbow Falls, and NTS 1:50,000 Mount Rae 82 J/10

Trailhead: Although there is a small area on the west side of Gorge Creek Trail (road) 1.2 km (0.7 mi) from the junction with Highway 546 that can conceivably be used to pull off, it's preferable to pull off to the left about 300 metres (0.2 mi) after the junction. **N.B.** Highway 546 west of the Sandy McNabb campground entrance, and Gorge Creek Trail, are closed December 1st—May 14th.

This short jaunt on the southwest ridge of Missinglink Mountain (an enigmatic name with no official explanation) includes an enjoyable saunter along the level top of a cliffband.

From the trailhead, walk north along the narrow dirt road for almost 1 km. There is little traffic, and the possibility of sighting a black bear. At the base of the southwest ridge, head up the open slope pocked with ground squirrel burrows. Those small mammals savour the abundant forage in their neighbourhood. Among the wildflowers to be found are three-flowered avens, puccoon, dwarf larkspur, shooting star, wild strawberry, yellow locoweed, a wild mint, and star-flowered Solomon's seal with its symmetrical leaves and exquisite blossoms. Fireweed, cow parsnip, wild rose, and shrubby cinquefoil also thrive in these conditions.

Near and above the cliffband are wolf willow, kinnikinnik, a fern species, a fleabane, forget-me-not, and a few clumps of spotted saxifrage. Limber pines with their characteristic windswept silhouettes grow in this zone too.

Views from the top of the cliff include the forested northern sides of Green Mountain (#43), and Junction fire lookout with Junction Mountain to its right. Bluerock Mountain (#45) lies to the west, while Surveyors Ridge and Mt. Ware (#47) rise to the northwest.

A game trail runs in from the edge of the cliff, the top of which is almost flat and is accommodatingly open. From the north end of the cliff, an open slope beckons above to the right. It's worth exploring this, but don't bother continuing north through forest to the cutline shown on maps. Rather, for an easy and enjoyable descent, backtrack to the end of the cliff and drop to the west on open slopes. A draw at the bottom quickly leads to the road, hitting it about 600 metres from where started up the ridge.

47 Surveyors Ridge and Mt. Ware

Map p. 262

Distance: 16 km loop

Trail/off-trail: 4—8 hr

Elevation gain: 545 m (1790 ft)

Maximum elevation: 2155 m (7070 ft)

Maps: Gem Trek 1:50,000 Bragg Creek and Elbow Falls, and NTS 1:50,000 Mount Rae 82 J/10

Trailhead: Turn west off Gorge Creek Trail {road} into Gorge Creek trailhead, 4.3 km (2.7 mi) north of the junction with Highway 546. **N.B.** Highway 546 west of the Sandy McNabb campground entrance, and Gorge Creek Trail, are closed December 1st—May 14th.

This route constitutes an enjoyable loop in seldom-visited country.

Head up Gorge Creek for just over a kilometre, then veer right (don't ford the creek) to go up the north fork. Keep left at the Y-junction in about another kilometre, and rise to a junction on the divide between this arm of Gorge Creek and the south fork of Volcano Creek.

(The summit of Volcano Ridge (#48) lies about 3.5 km away, first right to just past the pass, then left on an old road to climb to the high point at the south end of the curiously-named ridge. The walk there and then northeast along the ridge to Allsmoke Mountain is described in the next entry.)

Meanwhile, for Surveyors Ridge—having worked in land surveying at one stage, the author was attracted by this name—go left, then shortly after keep left again on an old road. Just before breaking into a meadow, pick up a narrow (cont. p. 96)

Cairn on Surveyors Ridge; Volcano Ridge and Allsmoke Mountain [#48] to the northeast.

(Cont. from p. 95) trail that links with another cutline road. Follow this to the north-west on a rising traverse, along which is a huge midden with tunnels: home to generations of red squirrels. At the T-junction with another cutline, turn left and head up.

Where the cutline dives down, it's time to forge a route *sans* trail by turning left on the ridge. Head toward the big cairn at the north end of Surveyors Ridge. From it, Calgary is in sight to the east, the canyon of Volcano Creek lies below to the north, and Forgetmenot Mountain (which blocks Moose Mountain from this spot) rises to the northwest.

To continue the ridgewalk, proceed southwest along the generally level top of Surveyors Ridge for almost a kilometre before beginning to drop. By going a little farther than makes for the most direct line and then climbing a little bit extra, to the little knoll at gr 584168, the descent southeast on a wide ramp will be over grassy slopes rather than in forest.

The ridge narrows and turns southwest at the bottom; a section of animal trail leads to a cluster of three dead trees above a steep dropoff. Next the route calls for another change of direction—southeast again—over a plateau toward Mt. Ware. The summit ridge of Mt. Ware is joined west of the cairn, from which there are surprisingly panoramic views. Bluerock Mountain (#45) to the west is the highlight of the vista, though lots of other peaks vie for attention.

To complete the circle, get off Mt. Ware (may have a short cliffband to negotiate) and head southeast until join the Gorge Creek trail, which follow out to the trail-head.

The name of Mt. Ware honours John Ware, an African-American who made his way to Alberta on a cattle drive from Texas in 1882 and stayed to become a respected pioneer rancher. He homesteaded in the Sheep River Valley in 1891 before leaving for the southeastern part of the province in 1902 when the foothills became too crowded for his taste.

Southwest from south base of Volcano Ridge; Bluerock Mountain [#45] on the right skyline, with Mt. Ware [#47] to its left and Surveyors Ridge [#47] to its right.

48 Volcano Ridge and Allsmoke Mountain Map p. 264

Distance: 17 km linear

Trail/off-trail: 4—8 hr

Elevation gain: 580 m (1900 ft)

Maximum elevation: 2120 m (6955 ft)

Maps: Gem Trek 1:50,000 Bragg Creek and Elbow Falls, and NTS 1:50,000 Mount Rae 82 J/10

Trailhead: Volcano Ridge parking area on the west side of Gorge Creek Trail {road}, 7.9 km (4.9 mi) north of Highway 546 via Turner Valley and 14.1 km (8.7 mi) south of Highway 549 via Millarville. **N.B.** Highway 546 west of the Sandy McNabb campground entrance, and Gorge Creek Trail, are closed December 1st to May 14th.

The first reconnaissance by the author to the summit of Volcano Ridge did not entice him onward, but second thoughts saw him return to enjoy a rewarding ridgewalk that is not too heavily treed after all.

A well-established trail leads west from the parking area, rolling gently through forest at first, later climbing steeply to a faint junction shortly before the saddle at gr 620180. Turn right here to undulate a bit more before commencing the steeper ascent up to the rounded knoll at the summit of Volcano Ridge [gr 616197].

Towers on the Calgary skyline break the horizon to the northeast, and a whole slew of other landmarks lies revealed in the 360-degree view. Salient features include: Surveyors Ridge and Mt. Ware (#47) to the southwest, with beyond them Bluerock Mountain (#45); and Forgetmenot Mountain (#52), Quirk Ridge (#51), and Moose Mountain (#50 and #58) to the northwest.

Surprisingly, elephanthead, a species usually associated with wetlands, grows near the top of this open, dry ridge. Rocky Mountain rhododendron, with its shrubby growth form, shiny green leaves, and waxy white flowers when in bloom, also thrives in the vicinity.

Of course, the length of Volcano Ridge running northeast to Allsmoke Mountain lies revealed, and it's a simple matter to check it out. Descend east at first, then turn northerly (crossing a cutline) and stride gradually up-and-down for almost 5 km, keeping in the open as much as possible. The south side of the summit of Allsmoke Mountain is treed, but—lo and behold, the effort is rewarded—the north side has an open area at the very top. The top of Allsmoke Mountain grants views of Nihahi and Compression ridges (#53) . There is an eyecatching waterfall at the confluence of Volcano and Threepoint creeks, its white cascades contrasting with the black walls of the gorge. (cont. p. 98)

(Cont. from p. 97)

Return could be made the same way, however a more direct alternative exists...albeit with routefinding required. Descend along the east ridge of Allsmoke Mtn. (some alders, a faint trail) to open meadows, where the ridge veers southeast. Follow it down, eventually moving into forested terrain. The going can get confusing with various cutlines, trails, and old roads: the objective is to get to the small meadow at the confluence on Ware Creek at gr 664215.

Here an old track solidifies, bending through 180 degrees to cross the tributary creek and climb up the west bank. It next turns south, then drops to the main branch in its gap between two hills. The going can be boggy and vague here, but it's better than bushwhacking! When hit a barbed wire fence with gate, the end is in sight.

Hit Gorge Creek Trail (gravel road) 2.4 km north of the trailhead; a "No Motorized Vehicles Beyond This Point" sign situated just in from the road helps in recognizing the spot.

The name of Volcano Ridge is a misnomer; there is very little igneous rock in the Rockies. The name may be connected with that of Allsmoke Mountain, which may have to do with Stoney people smoking out a black bear from its den.

View southwest from "Ranger Ridge" [#49].

Section 4 Northern Kananaskis Country

Summit of Moose Mountain from north peak; helicopter about to land at fire lookout.

49 Ranger Ridge

Map p. 263
Photo p. 98

Distance: 8 km loop

Trail/off-trail: up to 4 hr

Elevation gain: 265 m (870 ft)

Maximum elevation: 1660 m (5445 ft)

Maps: Gem Trek 1:50,000 Bragg Creek and Elbow Falls, and NTS 1:50,000 Bragg Creek 82 J/15

Trailhead: Allen Bill Pond day-use area, on the south side of Highway 66 (Elbow Falls Trail) 4.8 km (3.0 mi) west of the Kananaskis Country entrance sign.

This feature, whose unofficial name alludes to the ranger station below, is on the popular Fullerton Loop trail.

East of the easternmost parking area near Allen Bill Pond, the trail turns north to pass under Highway 66. The trail stays close to the river for a while (but not too close: it has been re-routed where floods caused washouts), then veers left. Go through a gate and keep left at a marked junction.

Shortly afterward, reach Fullerton Loop. The most direct approach to Ranger Ridge is to turn left again, climbing steeply (on stairs at first) to quickly gain the open ridge. This affords fine views south and west; to get a vista to the north, continue beyond the meadow section through forest.

The trail meanders along, with occasional glimpses of Moose Mountain, until turning east to descend and complete the loop. For more views, however, continue northwest on a path that contours for about 100 metres before petering out at the base of an open slope. Clamber up this to the top of the meadow and keep northerly to cross a cutline some 75 metres beyond the end of the first meadow.

Pushing through for approx. 150 metres from this cutline reveals a second meadow. Here is a panorama including Moose Mountain (#50), the top of Powderface Ridge (#54), Forgetmenot Ridge (#52) {with the wooded east aspect of Quirk Ridge (#51) in front}, and Volcano Ridge and Allsmoke Mountain (#48).

Return to the official trail and go back to the start by turning left to make a partial loop.

50 Moose Mountain and North Peak

Map p. 265
Photo p. 99

Distance: 18 km out-and-back with loop

Trail/off-trail: 4—8 hr

Elevation gain: 460 m (1510 ft)

Maximum elevation: 2438 m (7995 ft)

Maps: Gem Trek 1:50,000 Bragg Creek and Elbow Falls, and NTS 1:50,000 Bragg Creek 82 J/15

Trailhead: Turn north off Highway 66 (Elbow Falls Trail) onto Moose Mountain Road, 9.0 km (5.6 mi) west of the Kananaskis Country entrance sign. (**N.B.** This road is closed from 8 a.m. December 1st to 8 a.m. May 15th.) Drive 7.3 km (4.5 mi) to a gated fire road veering off to the north and park nearby.

This takes the well-established trail that is the usual approach to Moose Mountain, then throws in some off-trail ridgewalking for a bit more adventure.

The 7 km hike to the top of Moose Mountain goes easily in a couple of hours, and is popular because of its high start plus the great views. The 360-degree panorama is so sweeping that the summit was chosen as the site of a fire lookout. (For more information, including intriguing history, see **Fire Lookout Hikes in the Canadian Rockies**, Mike Potter, Luminous Compositions, 1998.)

The isolated position of Moose Mountain responsible for the excellent vistas was recognized by the Stoney people: their name for the peak, *Iyarhe Wida*, translates as "mountain by itself" or "island mountain." In addition to the many landmark peaks that can be picked out, several ridgewalks can be reconnoitred, including Jumpingpound Mountain East Ridge to Moose Mountain (#58), Jumpingpound Mountain (#56), Cox Hill (#57), Powderface Ridge (#54), and Nihahi Ridge and Compression Ridge (#53).

Among the many alpine wildflowers that can be found on this trip are purple saxifrage, spotted saxifrage, yellow mountain saxifrage, valerian, stonecrop, alpine bistort, roseroot, sawwort, umbrella plant, white mountain avens, and rock jasmine.

To proceed with the ridgewalk, descend to the northwest, steeply at first, then more gradually. From the dip [gr 517454], climb easily to the north peak [gr 515458]. Pushing on, descend about 300 m along the ridge before veering northeast down a well-defined spur with one cliffband that can be either downclimbed or skirted around. After about 500 metres of elevation loss, much of it along a cutline, hit a creek and veer right to pick up an old road at about gr 520473.

A longer option that the author hasn't yet checked out reaches a point a little downstream from here, at the base of what is known as "Lucky Valley," having stayed on the ridge over the subpeak at gr 508470 and dropped to the saddle at (cont. p. 102)

(Cont. from p. 101) gr 515485 before descending the draw.

On the described route, take the old road east until it bends northeast, then cut south to Moose Creek. Contour around the bottom of the spur [gr 526473], then angle toward the large rocky area at the base of the spur that leads back up to the Moose Mountain trail, which sports a small knoll at gr 537464. The going is open on the upper portion of this spur, happily since by now the ups-and-downs of this outing might make it feel as if trekking in Nepal.

Take the old road back to the start.

West-facing cliff at north end of Quirk Ridge; Jumpingpound Mountain [#56 & #58] on centre skyline and Prairie Mountain on right.

51 Quirk Ridge

Map p. 264

Distance: 13 km linear (or 18 km loop)

Trail/off-trail: 4—8 hr

Elevation gain: 435 m (1425 ft)

Maximum elevation: 1995 m (6545 ft)

Maps: Gem Trek 1:50,000 Bragg Creek and Elbow Falls, and NTS 1:50,000 Bragg Creek 82 J/15

Trailhead: Turn off Highway 66 (Elbow Falls Trail) onto the Cobble Flats day-use area access road, 21.8 km (13.5 mi) west of the Kananaskis Country entrance sign. Park off the road after 1.6 km (1.0 mi). **N.B.** Highway 66 (Elbow Falls Trail) is closed west of Elbow Falls {which is 13.7 km west of the K Country entrance sign} from December 1st to May 14th.

Quirk Creek and Quirk Ridge are intriguing, not least for their names, which derive from rancher John Quirk who homesteaded in the area. He called his spread "Kew," and used (what else?) a "Q" cattle brand.

This outing involves a ford of the Elbow River right away, a feat that requires judgement and timing (don't try it if there's a raging torrent!). Be aware that this ridge-walk lies within the McLean Creek Off-Highway Vehicle zone, so don't be surprised if noisy neighbours are encountered. In addition, expect cattle to be sharing the way.

Once across the Elbow, pick up the wide road that parallels it running north-east. This rises gently from the flats to turn southeast once around a forested spur, now in the valley of Quirk Creek. Soon the wide meadows of this stretch of the watercourse come into view, but the temptation to cut across them in a shortcut to the south end of Quirk Ridge leads into boggy ground. Rather, stay on the road until a junction at the grassy flats of Mac Creek.

Turn left on another road, cross the creek on a bridge, and begin the steady ascent up to the high point at the south end of the ridge [gr 584327]. The road ends shortly before the actual summit, but a good trail leads on to the top. The best views are had from a large table-like rock of purplish conglomerate situated in open meadow just below the rocks of the summit proper, which are surrounded by trees.

The superb panorama to the west takes in Forgetmenot Ridge to Forgetmenot Mountain (#52), and beyond on the horizon the quartet of Banded Peak, Outlaw, Mt. Cornwall, and Mt. Glasgow. To the northwest are Nihahi Ridge and Compression Ridge (#53), with Powderface Ridge (#54) below Nihahi Ridge. Further north can be discerned the ridges of Upper Canyon Creek (#55), "Tiara Peak" {accessible as an extension of "Porcupine Ridge" (#62)}, and Belmore Browne Peak (#59).

It is definitely feasible to continue the jaunt north, following a (cont. p. 104)

(Cont. from p. 103) well-defined trail over two bumps with open western aspects, then down to a saddle. The rocky bump at the north end of Quirk Ridge, and Moose Mountain further distant, soon appear; the second bump gives a superlative view up the Elbow Valley with its twisting channels. The trail rises again, but shortly after passing a junction where most traffic goes right, the ridgewalk continues straight, leaving the trail where it takes a sharp right turn.

Head northwest on a contour toward the aspen-filled dip at gr 572351, crossing a cutline en route. Then head west up through forest onto a level section crammed with spindly pines before veering northwest toward welcome rockier terrain. This soon leads to the most exciting part of this outing, the walk along the edge of the sheer cliff that comes after the high point at gr 565355 (which is marked by several cairns in various stages of collapse).

The most exposed bits, and places where trees perch on the very brink, can be easily avoided on the right. The cliff ends abruptly; the best descent is on steep mossy ground with a semblance of trail that wisely trends right to avoid more cliffs. This connects with a gentle slope (full of ant colonies) that could conceivably be followed north down to the Elbow. However, it looked "mangy," so the author elected to drop west—on scree at first—to the river, fortuitously coming to the water opposite the Beaver Flat campground.

The campground entrance off Highway 40 is 8.1 km by road east of the trailhead; there is a 5-km-long trail along the north side of the Elbow River starting 300 m west of the campground entrance.

North from Forgetmenot Ridge including Moose Mountain [#50 & #58] on centre skyline.

52 Forgetmenot Ridge

Map p. 266

Distance: 23 km out-and-back (or 25 km loop)

Trail/off-trail: 8—12 hr

Elevation gain: 705 m (2315 ft)

Maximum elevation: 2330 m (7640 ft)

Maps: Gem Trek 1:50,000 Bragg Creek and Elbow Falls, and NTS 1:50 000 Bragg Creek 82 J/15

Trailhead: Parking area near the end of Highway 66 (Elbow Falls Trail), opposite footbridge over the Little Elbow River. {This parking area is inside the Little Elbow campground, on the north side of the road some 400 metres (0.2 mi) west of the entrance kiosk and 24.9 km (15.4 mi) west of the Kananaskis Country entrance sign. If the gate to the campground at 24.0 km (14.9 mi) is closed, there is an alternate parking area to the left.} **N.B.** Highway 66 (Elbow Falls Trail) is closed west of Elbow Falls from December 1st to May 14th.

This route has a steep approach but once on the ridge the walking is an easy stroll over wide, gentle meadows, with grand views all round.

From the parking area, take the pedestrian bridge over the Little Elbow River, then turn left 400 metres from the start. Keep straight at the four-way junction 200 m further on, and ford the Elbow River in another 400 metres. (Caution: This can be a hazardous crossing.)

Veer right off the main trail 800 metres after the ford, at a junction marked by a large cairn on the south side of the trail. Head up a side drainage, climbing steeply on a faint path. Eventually top out at the end of a spur running northwest from Forgetmenot Ridge [gr 535293] and follow it more gradually up a treed slope to the southeast. Gain the main ridge in a little over a kilometre and head south on easy ground.

Ahead lies a classic ridgewalk of over 6 km, passing over a knoll [gr 548262] and bearing southeast en route to the summit of Forgetmenot Mountain [gr 564244]. The fact that this spot was once the site of a fire lookout indicates the panorama it gives, including Banded Peak, Mt. Glasgow, and Mt. Cornwall above the valley of the Elbow River to the west. Nihahi and Compression ridges (Ridgewalk 53) lie to the northwest, while Moose Mountain (reached via Ridgewalks 50 and 58) rises to the north.

The name of this ridge and mountain suggests the abundance of the sky-blue wildflowers of that species in the vicinity. Other of the many colourful blossoms adding their display on the ridge are spotted saxifrage, white mountain avens, dwarf larkspur, alpine bistort, rock jasmine, valerian, creeping beardtongue, golden (cont. p. 106)

(Cont. from p. 105) fleabane, moss campion, bladder locoweed, roseroot, mountain meadow cinquefoil, sawwort, Parry's townsendia, Jacob's ladder, alpine milkvetch, yellow mountain heather, stonecrop, umbrella plant, and silky scorpionweed.

Mammals found in the vicinity of Forgetmenot Ridge include hoary marmot, pika, and golden-mantled ground squirrel. Red-tailed hawks and common ravens are among the birds that may be sighted in the area.

Return can be made by backtracking, or—if up for more wandering—drop straight south from the summit to intersect the Threepoint Creek trail. Take it west, cut northwest on the direct trail to a ford of the Elbow River, then grind out the last stretch to the trailhead.

Sharp crest on Nihahi Ridge; Moose Mountain [#50 & #58] and Prairie Mountain on right.

Looking south from cairn at north end of Compression Ridge; Nihahi Ridge in centre and Forgetmenot Mountain [#52] on left.

53 Nihahi Ridge and Compression Ridge

Map p. 267

Distance: 22 km linear

Trail/off-trail: 8—12 hr

Elevation gain: 915 m (3000 ft)

Maximum elevation: 2545 m (8350 ft)

Maps: Gem Trek 1:50,000 Bragg Creek and Elbow Falls, and NTS 1:50,000 Bragg Creek 82 J/15

Trailhead: Far west end of Highway 66 (Elbow Falls Trail) at the Little Elbow campground, 26.2 km (16.2 mi) from the Kananaskis Country entrance sign {the last part of this access is a one-way road through the campground}. **N.B.** Highway 66 (Elbow Falls Trail) west of Elbow Falls, and Powderface Trail south of the Dawson trailhead at its north end, are closed from December 1st to May 14th.

Ridgewalking the entire extent of Nihahi and Compression ridges is a long outing that requires confidence on steep terrain. The Stoney name of the Nihahi Ridge is appropriate, meaning "rocky" or "steep cliff mountain."

An established trail gives access onto the south end of Nihahi Ridge: head west from the trailhead on an old fire road. Take the first trail to the right (there are a number of unofficial paths in the area), then turn left at a T-junction. Go right at the next intersection and climb into an open area interspersed with trees. Traverse to the south end of the ridge, angling up to a saddle. The defined trail ends a little farther above. To this point takes an hour or so, and gives fine views. To continue the ridgewalk, head north, at first on a few switchbacks in scree. A path contours below the ridgecrest on the east side, then after about a kilometre goes up through a gap.

Now begins the actual ridgewalking: a straightforward stretching of the legs, with occasional mild scrambling, over a series of bumps. Though with a dropoff on both sides (particularly the right), there isn't much exposure. The big factor on this trip is time, for the north end of Nihahi Ridge is still 7 km away from what has been termed the south summit at gr 482303.

Although it would appear from a distance to be an inhospitable location, many wildflowers grow here, among them such alpine specialties as silver rockcress, sawwort, alpine cinquefoil, bladder locoweed, spotted saxifrage, and purple saxifrage.

While travelling the ridge, each bump seems like it must be the end. Yet reaching it reveals another slightly higher point ahead beyond a dip, until finally arrive at the true summit of Nihahi Ridge at gr 458359 after a solid five hours from the trailhead. Mt. Sparrowhawk and the four peaks of Mt. Lougheed are visible, plus such other ridgewalks as Forgetmenot Ridge (#52), Powderface Ridge (#54), Jumpingpound Mountain (#56), Cox Hill (#57), and of course Compression Ridge to (cont. p. 108)

(Cont. from p. 107) the north.

If {understandably} the choice is to bring the day's exertions to an end, descent can be made northeast down to Prairie Creek and out to the narrow gravel road of Powderface Trail. However, the author can't vouch for the nature of this route as continuation was made in a big push to Compression Ridge. Another possibility, particularly if a vehicle shuttle isn't in the cards, is to drop southwest into Nihahi Creek and follow it south—eventually on trail—to the Elbow River, thence back to the start.

Before deciding whether to continue to Compression Ridge, it must be cautioned that doing these two together makes for a very long day (best attempted close to the summer solstice), and that this next section is more technically demanding.

From the summit of Nihahi Ridge, drop west to a saddle, then veer northwest for a little over 1 km before heading north for about 1.5 km. The crux of this outing comes shortly before the high point at gr 436381, in the form of a thin fin that is taken on the right, followed by a rib with considerable exposure.

Mt. Assiniboine is visible from this high point, which has the same elevation as the high point on Nihahi Ridge. Next the route heads east. Drop into a dip with several gendarmes that are turned on the right, except for the last one on which a scree ramp can be followed over the top. An arch with two holes lies along this section.

Now the east arm of Compression Ridge swings around to the north and descends a while before rising slightly to a cairn at its north end. This marks the end of the ridgewalk, an interesting, challenging route.

Descent to the wide flats of Canyon Creek and the final level stretch to Powderface Trail requires an hour or so, bringing to a close one of the more exhilarating ridgewalks in this book. {If desired, for example due to time or energy constraints, it should be possible to focus on Compression Ridge alone by going up Prairie Creek to gain the summit of Nihahi Ridge or perhaps the saddle at gr 450359. Another option is to do the above route in reverse.}

The name of the Compression Ridge alludes to its convoluted geology, but (despite intense moments) it actually represents a good place to decompress.

The author at gap above Powderface Pass, looking south to Bluerock Mountain [#45] on left and Banded Peak, Outlaw, Mt. Glasgow, and Nihahi Ridge [#53] on right.

54 Powderface Ridge

Distance: 9 km linear

Trail/off-trail: 4—8 hr

Elevation gain: 450 m (1475 ft)

Maximum elevation: 2205 m (7230 ft)

Maps: Gem Trek 1:50,000 Bragg Creek and Elbow Falls, and NTS 1:50,000 Bragg Creek 82 J/15

Trailhead: Small parking area off Powderface Trail, 5.9 km (3.7 mi) north of the junction with Highway 66 {which is 22.9 km (14.2 mi) west of the Kananaskis Country entrance sign on Hwy. 66}. **N.B.** Highway 66 (Elbow Falls Trail) west of Elbow Falls, and Powderface Trail south of the Dawson trailhead at its north end, are closed from December 1st to May 14th.

This outing is best done north to south, both in terms of elevation gain and of views. The name of Powderface Ridge honours Tom Powderface, a member of the Stoney people who lived with his family near Bragg Creek. The Stoney people call the ridge *Thidethaba Baha*, meaning "mule deer buck hill."

Head east from the parking area on the most direct route to the ridge, quickly connecting with a trail that starts farther north and lower down. Continue up to Powderface Pass at the head of Powderface Creek, whose valley lies to the east.

An enjoyable detour can be made to "Powderface Ridge North," a series of low, open hills culminating at gr 502366. This outing is renowned for wildflowers; the variety to be found includes prairie crocus, silver rockcress, shooting star, Jacob's ladder, spotted saxifrage, and kittentails. Bonsai-like lodgepole pines grow high on the ridges.

The main ridge lies south of Powderface Pass, so turn southeast and climb to a gap east of a knoll, where the first views south appear. The panorama includes Nihahi Ridge and Compression Ridge (#53) to the west, Quirk Ridge (#51) to the east, Forgetmenot Ridge (#52) to the south, and Moose Mountain (#50 and #58) to the north. Yamnuska and Devils Head stand out to the northwest.

Continue up through meadows to where the trail crosses over the ridge (or head straight up toward the rocky north end). Rather than leaving the ridge as soon as reaching it, stay high to enjoy the views. The ridgecrest stays quite level for about two kilometres, although the open going eventually ends and the way is over rockier, more forested terrain. Either keep to the ridge for the entire descent, or drop to the east at a suitable point to rejoin the trail that descends a draw below the saddle at gr 523320.

This outing ends at the junction of Elbow Falls Trail and Powderface Trail, where a second vehicle could be left to avoid a 6 km trudge back to the trailhead.

Expect mountain bikers on this one.

55 Ridges at Upper Canyon Creek

Map p. 266

Distance: 13 km loop

Trail/off-trail: 4—8 hr

Elevation gain: 835 m (2740 ft)

Maximum elevation: 2565 m (8415 ft)

Maps: Gem Trek 1:50,000 Bragg Creek and Elbow Falls, and Canmore and Kananaskis Village, and NTS 1:50,000 Bragg Creek 82 J/15

Trailhead: Small unofficial parking area on the south side of Powderface Trail 14.5 km (9.0 mi) north of the junction with Highway 66 and 400 metres (0.2 mi) south of the culvert crossing of Canyon Creek. **N.B.** Highway 66 (Elbow Falls Trail) west of Elbow Falls, and Powderface Trail south of the Dawson trailhead at its north end, are closed from December 1st to May 14th.

This loop ridgewalk takes to the heights around the northwest fork of upper Canyon Creek. Ten minutes or less after starting, where the road at the beginning disappears after crossing the creek, leave the rocky creekbed for the forest to the north. Soon hit a clearcut or a logging road and head west to a large clearcut. Head for the furthest north point of this cutblock, then trend left through trees again toward a grassy area below the ridge.

The angle steepens and the ground becomes rockier, but no major obstacles prevent access to the ridge. Now head north, then northwest, to the first high point [gr 436425]. Once ready to leave this vantage point, continue northwest, first dropping to a saddle (this bit is steeper than might be expected), then rising to gain a mostly level ridge with the second high point of this excursion [gr 427439].

Now head due west, then northwest again, toward a saddle. This once more proves more difficult than expected, due to oddly-shaped conglomerate towers straddling it that require a detour off the ridge to the left (not easy, but less steep than to the right). Once at the second saddle [gr 422442], head up the ridge toward the third high point [gr 413443]; the slabby bit that looks ominous from below is taken on directly (some exposure here) until a slightly overhung tier blocks the way...at this point, happily, it's possible to descend a small gully on the right and get back up on the ridgecrest.

Sheer towers preclude direct travel toward "Tiara Peak" (the only break in a series of linking routes that stretches for more than 25 kilometres of ridgewalking south to Forgetmenot Mountain and over 10 kilometres north to Mt. Baldy). This enjoyable circuit, however, goes on with a descent to the south to a third saddle, then the climb to the fourth and highest point of the day [gr 409434].

The views from here include Fortress Mountain, Mt. Galatea, Mt. Kidd, Mt.

Southeast from southeast end of Ridges at Upper Canyon Creek, including Compression Ridge [#53].

Bogart, Mt. Sparrowhawk, and Mt. Lougheed with its four peaks. In front of these peaks are Mt. Allan and Mt. Collembola, sites of Ridgewalks #64-#66. Nearer at hand are Wasootch Ridge (#63) and "Porcupine Ridge" (#62).

The Three Sisters and Mt. Rundle rise to the northwest, with Mt. Temple visible above the East End of Rundle [#84]. Black Rock Mountain and Devils Head (above Yamnuska) are readily identifiable to the north, while to the east are Cox Hill, Jumpingpound Mountain, Moose Mountain, Forgetmenot Mountain, Nihahi Ridge, and Compression Ridge—destinations of yet more ridgewalks.

Descent is to the southeast: although it looks intimidating from below, this goes without serious complications. After about two kilometres of enjoyable ridgewalking, arrive at trees and drop off the ridge to the right on scree. This leads quickly down to a tributary flowing from Bryant Lake (a remote tarn that is glimpsed from higher up), which soon joins the branch that rises at the "saddle of strange shapes." {How's that for alliteration?}

Now head southeast over rocks and on patches of trail to rejoin the main arm of Canyon Creek and return to the trailhead. There you have it, a fine loop ridgewalk.

56 Jumpingpound Mountain

Map p. 268

Distance: 13 km linear

Trail: 4—8 hr

Elevation gain: 495 m (1625 ft)

Maximum elevation: 2235 m (7330 ft)

Maps: Gem Trek 1:50,000 Bragg Creek and Elbow Falls, and NTS 1:50,000 Bragg Creek 82 J/15

Trailhead: At parking area north of Canyon Creek crossing on Powderface Trail, 15.2 km (9.4 mi) north of the junction with Highway 66 and 20.2 km (12.5 mi) south of the junction with Highway 68. **N.B.** Highway 66 (Elbow Falls Trail) west of Elbow Falls, and Powderface Trail south of the Dawson trailhead at its north end, are closed from December 1st to May 14th.

This ridgewalk follows a well-defined trail, and is popular with mountain bikers. Head east up Canyon Creek, then after a kilometre turn left and start climbing. Much of the initial bit is in forest, until after the junction with the direct trail described in Ridgewalk 58.

Once in the open it's a superb cruise along the virtually level ridgetop for about two kilometres. (The short detour to the summit of Jumpingpound Mountain is well worthwhile.) The outstanding views are to the west, including the four peaks of Mt. Lougheed, though the rest of the panorama is not to be sneezed at, including as it does the east ridge of Jumpingpound Mountain leading to Moose Mountain (#58) and Cox Hill (#57) ahead to the north—recommended as a continuation of this jaunt.

Among the many wildflowers growing along the way are the exquisite moss campion, white mountain avens, shooting star [at both low and high elevations], rock jasmine, forget-me-not, kittentails, and roseroot.

The trail descends north to a junction at gr 457487, from which it continues down to the northwest through forest to Powderface Trail. Rather than losing all that elevation, however, it's strongly suggested to connect with the Cox Hill ridgewalk as described in the following entry.

Ridgewalker feather Mills on Jumpingpound Mountain.

The author at cairn on Cox Hill [#57], with view west including four peaks of Mt. Lougheed.

57 Cox Hill

Map p. 268
Photo p. 113

Distance: 9 km linear

Trail: up to 4 hr

Elevation gain: 140 m (460 ft)

Maximum elevation: 2210 m (7250 ft)

Maps: Gem Trek 1:50,000 Bragg Creek and Elbow Falls, and NTS 1:50,000 Bragg Creek 82 J/15 and Jumpingpound Creek 82-O/2

Trailhead: The south end of this trail at the junction on the Jumpingpound Mountain (ridgewalk 56). If insistent on doing this Cox Hill ridgewalk alone, the elevation gain is about the same from either the Dawson or Lusk Pass trailheads on Powderface Trail (road), since although the latter starts higher it dips into a saddle from the junction with the Jumpingpound Mountain trip. **N.B.** Highway 66 (Elbow Falls Trail) west of Elbow Falls, and Powderface Trail south of the Dawson trailhead at its north end, are closed from December 1st to May 14th.

Cox Hill offers superb views, and the best way to get them is to combine its ascent with the traverse of Jumpingpound Mountain (#56). Mind you, the extended outing makes for a long day; it helps to have two vehicles available. (Be prepared to see mountain bikers tackling this trail.)

From the junction on Jumpingpound Mountain, lose something over 100 m of elevation as descending to the saddle at gr 461494. Then climb northwest onto the ridge of Cox Hill, which becomes more open and starts to allow some of those great views. The name is from an assistant of early surveyor A.O. Wheeler.

Mt. Kidd, Mt. Bogart, and Mt. Sparrowhawk are among the landmarks visible to the west, with Moose Mountain of course standing out to the southeast. The route to it along the east ridge of Jumpingpound Mountain (#58) is readily surveyed.

Golden-mantled ground squirrels frequent the summit of Cox Hill. The Stoney name for this feature is *Zotha Odabi Baha*, meaning "many marmots hill." Wildflowers along the open tops on this trip include Jacob's ladder, yellow mountain heather, alpine buttercup, and spotted saxifrage. On the descent through the forest can be found yellow columbine, baneberry, purple clematis, lungwort, bracted honeysuckle, and bunchberry.

The long downhill grade from the summit of Cox Hill leads northeasterly to the Dawson trailhead on Powderface Trail, which is 3.1 km (1.9 mi) south of the junction with Highway 68.

58 Jumpingpound Mountain East Ridge to Moose Mountain

Distance: 18 km out-and-back (or 19 km loop)

Trail/off-trail: 8—12 hr

Elevation gain: 610 m (2000 ft)

Maximum elevation: 2438 m (7995 ft)

Maps: Gem Trek 1:50,000 Bragg Creek and Elbow Falls, and NTS 1:50,000 Bragg Creek 82 J/15

Trailhead: Parking area on the west side of Powderface Trail, 18.3 km (11.3 mi) north of the junction with Highway 66 and 17.1 km (10.6 mi) south of the junction with Highway 68. **N.B.** Highway 66 (Elbow Falls Trail) west of Elbow Falls, and Powderface Trail south of the Dawson trailhead at its north end, are closed from December 1st to May 14th.

This is an unconventional approach to the summit of Moose Mountain, with all manner of possibilities once there.

The direct trail leads to the summit of Jumpingpound Mountain in an hour or so, where a break is in order to take in the expansive views. Included (cont. p. 116)

Along east ridge of Jumpingpound Mountain to Moose Mountain.

(Cont. from p. 115) in the panorama are such other ridgewalks as the Jumpingpound Mountain traverse (#56), Cox Hill (#57), Powderface Ridge (#54), Forgetmenot Ridge (#52), and Nihahi Ridge and Compression Ridge (#53).

This route heads northeast from the top of Jumpingpound Mountain, first descending over grassy slopes. Then roll over one knoll to a high point at gr 484473 (rockpiles mark the way, with bits of path).

Now go due east for almost a kilometre, then turn southeast to the bump at gr 494465. Don't be tempted to drop off the ridge, as a path seemed to; rather, keep going on dry, rocky ground with widely-spaced trees. Drop easily through an open grassy area to a dip, then head up to a high point at gr 502464.

Go a little further south before veering east down a steep slope to the saddle [gr 505462] that has a road angling from the north into the old well site. Next up is the slope climbing to the north summit of Moose Mountain [gr 515458], following which is the rocky connecting ridge to the summit (steep section just before the top).

As expected given the fire lookout there, the top of Moose Mountain reveals a spectacular panorama. Among the many landmarks are distant views of Mt. Assiniboine and Mt. Temple. Wildlife that can be seen on this outing includes pikas, hoary marmots, and even mountain goats, which have been reintroduced in the area.

Return the same way, or try the option if time and energy permit.

Option

Lose elevation quickly to the mini-plateau below to the southwest, then traverse southeast to the saddle at gr 520438. (Side trips could be made to the peaks on either side.) Once at the small bump at gr 523436, head south to the southernmost peak of Moose Mountain, then lose height—staying on the ridge—to a small knob [gr 525420].

From here it's steep scree down to Canyon Creek, especially at the end, where there are also some friction slabs and one small rockband. A campground with a large triangle of rocks around a fireplace can serve as "drop zone" (the angle makes it feel a bit like parachuting).

This long day ends with a fairly long haul up Canyon Creek, probably requiring at least one ford before joining the old road on the north side of the valley.

{Another, more direct, alternative (which the author has not done) takes a southwest line from the northwest end of the summit ridge of the peak at gr 516442. Aim for the notch at gr 505432, at which point a trail of sorts should lead into the drainage to the north and down to a crossing of Moose Mountain Creek on a piece of old road that links up with the old road north of Canyon Creek.}

59 Belmore Browne Peak and North

Map p. 269

Distance: 19 km linear

Trail/off-trail: 8—12 hr

Elevation gain: 690 m (2265 ft)

Maximum elevation: 2445 m (8020 ft)

Maps: Gem Trek 1;50,000 Canmore and Kananaskis Village, and NTS 1:50,000 Bragg Creek 82 J/15, Spray Lakes Reservoir 82 J/14, Canmore 82-O/3, and Jumpingpound Creek 82-O/2

Trailhead: Park off Powderface Trail 14.5 km (9.0 mi) south of the junction with Highway 68 (Sibbald Creek Trail) and 20.9 km (13.0 mi) north of the junction with Highway 66; the corridor near the start of the approach route can be seen to the southwest. **N.B.** Highway 66 (Elbow Falls Trail) west of Elbow Falls, and Powderface Trail south of the Dawson trailhead at its north end, are closed from December 1st to May 14th.

The reward of hiking through the leftovers of logging operations at the southwestern headwaters of Jumpingpound Creek is a glorious extended ridgewalk to the north. From the trailhead, pick up a former road through a corridor that (cont. p. 118)

Belmore Browne Peak (on left) from peak to northwest; Ridges at Upper Canyon Creek [#55] and Compression Ridge [#53] on right.

(Cont. from p. 117) leads to the first clearcut, then crosses the creek to a second clearcut. Where the road veers left to cross the creek again, keep straight on a cutline that goes over a spur to rejoin the creek higher up.

Now follow up the main creekbed (not taking any turns to the right) to where it bends left and opens out. Head west up the steep forested slope, which eventually becomes a rocky rib. Keep up this to the ridge at gr 406455, not far north of "Tiara Peak" and the extension of Ridgewalk 62 on "Porcupine Ridge" (which is now in view).

On this trip, however, face north and go! First down to a dip, then up and over the bump at gr 405463, which presents some scrambling challenges to get down through rockbands on its north ridge. Arrive at a hub [gr 406465], where an easy detour east leads to the summit of Belmore Browne Peak, which looks dramatic from other perspectives. Mind, the stroll is a little complicated by the existence of a double summit, necessitating a short descent to get around the gap and onto the true easternmost top.

The name of this peak honours Belmore Browne, an American-born artist renowned for paintings that conveyed the mystery of wilderness in their atmospheric effects. He lived in Banff from 1921 to 1940 and later on what is now the Rafter Six Ranch near Seebe, visiting this region frequently. He so loved the area that upon his death his ashes were cast to the wind on this peak rather than on any other of the mountains he had ascended in an illustrious climbing career (including Mt. McKinley, now called by its Native name Denali).

Returning to the hub, drop to the saddle to the northwest and head up to the pyramidal peak [gr 403470]: an easy ascent for a feature that looks so formidable from the west. Continuing the ridgewalk, veer northeast off the summit to descend to a dip at the head of the northeast fork of Porcupine Creek. It is possible to leave the route in either direction here, down Porcupine Creek or into the draw to the north leading to the north side of the Baldy Pass trail.

To go for the gusto, however, turn northwest over a ship-shaped prominence to another dip [gr 395485]. Now the crux of the route presents itself: proceed up from the saddle, then change direction 90 degrees to head southwest up a steep face that requires hands-on scrambling over the final stretch to get to the summit at gr 385485.

From this top, a roller-coaster ride of a dip sweeps northwest down to a saddle with a slabby bit that can be tackled by holding onto the sharp crest and walking along using friction holds. Up next is the unnamed peak south of Baldy Pass, from which several options are available. Either follow the descent route of Ridgewalk 60, or the longer ascent route of that same description, or—the way that leads back closest to the trailhead—head down the north side of the pass.

The winding trail soon joins an old logging road and keeps straight at a junction with a road to the right. Continue about 2 km to a junction with a less well-defined path to the right, where turn off to take this connector to the Lusk Pass trail. When that is reached, turn right again and follow it along a course that is level at first before rising steadily to the forested pass. Pass a backcountry campground soon after the high point, then descend quickly to Jumpingpound Trail {road} at the Lusk Pass trailhead, 3.5 km (2.2 mi) north of the start of this outing. This marks the end of a long, ambitious, yet rewarding effort.

60 Baldy Pass to Unnamed Peak to South

Map p. 269

Distance: 9 km loop

Trail/off-trail: 4—8 hr

Elevation gain: 905 m (2970 ft)

Maximum elevation: 2325 m (7625 ft)

Maps: Gem Trek 1;50,000 Canmore and Kananaskis Village, and NTS 1:50,000 Spray Lakes Reservoir 82 J/14

Trailhead: Baldy Pass trailhead on the west side of Highway 40, 10.3 km (6.4 mi) south of the entrance to Kananaskis Country.

This is a shorter and simpler variation from Baldy Pass than the ridgewalk to Mt. Baldy, and reaches a summit over 130 metres higher even though it is not officially named.

Take the Baldy Pass trail, which starts on the east side of the highway, to its high point. This is 30 metres of elevation gain above the low point in the saddle (which is where Ridgewalk 61 to Mt. Baldy takes off). Now head southwest, first through sparsely treed terrain, then skirting right at the bottom of a rockslide. Once past the boulders, head up the open slope as far as possible before heading into forest.

There are sections of faint path on the ridge, which eventually joins talus to the right. Plug up the steep angle to the small cairn at the top. This allows views to the east, including Ridgewalks 57, 56, and 58 {Cox Hill, Jumpingpound Mountain, Moose Mountain}. Of course, much of the route of (cont. p. 120)

Southeast from unnamed peak south of Baldy Pass to peaks north of Belmore Browne Peak [#59] and "Tiara Peak" [#62] (centre) and "Porcupine Ridge" [#62] (right).

119

(Cont. from p. 119) Belmore Browne Peak and North (#59) can also be scrutinized. In addition, "Porcupine" and Wasootch ridges (#62 and #63) are visible to the south.

As well, the vista to the west takes in the expected panorama, featuring such landmarks as Mt. Lougheed, Mt. Rundle, and Mt. Fable. To the north are Yamnuska, Devils Head, and Black Rock Mountain.

Forging a traverse of this unnamed peak, descend to the west, initially on slabby terrain. A small knoll after the dip at gr 369490 is easily turned on the left. Then, rather than pushing through forest on the true continuation of the ridge toward Porcupine Creek, it's feasible to drop west where the going gets trickier. Take mostly open scree, perhaps angling right down through trees to join a prominent gully. No matter how tackled, connect with the Baldy Pass trail slightly north of the jog that leads out to Highway 40, thus completing a nice little circuit.

Ridgewalker John Blum on ridge from Baldy Pass to Mt. Baldy; unnamed peak south of Baldy Pass [#60] on right, and peaks north of Belmore Browne Peak [#59] on left and centre.

61 Baldy Pass to Mt. Baldy

Map p. 269

Distance: 11 km linear

Trail/off-trail: 4—8 hr

Elevation gain: 770 m (2525 ft)

Maximum elevation: 2192 m (7191 ft)

Maps: Gem Trek 1;50,000 Canmore and Kananaskis Village, and NTS 1:50,000 Spray Lakes Reservoir 82 J/14 and Canmore 82-O/3

Trailhead: As for Ridgewalk 60, Baldy Pass to Unnamed Peak to South.

This is a longer excursion than Ridgewalk 60 to the unnamed peak south of Baldy Pass, albeit to a lower elevation. It includes one potentially tricky section, as well as a bit of steep scrambling to gain the summit plateau of Mt. Baldy.

From the large cairn where the trail first arrives at Baldy Pass, head up northwest on the ridge (path at first). Limber pines grow on this section, as do pikas. Wildflowers to be found include white mountain avens, rock jasmine, roseroot, and purple saxifrage.

The route passes over small bumps before reaching the first well-defined high point [gr 376512]. Descend slightly before rising to the next high point [gr 373518]. Continuing along the narrow ridge to the north is fine in dry conditions; however, if snow-covered (as on the author's first visit), a flanking maneuver down to the west may be called for [beware of avalanche hazard].

Ahead is another dip in the ridge, then the formidable-looking summit block of Mt. Baldy. This is negotiated by traversing out right at the cliff, then scrambling up a steep section of the eastern aspect to arrive at the southern end of the plateau above.

The final bit to the cairn is an easy stroll; the top of Mt. Baldy is a good place to take in the views, including of the Barrier Lake reservoir far below. The sheer south face of Yamnuska rises above the site of the Barrier Lake fire lookout to the northwest. Different 'peaks,' in the form of skyscrapers, indicate the location of Calgary far out on the prairies.

Descent is via the southwest ridge on a well-trodden path: this is the most direct route to the summit. The gendarme about a third of the way down can be turned on the left if desired; one little bit of climbing is called for lower down in order to stay on the ridge.

62 "Porcupine Ridge"

Distance: 16 km loop

Trail/off-trail: 8—12 hr

Elevation gain: 895 m (2935 ft)

Maximum elevation: 2300 m (7545 ft)

Maps: Gem Trek 1;50,000 Canmore and Kananaskis Village, and NTS 1:50,000 Spray Lakes Reservoir 82 J/14 [and, for "Tiara Peak," Bragg Creek 82 J/15]

Trailhead: Park well off Highway 40 on the east shoulder on the north side of Porcupine Creek, 11.7 km (7.3 mi) south of the entrance to Kananaskis Country.

"Porcupine Ridge" has several daunting gendarmes seen from the distance in various directions, but once on the ridge they are avoided or can be easily turned. However, there is one unexpectedly nervy section of exposed scrambling that some may prefer to circumvent by a lower route.

Head up the drainage from Highway 40, initially on an old road that comes to an end shortly before a footbridge over Porcupine Creek. A footpath continues on the north side, passing round the forested bulge at the bottom of the southeast ridge of the unnamed peak south of Baldy Pass.

A rock wall forces a crossing to the south side at the forks of the two main branches of the creek: this is the desired side in any case. After only about 250 metres of travel up the south fork, cross the creek again to get onto the beginning of "Porcupine Ridge." Although the western part of the ridge is shown in green on the "Spray Lakes Reservoir" map, much of it is actually completely devoid of tall vegetation. A sparsely treed rocky section near the start of the ridge gives a view west over the narrows to Mt. Lorette. Though more heavily forested, the next stretch is easily negotiated, leading to the first truly open bit. This rises to rocky outcrops, reached a little more than an hour from the start. The Three Sisters are in view through the gap of Skogan Pass, while Barrier Lake and the sheer south face of Yamnuska are in view to the northwest.

A slabby bit encountered soon afterward is readily climbed on good holds to easy ground. After a treed slope, reach a gendarme that is skirted below at the base of its north aspect (another gendarme is off the ridge proper). After passing above a ridge with gendarmes running off to the southwest, the crux of the outing appears suddenly at about gr 376464. This comes in the form of about 10 metres of sharp crest with loose rock, and drop-offs on either side. Most will either crouch down to carefully traverse this bit, or perhaps skirt below it on the south side.

A little more than three hours of ridgewalking sees the high point of "Porcupine Ridge" gained [gr 396456]. Shortly before reaching this culmination, it is advis-

"Porcupine Ridge" from approach to "Tiara Peak," looking west including Mt. Allan [#64 & #65] and Mt. Collembola [#66] beneath four peaks of Mt. Lougheed, The Three Sisters, and Mt. Lorette to right of Skogan Pass.

able to stay on the ridge before it takes a jog northwest. This avoids scree-churning across the slope to the saddle before the high point. Views from the apex of "Porcupine Ridge" take in Mt. Bogart, Mt. Sparrowhawk, and the four peaks of Mt. Lougheed. Mt. Allan and Mt. Collembola, the destinations of Ridgewalks 64-66, lie in front of those distinctive landmarks. Wind Ridge (#77) is now seen below the Little Sister.

Descent can be made south down the gully to the main south fork of Porcupine Creek. At first it is "The Ballet of the Rockhopper," but with flagging energy and diminishing rock size, things soon deteriorate to "The Trudge of the Gravel Grinder." At the end of the flats, the creek pinches in and meanders about, likely requiring several crossings that are just too narrow to want to take the boots off for a ford but just too wide to manage by leaping from rock to rock.

An optional extension requiring lots of energy and experience on dicey terrain is to climb "Tiara Peak" from the high point of "Porcupine Ridge." This involves an extra 3 km of travel and 240 m (785 ft) of elevation gain.

Head southeast down to a saddle, deking down to the left at the gable end and passing two small arches. Then grind up the slope to just north of the peak (which point is not far from the access point to this ridge of Ridgewalk 59). Now with views to the east including Moose Mountain, scoot beneath the imposing east face of "Tiara Peak" and around beneath the cliffs on its south side. [Here it becomes clear why connecting with Ridgewalk 55 is problematic.]

Immediately after a slabby section (friction moves required), head up the southwest side of the peak. The top gives an excellent overview of Belmore Browne Peak and the peaks to the north and west (Ridgewalk 59). In addition, it represents a vantage point over the route of Ridgewalk 55 above Upper Canyon Creek. Also in sight on the horizon to the west are the summits of Deltaform, Hungabee, and Temple.

Descend via the southwest slopes, through a rockband beneath the slabby section encountered earlier. Next enjoy a "scree-amer" to treelimit, after which the rocks become larger and the going slower. A canyon on the watercourse is bypassed on the right; shortly afterward, hit the big debris flow of the standard descent route.

63 Wasootch Ridge

Map p. 270

Distance: 16 km loop

Trail/off-trail: 8—12 hr

Elevation gain: 890 m (2920 ft)

Maximum elevation: 2320 m (7610 ft)

Maps: Gem Trek 1;50,000 Canmore and Kananaskis Village, and NTS 1:50,000 Spray Lakes Reservoir 82 J/14

Trailhead: Turn off Highway 40 to the Wasootch Creek day-use area, 12.3 km (7.6 mi) south of the entrance to Kananaskis Country.

This well-defined ridge extends for over four kilometres between the parallel drainages of Wasootch Creek and the south branch of Porcupine Creek.

Access is simple: from the parking area, head directly up the rough trail. Pass above the popular rockclimbing area—the slabs are out of sight but climbers may be heard below. Continue, initially through forest, on the treadworn route. It peters out, although several cairns signal the persistence of some hikers.

Pushing on, the route opens into a fine ridgewalk (photogenic limber pines) with some scrambling. If preferred, exposed bits can be circumvented by sidehill gouging on scree. The high point at gr 375436 allows views out to the foothills and around the amphitheatres at the heads of Wasootch and Porcupine creeks. Mt. McDougall to the south is prominent among the nearby peaks. More distant landmarks include Mt. Bogart, Mt. Sparrowhawk, Mt. Lougheed with its four summits, Mt. Rundle above Skogan Pass, and Mt. Lorette. More to the north are features such as the top of Devils Head, Yamnuska, Barrier Lake, and Mt. Baldy.

Other ridgewalks that can be scouted from this location include "Porcupine Ridge" (#62), part of the route to the unnamed peak south of Baldy Pass (#60), and parts of the Mt. Allan Centennial Ridge and Mt. Collembola routes (#64 and #66).

Among the many wildflowers that enliven the route are rock jasmine, white mountain avens, spotted and purple saxifrages, roseroot, sawwort, Jacob's ladder, the unusual double bladderpod, and moss campion.

Return is made by first descending toward the saddle at gr 384432, which sports a rock outcrop. The best scree for the drop south into Wasootch Creek is found shortly before the lowest point in the saddle. The bottom part of this quick loss of elevation is through open forest. There is a small canyon on the creek before wide flats are reached. Here it could be said that there is a price to pay for the easy start, since ahead lies over 6 km of tiring travel over water-strewn boulders to get back to the trailhead. Still, human nature being what it is, these travails will fade into the background while the joys of the panoramic ridgewalk will be retained as vivid memories.

Gnarled limber pine on Wasootch Ridge; "Tiara Peak" [#62] on centre skyline.

Ridgewalker John Blum beneath rock towers on Mt. Allan Centennial Ridge [#64]; summit of Mt. Allan on right and peaks of Mt. Lougheed to west.

64 Mt. Allan Centennial Ridge

Map p. 271
Photo p. 125

Distance: 16 km out-and-back [or see options]

Trail: 4—8 hr

Elevation gain: 1335 m (4380 ft)

Maximum elevation: 2820 m (9250 ft)

Maps: Gem Trek 1;50,000 Canmore and Kananaskis Village, and NTS 1:50,000 Spray Lakes Reservoir 82 J/14

Trailhead: The Ribbon Creek day-use area, reached by turning west off Highway 40, 18.5 km (11.5 mi) south of the entrance to Kananaskis Country, turning left 800 metres (0.5 mi) from the junction, turning right after 250 metres, and continuing past the youth hostel to the end of the road in a further 500 metres. **N.B.** This trail is closed from April 1st to June 21st each year to protect newborn bighorn sheep lambs born on this and adjacent ridges.

This, the highest maintained trail in Canada, was established by the Rocky Mountain Ramblers to mark the country's one hundredth anniversary in 1967. It passes beside spectacular pinnacles and grants panoramic views.

The trail heads north from the parking area, then in 300 metres turns west and follows a well-marked route through a maze of old roads and trails. After about half an hour there are views south over the clearing of a former mine site to the precipitous cliffs of Mt. Kidd. Then the trail plunges back into the forest, climbing more steeply now to at last rise above the trees and begin numerous switchbacks.

A more gradual section following a small knoll with subalpine larches below precedes a cliffband skirted on the right. "Olympic Summit," named in connection with a ski run used in the 1988 Winter Games, lies ahead. This rounded top gives a breather; beyond, a short descent precedes the resumption of the steady climb. A highlight of this section is the collection of freestanding rock towers just off the ridge to the left (the trail wends beside them, allowing for eyecatching photographic compositions).

The route continues, steepening toward the end, to the summit of Mt. Allan, whose name honours Dr. John A. Allan, a geologist and university professor who did much field work in the Rockies. The top of Mt. Allan and the culmination of Centennial Ridge is a fine place to soak up the impressive views, including the nearby four peaks of Mt. Lougheed and the sweeping cliffs of the gap between it and Mt. Sparrowhawk. The inspiring vista includes other ridgewalks such as Baldy Pass to Mt. Baldy (#61) and Wind Ridge (#77).

The choices from the summit of Mt. Allan are to return via Centennial Ridge, descend to the north (Ridgewalk 65), or—if experienced in off-trail travel and so inclined energy-wise—traverse Mt. Collembola (#66).

65 Mt. Allan North Ridge

Map p. 271

Distance: 11 km linear

Trail: up to 4 hr (descending)

Elevation gain: nil from summit

Maximum elevation: 2820 m (9250 ft)

Maps: Gem Trek 1;50,000 Canmore and Kananaskis Village, and NTS 1:50,000 Spray Lakes Reservoir 82 J/14 and Canmore 82-O/3

Trailhead: Summit of Mt. Allan, reached via the Centennial Trail (ridgewalk 64). The north end of this trail is near Alpine Resort Haven (see trailhead info for Ridgewalk 76, Pigeon Mountain). **N.B.** Most of this trail is closed from April 1st to June 21st to protect bighorn sheep lambs born in the area and finding their first legs.

This trail serves as a continuation of the Centennial Ridge trail, enabling a traverse of Mt. Allan (making for a longer day and ending up far from the start at Ribbon Creek).

The descent from the summit begins easily on open slopes. After a subsidiary summit where the ridge bends northeast, a mild difficulty rears up in the form of a series of pinnacles. Follow the diamond-shaped orange markers in cairns (cont. p. 128)

Mt. Allan North Ridge in foreground, from Mt. Collembola [#66]; peak of Mt. Lougheed on left, The Three Sisters in centre, and Mt. Rundle [#84] on right with Wind Ridge [#77] below.

(Cont. from p. 127) to drop off the crest to the left and squeeze through an opening before regaining the ridge proper.

The descent resumes its straightforward course until a gable end appears, at which point the trail doubles back a bit to the east before scooting down a series of grassy ledges. Then slither down a steep slope with a few trees to arrive in the basin between Mt. Allan and Mt. Collembola.

Here keep on a contour to intersect the bottom of the northwest ridge of Mt. Collembola (an optional exit from the traverse of Ridgewalk 66), then veer left, now on a road through forest. Go right-left-right at the next three main junctions to reach the trail parallel to the powerline right-of-way climbing over Skogan Pass, where keep left to reach the parking area near Alpine Resort Haven.

Wildflowers that enhance this outing include such alpine specialties as moss campion, alpine spring beauty, kittentails, mist maiden, sawwort, spotted saxifrage, silky scorpionweed, rock jasmine, white mountain avens, valerian, roseroot, and white mountain heather. As well as bighorn sheep, elk may be sighted on the extensive grassy meadows. Lady beetles often add a small splash of colour even on the tops.

Rarely is this trail done in the reverse direction to that described.

Mt. Collembola from Mt. Allan [#64 and #65].

66 Mt. Collembola

Distance: 15 km linear

Off-trail/trail: 4—8 hr

Elevation gain: nil from summit Mt. Allan

Maximum elevation: 2820 m (9250 ft)

Maps: Gem Trek 1;50,000 Canmore and Kananaskis Village, and NTS 1:50,000 Spray Lakes Reservoir 82 J/14

Trailhead: Summit of Mt. Allan, reached via Ridgewalk 64 (or, rarely, Ridgewalk 65). **N.B.** The trails on Mt. Allan are closed from April 1st to June 21st to protect bighorn sheep lambs born in the area and finding their first legs.

The traverse of Mt. Collembola offers a more adventurous alternative from the top of Mt. Allan than either of the established trails from the summit.

The beginning is a bit discouraging, involving as it does the loss of about 200 metres of elevation. En route to the saddle at gr 255467, pass the same strata with pinnacles that continues to the north ridge of Mt. Allan.

Once on Mt. Collembola proper, things look up with the feeling of tackling a less-trodden route. Reaching the subpeak southeast of the summit is straightforward; however, getting off it to continue the traverse takes a bit of routefinding and scrambly downclimbing.

More of the same follows upon leaving the summit, after which things calm down on a level spur. Where this rolls over down to the northwest (optional connection to Ridgewalk 65, Mt. Allan North Ridge; or complete the loop if chose to go up Mt. Allan that way), head due east down a steep grassy ridge. From above, pick out a cutline running east-west and aim to join this after crossing a streambed (may take some scouting around on the treed slope).

This somewhat overgrown swath eventually connects with the wide road in the general vicinity of Skogan Pass...now it's simply a matter of slogging out down past the Nakiska downhill ski area back to the trailhead.

By the by, the unusual name of this feature commemorates—if that's the right word—the humble "snow flea" or springtail, a primitive but well-adapted organism that thrives in the harsh conditions of the alpine zone such as on top of this mountain.

67 Old Baldy

Map p. 269

Distance: 14 km loop

Trail/off-trail: 4—8 hr

Elevation gain: 860 m (2820 ft)

Maximum elevation: 2385 m (7825 ft)

Maps: Gem Trek 1;50,000 Canmore and Kananaskis Village [Old Baldy marked incorrectly], and NTS 1:50 000 Spray Lakes Reservoir 82 J/14

Trailhead: Evan-Thomas Creek day-use area, whose entrance is to the east off Highway 40, 22.8 km (14.1 mi) south of the entrance to Kananaskis Country.

This loop makes for interesting travel and represents another of the fine ridge-walks in the Kananaskis Valley area.

Start up the Evan-Thomas Creek trail, then turn left onto a side path 300 m past its junction with the Wedge Connector trail. (This is marked with two cairns, distinguishing it from the horse trail shortly before, and follows beside a creek coming in from the east.) Take the rough route up the valley, keeping north past a branch to the east. A series of easy creek crossings leads to a steep climb onto a terrace above the east bank, then a turn toward an ephemeral tarn.

Climb north on open slopes to the notch at gr 353412, then head west over gentler ground to the high point of Old Baldy at its north end [gr 344410]. Although a minor peak, this summit grants superb views, including of the unnamed outliers of Mt. McDougall that march off to the north. To the northwest are Mt. Allan and Mt. Collembola (#64-66), with Mt. Lougheed's four peaks beyond. Mt. Kidd is across the valley to the west, while the feature known simply as The Wedge reveals its trademark profile to the southwest. Fortress Ridge (#70) can be seen between the two; just east of The Wedge are the Mackay Hills, traversed on Ridgewalk 68.

There are lots of wildflowers on this trip, including silver rockcress, alpine forget-me-not, kinnikinnik (bearberry), red paintbrush, Jacob's ladder, stonecrop, spotted saxifrage, and shooting star. Among the wildlife that may be sighted, or of which sign can be seen, are elk, bighorn sheep, black bear, bushy-tailed woodrat, and grouse.

Although descent can be made to the west, it is a confusing thrash; much more interesting is to continue south and southwest along the ridge. On grassy slopes at first, there are later some stretches of big rocks; much of the remainder of the way down is in the trees. There are lots of small lodgepole pines (curiously, an apparently isolated bit of blazed trail might be encountered) and several small rockbands to negotiate before the final steep section down through open forest to the approach creek. Back on the path about 1.5 km from the Evan-Thomas Creek junction, take it out to the trailhead.

Ridgewalker John Blum on Old Baldy; Mt. Lorette on left and Fisher Range on right.

West on Ridgewalk 68 from saddle southeast of Mt. Mackay (on right) to (l to r) The Fortress, Gusty Peak, Mt. Galatea, and The Tower with part of Fortress Ridge [#70] below, and eastern aspect of The Wedge.

68 Mackay Hills

Distance: 20 km loop

Trail/off-trail: 8—12 hr

Elevation gain: 930 m (3050 ft)

Maximum elevation: 2455 m (8050 ft)

Maps: Gem Trek 1:50,000 Canmore and Kananaskis Village and NTS 1:50,000 Spray Lakes Reservoir 82 J/14

Trailhead: Evan-Thomas Creek day-use area, whose entrance is to the east off Highway 40, 22.8 km (14.1 mi) south of the entrance to Kananaskis Country.

This ridgewalk has a mundane beginning and an anything-but-mundane end (unfortunately, not in a positive sense). The middle section, though, is highly rewarding.

Start this outing with a plod on the old road up the valley of Evan-Thomas Creek, mostly in the trees. Two fords, almost 10 kilometres, and about two and a half hours later, arrive in the vicinity of Cloudburst Pass (having kept right at the junction with the trail continuing toward Evan-Thomas Pass).

Now commences the fun stuff: turn north and head up, through trees at first, then on open grassy slopes. The seldom-seen sheer rocky east face of The Wedge soon looms into view, with more expansive vistas unveiled from the knoll at gr 343334 (earned after ascending over 300 metres in a kilometre).

The panorama from this first of the Mackay Hills includes, to the west, The Fortress (looking particularly dramatic from this angle), Gusty Peak, Mt. Galatea, and The Tower. To the southeast is Fisher Peak, which gives the name to the entire Fisher Range, while to the southwest lies Opal Ridge (#69).

As well, to the north sits Old Baldy (#67), its southeastern cliffs apparent. Finally, farther off to the northwest are Mt. Allan and Mt. Collembola, venues for yet more ridgewalks (#64-66). On leaving the first knoll, descend slightly and gently to a dip graced with a grove of subalpine larches, then climb to the second hill [gr 335338].

From here, what is termed Mt. Mackay {even though it looks more-or-less equal in elevation to this second height} comes in sight, seemingly an easy stroll away. However, the northwest ridge of the second peak throws out some challenges, requiring that careful attention be paid on its descent. Once past the tricky bits, it is a straightforward plug up to the top of Mt. Mackay.

After savouring the panorama, be aware that the enjoyable part of the day is coming to a finish. Among a variety of options, all less than appealing, the author chose to bail west off the north ridge at treelimit, down into the drainage running north from the saddle between Mt. Mackay and The Wedge. This untracked valley presents unpleasant obstacles in the shape of windfall, alders, and doghair stands of lodgepole pine.

Perseverance will see the Wedge Connector trail at last stumbled upon, at which point a right turn will lead back to Evan-Thomas Creek and the outbound trail. Highway 40, which may be quite welcome by this stage, is actually closer if a left is made, which leads toward the Wedge Pond picnic area.

Having done this route, the following will address curiosity as to the names of the various features...Evan-Thomas was a British naval officer in World War I, Cloudburst was a coal company active in the area in the 1950s (a poetic name for a mining outfit, eh?), and Mackay was a prospector in the area around 1910.

North along Opal Ridge [#69] to The Wedge; Mackay Hills [#68] to right.

69 Opal Ridge

Map p. 271
Photo p. 133

Distance: 8 km linear

Trail/off-trail: 4—8 hr

Elevation gain: 1015 m (3330 ft)

Maximum elevation: 2600 m (8530 ft)

Maps: Gem Trek 1:50,000 Kananaskis Lakes and NTS 1:50,000 Spray Lakes Reservoir 82 J/14

Trailhead: Parking area at Fortress Junction, east off Highway 40, 37.3 km (23.1 mi) south of the entrance to Kananaskis Country.

Although the southern end of Opal Ridge looks daunting from below, it is straightforward. There's just the matter of getting up to it, which entails a steep grind of over 1000 metres elevation gain. Then follows some two kilometres of superb walking.

From the trailhead, pick a way up the wet slope to the powerline, then turn left on the access road. Cross a drainage, then head up right (possible flagging tape) and begin to grind it out. Don't, however, neglect the views that quickly appear: there are several brief respites in the steep grade that make for natural rest spots.

Another highlight along the way is an outcrop of large horn coral fossils. The high cliffs ahead seem impregnable, but a piece of sheep trail sneaks through an unexpected gap and traverses right to gain the dip at gr 315281. Now things settle down to the ridgewalk proper with a turn to the south and a climb up a gentler slope to the first of three bumps at gr 314275.

This gives views of the Mackay Hills (#68) just east of north, and even brings into sight the glaciated summit of Mt. Joffre off to the southwest. The slabby grey limestone peaks of the Opal Range make for a striking skyline to the southeast. The traverse to the southernmost of the three bumps and beyond gives an airy feeling, the Kananaskis Valley far below on the right and the valley of Rocky Creek on the left. To descend, drop east on mainly grassy slopes to the saddle at the head of Rocky Creek, then start what can be a rather convoluted descent of the drainage of Grizzly Creek.

Head steeply down into the notch, then get across to the south side of the drainage to pick up a path that traverses high across rocky slopes. Where the rocks run out, continue into trees (don't go down to the creek) and bend southwest—contouring as much as possible rather than going up. Come out above an open slope that leads directly down to the Grizzly Creek parking area, albeit with several small rockbands to negotiate.

70 Fortress Ridge

Map p. 272

Distance: 11 km out-and-back (or 9 km with loop)

Trail/off-trail: 4—8 hr

Elevation gain: 250 m (820 ft)

Maximum elevation: 2365 m (7755 ft)

Map: NTS 1:50,000 Spray Lakes Reservoir 82 J/14

Trailhead: Turn west off Highway 40 at Fortress Junction, 37.3 km (23.1 mi) south of the entrance to Kananaskis Country, and take the road to its end at the upper parking area of Fortress Mountain downhill ski area.

From the trailhead, take the service road that heads north (rather than the ski run to the northwest) and follow it over the rise. It turns southwest and traverses down into the headwaters of Aussie Creek, then climbs up the west side of the drainage to the ski facilities at the south end of Fortress Ridge.

Now, away from further development, begins the ridgewalk proper. Walk up the gentle first incline to the highest elevation on this outing. Easy to reach, it nevertheless grants an impressive vista including of course The Fortress with (cont. p. 136)

Ridgewalker Paul Zibotics (right) and thr author at the high point of Fortress Ridge, with The Fortress above.

(Cont. from p. 135) its folds of sedimentary rock. Also in sight are steep-walled unnamed outliers of Mt. James Walker above the basin at the head of Aussie Creek, Gusty Peak northwest of The Fortress, and the high pyramid of Mt. Galatea.

A small dip leads to the second high point, then a more pronounced descent precedes the rise to the third high point. Now the character of the trip changes a bit, for there is some scrambling to get down to the third dip. That done with, it's a simple haul up to the fourth high point that marks the sudden north end of the ridge. This spot gives a bird's-eye view into Galatea Creek and to Guinns Pass, which leads to Ribbon Creek.

A virtue of Fortress Ridge, which can be enjoyed at leisure as reversing the route, is the abundance of wildflowers in season. Among those that can be seen are spotted saxifrage, moss campion, roseroot, white mountain avens, felwort, red paintbrush, creeping beardtongue, stonecrop, golden fleabane, valerian, mountain fireweed (river beauty), western anemone, alpine speedwell, fringed grass-of-Parnassus, glacier lily, and forget-me-not.

An alternate, more direct return can be made from the south end of the ridge by going steeply down to Aussie Creek and then steeply up to the spur on the other side just before the trailhead.

The author on King Creek Ridge, with view south to Mt. Wintour and the Kananaskis Lakes with peaks beyond.

71 King Creek Ridge

Map p. 272

Distance: 7 km loop

Off-trail/trail: 4—8 hr

Elevation gain: 730 m (2395 ft)

Maximum elevation: 2420 m (7940 ft)

Maps: Gem Trek 1:50,000 Kananaskis Lakes and NTS 1:50,000 Kananaskis Lakes 82 J/11

Trailhead: King Creek day-use area, west off Highway 40, 45.8 km (28.4 mi) south of the entrance to Kananaskis Country and just north of the spur road west to Kananaskis Lakes.

This short loop holds the reward of expansive views over the Kananaskis Valley and dramatic peaks of the Opal Range.

From the parking area, walk back to Highway 40 and cross to the north bank of King Creek on the pavement. Cut back east on a short stretch of old road, then head up left on one of the steep, vague trails. Above, on grassy slopes, follow bits of path (some better defined than others, some marked with cairns) to gain the summit ridge.

Turn left (north) and climb more gradually, through trees at first, to the high point at gr 337222. A second, almost equally high, bump lies some 250 metres further along. These spots are excellent vantage points, especially for Mt. Wintour with its narrow profile and for the vertically tilted strata of the peaks of the Opal Range.

The Kananaskis Lakes sparkle deep blue in the valley to the south, with the mountains backing them culminating in glaciated Mt. Joffre. The Spray Mountains rise to the west, while the top of Fortress Mountain and Fortress Ridge (#70) are visible to the northwest.

Among the many wildflowers to be found on this outing are common harebell, white camas, nodding onion, red paintbrush, fireweed, stonecrop, rock jasmine, golden fleabane, yellow mountain heather, spotted saxifrage, valerian, Jacob's ladder, alpine forget-me-not, creeping beardtongue, and moss campion.

To make a circuit, drop east from between the two summit knolls to the saddle [gr 342225] between King Creek Ridge and Mt. Hood. Turn south and follow the valley of the north branch of King Creek back to the trail at the confluence of the two branches [gr 348204]. Keep in mind that this is prime grizzly bear habitat.

Head west through the canyon, rockhopping or wading where necessary, to pick up the established interpretive trail that leads back to the start. A highlight of the canyon is the presence of dippers, small, plump, grey birds that glean food in wild, clear streams, and that sing cheerfully year round.

72 Pocaterra Ridge

Map p. 272

Distance: 9 km linear

Trail/off-trail: 4—8 hr

Elevation gain: 460 m (1510 ft)

Maximum elevation: 2670 m (8760 ft)

Maps: Gem Trek 1:50,000 Kananaskis Lakes and NTS 1:50,000 Mount Rae 82 J/10 and Kananaskis Lakes 82 J/11

Trailhead: The parking area on the west side of Highway 40, 400 metres (0.2 mi) south of Highwood Pass, which is 63.2 km (39.2 mi) south of the entrance to Kananaskis Country and 38.4 km (23.8 mi) northwest of Highwood Junction. **N.B.** Highway 40 between the Kananaskis Lakes spur road and Highwood Junction is closed Dec. 1st—June 15th.

This is an enjoyable ridgewalk among rugged peaks, one whose easy access seems out of proportion to its scenic rewards. Be aware that grizzly bears frquent this area.

From the trailhead, take the start of the short Highwood Pass Meadows interpretive trail, then—where it turns right—leave it to the left. Follow the increasingly well beaten trail to a narrowing of the clearing near a boulder, where it dekes into the trees. Keep to it into the basin to the west. Rather than heading south to Grizzly Pass, veer northwest to Little Highwood Pass nestled at the base of the grey cliffs of the Elk Range. From the pass, climb east to the high point of Pocaterra Ridge [gr 403068].

From the high point, the ridge undulates over three subpeaks, extending over 3 km to the northwest. In the rocky basin between the ridge and the Elk Range is Rockfall Lake, which feeds a north-flowing tributary of Pocaterra Creek.

Silver-leaved scorpionweed, white mountain avens, rock jasmine, forget-me-not, kittentails, purple saxifrage, bladder locoweed, alpine cinquefoil, and even prairie crocus are among the hardy wildflowers that grow on the ridge.

A steep descent can be made to the east toward the highway, with a short ford of Pocaterra Creek before reaching the pavement.

Pocaterra Ridge and the nearby creek are named after George Pocaterra (1882-1972), a pioneer rancher, guide, and prospector who established the Buffalo Head ranch on the Highwood River, later sold to writer R.M. Patterson.

South end of Pocaterra Ridge (right) from the south; Elk Range on left.

East from the north end of Highwood Ridge [#73] to Ptarmigan Cirque and Mt. Rae.

139

73 Highwood Ridge

Map p. 260
Photos p. 7 and p. 139

Distance: 6 km linear to southeast end

Trail/off-trail: up to 4 hr

Elevation gain: 490 m (1605 ft)

Maximum elevation: 2700 m (8855 ft)

Maps: Gem Trek 1:50,000 Kananaskis Lakes and NTS 1:50,000 Mount Rae 82 J/10

Trailhead: The parking area on the west side of Highway 40, 400 metres (0.2 mi) south of Highwood Pass, which is 63.2 km (39.2 mi) south of the entrance to Kananaskis Country and 38.4 km (23.8 mi) northwest of Highwood Junction. **N.B.** Highway 40 between the Kananaskis Lakes spur road and Highwood Junction is closed Dec. 1st—June 15th.

This ridgewalk can allow a certain amount of smugness as cruising along the tops while looking way down to tiny vehicles on Highway 40.

Take the same start as for Pocaterra Ridge (#72), but upon reaching a small creek take a faint path marked with red and white tape that leads up to the north end of the target ridge.

Soon break out of the trees (including larches) and keep going, over grassy patches and a few rock steps. Lots of alpine wildflowers adorn the route: forget-me-not, kittentails, Parry's townsendia, spotted and purple saxifrages, mist maiden, roseroot, sawwort, and (a favourite of high country ramblers) moss campion. The high point [gr 423057] "falls to conquest" in just over an hour.

Ahead lies over three kilometres of superb sauntering, first over wide vegetated terrain, then on rockier ground toward the southeastern end. The route rolls over a series of knolls, with a final rise marking the end of the ridge. Pikas, least chipmunks, Clark's nutcrackers, water pipits, and rosy finches can be observed along the way.

Grizzly Ridge (#74) is of course nearby; Mt. Lipsett (#34) and Odlum Ridge (#35) are also in view. The progress of scramblers on Mt. Tyrwhitt and Mt. Rae can be followed.

A quick descent can be made to the highway, but the recommended course is to join the Grizzly Ridge route (#74) to return to Highwood Pass.

74 Grizzly Ridge

Distance: 8 km linear

Off-trail/trail: 4—8 hr

Elevation gain: 55 m (180 ft)

Maximum elevation: 2755 m (9035 ft)

Maps: Gem Trek 1:50,000 Kananaskis Lakes and NTS 1:50,000 Mount Rae 82 J/10 and Kananaskis Lakes 82 J/11

Trailhead: Southeast end of Ridgewalk 73, Highwood Ridge.

This route is described as a continuation from the southeast end of High-wood Ridge (#73). Head down to the notch of the creek draining "Paradise Valley," then steeply up to the southeast end of Grizzly Ridge. After this bit, enjoy a gentle amble toward Grizzly Pass.

There is a section with boulders, covered in black and light green lichens, that can be fun to balance from one-to-the-other in emulation of the bighorn sheep that frequent the ridge. Elk also occur in this habitat. Further, the author can vouch for the accuracy of the name of the ridge and the pass: once on descending from the scramble up Mt. Tyrwhitt, large prints in the snow on the north side of Grizzly Pass showed that a bear had passed in the time since earlier standing on the pass.

And that wasn't it for the incident...another scrambler had just taken footage of the bear in the meadows below and showed it to the author on the preview screen of his video camera. Yours truly only descended further after watching with binoculars as the bruin made its way onto Pocaterra Ridge. (As another footnote, that (cont. p. 142)

Bighorn sheep ram below the north end of Grizzly Ridge.

(Cont. from p. 141) caution was not shown by the people who unwisely and illegally had camped overnight in the same meadows. Fortunately, they had packed up and left in time, but things could easily have ended up differently.)

An optional extension, which adds 1 km distance and 30 metres elevation gain, can be made to the high point at gr 414055. (Connecting to the high point of Highwood Ridge is not advised due to the broken nature of the ridge.) Drop to Grizzly Pass to join the defined trail leading down to the aforementioned meadows and back to the trailhead.

Cloud sweeps over McConnell Ridge below the Barrier Lake fire lookout.

South from south ridge of Pigeon Mountain [#76], including Mt. Collembola [#66] (centre), and to its right Mt. Allan [#64 & #65] and a peak of Mt. Lougheed.

75 McConnell Ridge to Barrier Lake Fire Lookout

Map p. 272

Distance: 12 km out-and-back, or 12 km loop

Off-trail/trail: 4—8 hr

Elevation gain: 690 m (2265 ft)

Maximum elevation: 1995 m (6545 ft)

Maps: Gem Trek 1;50,000 Canmore and Kananaskis Village, and NTS 1:50,000 Canmore 82-O/3

Trailhead: Parking area on the south side of the Trans-Canada Highway, accessible from the eastbound lane only, 2.7 km (1.7 mi) east of the Lac des Arcs overpass. (The trailhead can be seen from the westbound lane, 6.1 km (3.8 mi) west of the Exshaw/Bow Valley Provincial Park exit overpass.)

This *is* a ridgewalk but it's not one that the author recommends. Most of the ridge is forested and so gives limited views, most of the forest is thick young growth so there is a lot of bushwhacking, at the end there is steep rock that requires rather daunting scrambling, and the fire lookout at the top is much more easily reached via an established trail.

If nevertheless desirous of doing this route, head up the Quaite Valley logging road about 500 metres, then leave it to climb up to the east. Initially in trees, the terrain becomes more open but includes slabs that can be skirted or taken straight on. A plateau partway up obstructs progress with doghair pines that make it tricky to keep oriented, plus threaten to poke an eye (as well as not being the place for an arachniphobe).

Eventually the forest becomes more open and there are meadows below the ridgecrest. The 'summit' at the northwestern end of the ridge sports a small plywood shed with green tarpaper roof, and three nearby antenna masts, but mostly uninspired views taking in heavy industrial development. The constant sound of traffic on the Trans-Canada Highway carries up to the spot, as well as occasional aural blasts from planes and trains.

The subsequent going is less than ideal, following scraps of trail at first, then descending to a dip before going over a bump to another dip (all the while mainly wandering among tree trunks). The final approach to the lookout is a steep grovel up scree and smooth rock, topping out almost right at the building (which is a private residence as well as workplace).

It will be more appealing—though not a highly scenic option either—to return via trail down the easterly ridge from the lookout, then to Jewell Pass and out via Quaite Valley.

76 Pigeon Mountain

Map p. 273
Photo p. 142

Distance: 16 km out-and-back with loop

Trail/off-trail: 8—12 hr

Elevation gain: 990 m (3245 ft)

Maximum elevation: 2395 m (7855 ft)

Maps: Gem Trek 1:50,000 Canmore and Kananaskis Village, and NTS 1:50,000 Canmore 82-O/3

Trailhead: Parking area near Alpine Resort Haven, reached by taking the Dead Man's Flats exit off the westbound lane of the Trans-Canada Highway and turning right in 0.5 km (0.3 mi). Turn right again at 0.6 km (0.4 mi), as if returning to Calgary; keep straight where turn left to do so {exit from eastbound lane of TCH joins here}. The road turns to gravel at 1.7 km (1.1 mi); keep on uphill until turn right at 2.8 km (1.7 mi) just before the Alpine Resort Haven entrance. Park before the gate in another 0.1 km (0.1 mi).

Although the approach to this ridgewalk is not very appealing, the reward makes it worthwhile.

From the trailhead, go south about 200 metres and turn left to tromp along old road, mostly the powerline right-of-way, with short detours into forest. At a cairn before a pronounced dip, turn left and go up several switchbacks. Finally reach the unmarked junction with the steep footpath to Pigeon Mountain, after over 5 km of uninspiring travel.

Soon leave the trees to ascend through vast meadows carpeted with wildflowers in season: prairie crocus, shooting star, forget-me-not, and kittentails—easily overlooked, but every bit as cute as the name suggests. Bighorn sheep frequent this area, which is apparent from their droppings even if the animals themselves aren't sighted.

The trail takes a good line to reach the saddle in the summit ridge, where it peters out after a couple of cairns. However, it's easy to continue to the summit of Pigeon Mountain. At 2395 metres, it's not very high but it has impressive cliffs below to the east and it gives good views. Highlights include Mt. Collembola (#66), Mt. Allan (#64 and #65), the four peaks of Mt. Lougheed, and even the top of Mt. Assiniboine.

Immediately to the east is the cirque-like valley of McGillivray Creek, with Mt. McGillivray (named after a fur trader who passed below in 1801) and unnamed higher peaks to the southeast. Other ridgewalks that can be identified are Mackay Hills (#68), Wind Ridge (#77), and Mt. Rundle Southeast Ridge (#84). There's not much percentage in continuing the 700 metres northwest to the low point at the end of the summit ridge...all it does it give a closer view of a shed on a spur below and the sight of more of the infrastructure in the heavily developed Bow Valley.

But once back at the saddle, it is recommended (it's really the whole point of this outing) to proceed southeast along the extension of the ridge. A subpeak with a shed at top is most easily gained by scrambling up over shaly rocks on the west side. From there it's a cruise down a wide, grassy ramp favoured by horned larks: small birds with black markings on head and throat; the terrain is much like the arctic tundra where many of them breed in summer.

Keep veering left [there are cliffs to the right, and rocky slopes] for the easiest descent. Classic examples of tree islands occur where the open areas are being colonized. Eventually return to forest with open patches and work down to the old road, where head right to rejoin the way up. {An option for a quick return is to mountain bike to the cairn or to the Pigeon Mountain junction, and fly back down those dreary kilometres.}

Southeast aspect of Wind Ridge [#77].

77 Wind Ridge

Map p. 273
Photo p. 145

Distance: 16 km out-and-back, or 16 km loop

Trail/off-trail: 4—8 hr

Elevation gain: 765 m (2510 ft)

Maximum elevation: 2170 m (7120 ft)

Maps: Gem Trek 1:50,000 Canmore and Kananaskis Village, and NTS 1:50,000 Canmore 82-O/3

Trailhead: As for Ridgewalk 76, Pigeon Mountain.

Wind Ridge is a classic outing now protected as part of a Natural Area following controversy regarding proposed development in the early 1990s.

The approach to the ridge is involved, so here follows detailed instructions: Head south from the trailhead on an old road, soon passing under a powerline and keeping straight where the trail to Skogan Pass and Pigeon Mountain (#76) goes left. Follow to the right round a cleared area for 700 metres to a crossing of Pigeon Creek via culverts, then keep right and 100 metres later cross Wind Creek on a bridge. Turn left at the intersection a mere 50 metres further on, then keep straight at a junction 500 metres later.

Reach another intersection in 900 metres, where keep straight and continue another 400 metres. Here is yet another junction, where keep straight and reel off another 500 metres. Keep right, then straight only 30 metres further. Now commence a steep climb among big Douglas-firs for about 1.5 km, where turn hard left. (Red arrows mark many of these junctions.)

Now on a level road, all the navigational to-and-fro is at an end. Contour around a spur and through a stand of trees to break out onto open slopes with views of West Wind Valley and the peaks around it, most spectacularly Windtower. The old road swings up north and narrows to footpath width as the ridge is finally attained. The south side of Wind Ridge surprises with its cliffs and meadows, features not present on the more-often-seen north side.

Now head west to ascend to the high point [gr 198533], with one minor bit of scrambling en route. There is a chimney left of where the trail reaches the crux rockband, but the better choice is just to the right. Clamber up about 2.5 metres to gain a ledge that trends to the right onto easier ground again.

On the flat top, views are to the north and northwest, including up the wide valley of the Cascade River: from here it seems the most obvious route further into the mountains, while the Bow River as it turns west around Mt. Rundle appears inconspicuous. It is the peaks in the immediate vicinity, though, that hold the most appeal. There's Windtower, as earlier mentioned, and the four summits of Mt. Lougheed. The summits of the Three Sisters have made their appearance too.

Also in view are inviting ridges on Mt. Allan (its north ridge #65), Mt. Collembola (#66), and Pigeon Mountain (#76). Tent Ridge (#80) lies below Mt. Birdwood and Mt. Smuts through West Wind Pass, while the ridges in the vicinity of "Tiara Peak" (#59 and #62) can be seen to the southeast over Skogan Pass.

Other attractions come in the shape of wildflowers, of which (to put it succinctly) there are lots...here's a good place to take a compact guidebook. [That's a plug {shameless, eh?} for the author's **Central Rockies Wildflowers**, also published by Luminous Compositions.]

To make a circuit, descend gradually southwest to the saddle at gr 189524, then descend southeast through meadows toward West Wind Creek. A trail will eventually be found leading downstream. Return to the start.

The name of the ridge is self-explanatory, yet that doesn't mean there isn't some intrigue here. It all stems from the fact that the original name for Mt. Lougheed was Wind Mountain, but that was changed in 1928 to honour politician James A. Lougheed. To further confuse matters, in 1986 the name Wind Mountain was reinstated but applied to the feature between the southeastern peak of Mt. Lougheed and Mt. Allan.

P.S. Be aware that there is lots of helicopter traffic in the vicinity, including many flights above West Wind Pass.

West from Reads Tower [#78] over Spray Lakes Reservoir to (l to r) Mt. Assiniboine, Mt. Nestor, and Old Goat Mountain.

78 Reads Ridge and Red Ridge

Map p. 273
Photo p. 147

Distance: 12 km linear

Unofficial trail/off-trail: 4—8 hr

Elevation gain: 925 m (3035 ft)

Maximum elevation: 2630 m (8625 ft)

Maps: Gem Trek 1:50,000 Canmore and Kananaskis Village and 1:100,000 Banff & Mt. Assiniboine, and NTS 1:50,000 Spray Lakes Reservoir 82 J/14

Trailhead: Sparrowhawk day-use area off Highway 742 (Smith-Dorrien/ Spray Trail), 23.1 km (14.3 mi) south of the Canmore Nordic Centre entrance and 39.0 km (24.2 mi) north of the junction with the spur road to Kananaskis Lakes.

This ridgewalk follows the approach used by scramblers heading for Mt. Sparrowhawk from the west, then strikes off to climb an easy slope to the summit of Reads Tower, otherwise ringed by impressive cliffs. The continuation leads to an adjacent ridge, making for an enjoyable, challenging loop.

Cross Highway 940 from the trailhead and climb up the bank to find the trail on the north side of what is known as Sparrowhawk Creek. (As a cautionary note, to the effect that bears can be anywhere, only about 50 metres along this path on his first attempt at this route the author was bluff-charged to within 5 metres by a grizzly sow with cub. Be aware!)

Where the trail veers right as it parallels the creek, climb to the left. First head up through trees (some flagging tape), then cross a shallow gully to join open slopes above the next drainage north. Continue up to the mini-knoll at gr 202439. Scramblers pass beneath the north face of Reads Tower here, but to go for its top simply push on up its southwest slopes after the slight drop.

There is loose stuff at the start, but the going is mostly quite good with mid-sized blocks and some slabby bits. From the top of Reads Tower the views include Mt. Assiniboine and neighbouring Mt. Eon to the west, and of course Spray Lakes Reservoir below.

The names for the ridge and tower come from Ken Read, the skier who was associated with the doomed proposal to put in a downhill course on these slopes for the 1988 Winter Olympics.

Descent could be made the same way, or once off the tower it may be feasible (the author hasn't confirmed this) to keep heading southwest right down to Sparrowhawk Creek, where the trail on its north side will lead back out to the trailhead.

But the most fun is to combine with Red Ridge: the names even go together! From the summit of Reads Tower, descend at the edge of the southwest ridge until find a place to cut down into the drainage to the left. The first big break in the cliffband will go with care (steep chute with lots of loose rock); other less dramatic choices exist lower down.

Traverse rugged terrain on a gradual descent to hit Sparrowhawk Creek as high as possible. There are myriad possibilities: one is to cross the drainage from the saddle northeast of Reads Tower and skirt the base of the slope to the east. Later turn left to traverse on an open slope with a few weathered tree skeletons. Go on or below grey slabs to get onto a ribbon of turf embroidered by small, wind-flagged subalpine fir. Next cross a boulderfield using a series of three giant boulders as 'railings.'

Continue southeast up the drainage of Sparrowhawk Creek to the tarns at its source, then slog west up scree in the chute left of a rock outcrop (the chute to the right has a tight spot best avoided). Reach the saddle at gr 214410, then head right up easy ground to the high point of Red Ridge (so called because of the colour of its rocks). The summit cairn grants a view of the steep western aspect of Mt. Bogart and back down to the colourful tarns. Of course, Spray Lakes Reservoir and the peaks beyond it lie to the west. Take some time to savour the scene.

On the descent, the terrain varies from grassy slopes to mid-sized rocks (to which lichens have taken a liking = slippery when wet) to broken boulders that call for a bit of scrambling. Several notches break the ridge, but nothing that can't be circumvented. Eventually drop to the creek below to the southwest, where a sketchy trail can be picked up on the north side. This leads out to Highway 40 at the Spray Lakes dayuse area, 1 km south of the trailhead.

Over Spray Lakes Reservoir from Red Ridge.

79 Ridge North of North Buller Pass

Map p. 274

Distance: 16 km out-and-back

Trail/off-trail: 4—8 hr

Elevation gain: 940 m (3085 ft)

Maximum elevation: 2755 m (9035 ft)

Maps: Gem Trek 1:50,000 Canmore and Kananaskis Village, and NTS 1:50,000 Spray Lakes Reservoir 82 J/14

Trailhead: Buller Mountain day-use area off Highway 742 (Smith-Dorrien/Spray Trail), 31.8 km (19.7 mi) south of the entrance to the Canmore Nordic Centre and 30.3 km (18.8 mi) north of the junction with the spur road to Kananaskis Lakes.

This ridgewalk leads to an unnamed mountain that nevertheless has a summit register, and which gives superb views.

Take the Buller Pass trail starting across the road from the spur leading into the day-use area, and hike about 4 km to a junction [gr 193378] shortly after crossing the south fork. (This intersection is approx. 1 km beyond the point where the trail crosses to the south bank of Buller Creek near the base of the northwest ridge of Mt. Engadine.) Turn left here to head up toward North Buller Pass, on a defined trail for the first kilometre.

The path becomes sketchy after crossing to the north side of this north fork, but the route is straightforward to the pass. From the saddle, head north up the open ridge toward a subpeak [gr 211395]. Skirt the cliffband on the east, and grovel up steep, loose scree if the summit of this feature is a goal. Otherwise, keep traversing until on an easy ridge again, and descend slightly to a saddle [gr 213397].

The easy, gradual slope north leads to the summit of the day's objective [gr 214404], a seldom-visited peak that rewards with excellent vistas. Mt. Assiniboine and its satellites, Eon Mountain and Mt. Aye, stand off to the west, while much closer in the opposite direction rises Mt. Bogart. Both Red Ridge and Reads Ridge (#78) lie below to the north. The Spray Lakes Reservoir fills the valley to the northwest; immediately below to the northeast are the colourful Sparrowhawk Tarns. Another attractive body of water, Ribbon Lake, is in the green valley to the southeast.

Backtrack to North Buller Pass and return by reversing the approach, or—if full of energy and desirous of further wandering—head for the unnamed saddle at gr 210383. From there, it's easy to go up the east ridge of the peak at gr 205383; it offers a fine vantage upon the sheer cliffs of Mt. Buller. Back at the saddle, drop south to join the main Buller Pass trail and take it out to the start.

Note that the peak between the two passes is a demanding scramble: the north ridge is unknown ground to the author; the south ridge from Buller Pass is steep and exposed near the summit.

This ridgewalk can also be done as a side trip from the backcountry campground at Ribbon Lake, reached via the 13 km trail up Ribbon Creek.

North along Ridge North of North Buller Pass; Mt. Sparrowhawk on left and Mt. Bogart on right.

View of Tent Ridge [#80] and peaks to south from north end of west arm of the horseshoe.

80 Tent Ridge

Map p. 273
Photo p. 151

Distance: 9 km loop

Trail/off-trail: 4—8 hr

Elevation gain: 670 m (2200 ft)

Maximum elevation: 2550 m (8365 ft)

Maps: Gem Trek 1:100,000 Banff & Mt. Assiniboine and NTS 1:50,000 Spray Lakes Reservoir 82 J/14

Trailhead: Small parking area on the east side of the spur road to Shark Mountain helipad and Watridge Lake trailhead, 1.8 km (1.1 mi) west of the junction with Highway 742 (Smith-Dorrien/Spray Trail). {The junction is 35.5 km (22.0 mi) south of the Canmore Nordic Centre entrance and 26.6 km (16.5 mi) north of the junction with the spur road to Kananaskis Lakes.}

This ridgewalk makes for an enjoyable circuit in a spectacular landscape. The only downside is some tricky routefinding to get onto the ridge. Happily, given proposals for massive development, this area is part of the Spray Valley Provincial Park established in 2000.

From the parking spot, go back along the road a little way, then turn right onto an old logging road. Take this into a cutblock. About 20 minutes from the start, turn hard right on a skid trail just before an old weather station (the choice of right skid track is a bit of a gambling proposition among the numerous options). This leads to a faint path along the upper edge of the cutblock, which goes into the forest—in 1997 there was a marker along the way in the form of a tin can atop a small dead tree {the label for "Town House Peach halves" was still legible at the time}.

Fresher flagging tape also indicates the rather vague path, which eventually meets a better trail at a T-junction. Turn left, then right after about 100 metres...keeping straight following the tape leads to another cutblock. The proper choice comes to what is known as Monica Brook and follows beside it to a beautiful basin with meadows, larches, wildflowers, and a shallow pond.

From the pond (or perhaps preferably earlier), cut left to gain the north end of the eastern part of the horseshoe. This enjoyable step features such colourful flora as moss campion, rock jasmine, mist maiden, and three species of saxifrage: yellow mountain, spotted, and purple. There are mats of bearberry on the level bits.

A small radio mast marks the high point of this arm [gr 154311]. Next is the saddle to the west, which takes less than five minutes to reach. Then climb up to the high point at gr 146308, from which there is a magnificent panorama. The most impressive views are those of the nearby steep peaks of Mt. Smuts, Mt. Birdwood, The Fist, Mt. Sir Douglas, Mt. Robertson, Commonwealth Peak, and Mt. French. But it's also possible to recognize such distant summits at Mt. Rundle, Cascade Mountain, and even Mt. Ball.

The author had two sightings on Tent Ridge itself: of an immature golden eagle, which although truly welcome was not unexpected, and of an upland sandpiper, which was more unusual. That species, presumably already migrating south in late August, has a long neck and large dark eyes.

The north end of Tent Ridge gives a fine view of Spray Lakes Reservoir, although as a dam-created body of water its aesthetic appeal is reduced. Much more wild, Mt. Assiniboine lies off to the west.

The descent is again somewhat involved, entailing first a descent northeast off the ridge and then locating a trail in the draw (referred to as Gawby Gulch). This later veers left into a cutblock, down which old roads go to a bigger road. Turn left here—right dead-ends—then right at the junction with a major logging road leading to Shark Lake. Hit the main road just west of the trailhead.

Rummel Lake below The Tower and Rummel Pass, from the north end of Ridge Southwest of Mt. Galatea [#81].

153

81 Ridge Southwest of Mt. Galatea

Map p. 274
Photo p. 153

Distance: 14 km out-and-back with loop

Trail/off-trail: 4—8 hr

Elevation gain: 790 m (2590 ft)

Maximum elevation: 2700 m (8855 ft)

Maps: Gem Trek 1:50,000 Kananaskis Lakes and 1:100,000 Banff & Mt. Assiniboine, and NTS 1:50,000 Spray Lakes Reservoir 82 J/14

Trailhead: Chester Lake parking area off Highway 742 (Smith-Dorrien/ Spray Trail), to the east 41.9 km (26.0 mi) south of the Canmore Nordic Centre entrance and 20.2 km (12.5 mi) north of the junction with the spur road to Kananaskis Lakes. {The junction is 2.2 km (1.4 mi) along the spur road from Highway 40.}

This outing settles for the subpeak on the well-defined ridge southwest of the summit of Mt. Galatea, but what it lacks in elevation it makes up with a superb jaunt.

Head up the heavily used trail to Chester Lake, but don't leave it too soon as that causes unnecessary elevation loss. Wait until shortly before the lake—at a point more or less on the line between the saddle southwest of Mt. Chester and the saddle east of this ridge, and near several small ponds to the right—to cut off-trail to the left. (Follow faint paths where possible to avoid trampling.)

The initial meadow leads to a narrow band of trees, beyond which is a tarn with grey boulders near its northwest corner. Go around the west side, then skirt the west side of a large meadow to avoid willow-bashing. This leads to several open swaths leading up to the ridge, of which the one farthest west leads to the crest soonest. [The trail used later on this trip may be found; if so, it can be followed for a while before striking up, but it's no big deal if it remains incognito until near the end of the day.]

Once on the ridge proper, simply follow it north to the summit at gr 203314. What could be called a 'scree' pole comes in handy on the lower section. Although there are cutblocks in evidence, the view is otherwise not shabby, crowned with the asymmetrical (from this direction) profile of Mt. Assiniboine. The ridge southwest of Mt. Chester (#82)—similar in appearance to this ridge—is nearby, while Tent Ridge (#80) lies due west.

Bighorn sheep frequent this ridge, attracted by a veritable salad bar. Among the numerous species of wildflowers to be seen are such alpine delights as rock jasmine, roseroot, sawwort, alpine hawksbeard, and moss campion.

A bonus of this outing is the descent northwest along the surprisingly sharp ridge, with dramatic cliffs on the east. Another enticement is the view of Rummel Lake, gradually revealed on the way down, as is the lofty grey, slabby summit of Mt. Galatea.

The north end of the ridge drops abruptly to Rummel Creek, but the recommended exit is to angle down south into an obvious draw. Apart from some shintangle and slide debris, the going is clear. Be aware that grizzly bears like the meadows on these slopes and in the draw.

Pick up a faint path that leads southeast through the draw, but don't continue down south at its end. Rather, cut left to intersect game paths that coalesce into a trail (some chainsaw cutting, flagging tape), which leads back to the meadow used to gain the ridge. Wind back down the Chester Lake trail to finish a rewarding trip.

View north from north end of Ridge Southwest of Mt. Chester [#82], including Ridge Southwest of Mt. Galatea [#81] (left), Mt. Galatea, Gusty Peak, and Chester Lake.

South from Snow Peak over Burstall Pass and South Burstall Pass to Mt. Sir Douglas, with ridge south of Burstall Pass on right [#83].

82 Ridge Southwest of Mt. Chester

Map p. 274
Photo p. 155

Distance: 11 km loop

Trail/off-trail: 4—8 hr

Elevation gain: 750 m (2460 ft)

Maximum elevation: 2660 m (8725 ft)

Maps: Gem Trek 1:50,000 Kananaskis Lakes and NTS 1:50 000 Spray Lakes Reservoir 82 J/14

Trailhead: As for Ridgewalk 81, Ridge Southwest of Mt. Galatea.

Like the nearby ridgewalk southwest of Mt. Galatea (#81), this outing does not bag a summit, but it does make for an enjoyable ramble.

The best way to approach this jaunt is in a south-to-north direction, so from the trailhead go only about 100 metres along the Chester Lake trail, then veer right before the bridge. Now on the Blue cross-country ski trail, head easterly. Cross a drainage in about 1 km, and keep straight at the intersection with Orange. In another 500 m or so, head left on Yellow at the junction where the Blue/Yellow comes up from below.

The trail now bends northerly before turning to cross Headwall Creek and head south briefly before the junction with the trail up the creek. Turn left and proceed some 300 metres to where the open slope of the ridge above to the northwest beckons. Leave the trail, cross the creek, and head up the steep, grassy slopes. Many wildflowers provide ample inspiration, and ample reason to pause for a breather.

There is one gully that may have to be negotiated; another concern is the strong possibility of grizzly bears in the area, so be alert for sign and make lots of noise. The high point of the day is the knoll [gr 219290] just above the saddle east of Mt. Chester that is used by scramblers heading for the peak.

Rather than taking the gully on the north side of the saddle {unless lightning threatens, in which case it serves as a quick escape route, as the author took advantage of on one occasion}, this ridgewalk stays high. Drop northwest, on bare terrain at first. Midway along is a level grassy section with an out-of-the-ordinary perspective upon Chester Lake. The final descent to the valley is steep, with some trees.

Although it is a bit longer, it is preferable to head east to the base of the draw below the above-mentioned saddle. There pick up the scrambler's trail that connects to the lake itself. This avoids trampling fragile (and wet) meadows, and even allows a stop at an outhouse if necessary. Besides, it's enjoyable to relax a while at the edge of the turquoise water before taking the well-established trail back to the start.

83 Ridges at Burstall Pass

Distance: 22 km out-and-back (with both options)

Trail/off-trail: 8—12 hr

Elevation gain: 895 m (2935 ft)

Maximum elevation: 2800 m (9185 ft)

Maps: Gem Trek 1:50,000 Kananaskis Lakes and 1:100,000 Banff & Mt. Assiniboine, and NTS 1:50,000 Spray Lakes Reservoir 82 J/14 and Kananaskis Lakes 82 J/11

Trailhead: Burstall Pass trailhead to the west off Highway 742 (Smith-Dorrien/ Spray Trail), to the west 41.9 km (26.0 mi) south of the Canmore Nordic Centre entrance and 20.2 km (12.5 mi) north of the junction with the spur road to Kananaskis Lakes. {The junction is 2.2 km (1.4 mi) from Highway 40.}

These two ridges near Burstall Pass are well worth exploring, and can readily be combined in a day's outing. To start, take the trail to the pass, reaching it after 8 km and less than two hours. The first option is to go up the prominence to the north, unofficially known as Snow Peak [gr 139256]. The going is easy at first, but becomes more difficult on steep scree and loose rocks. Many wildflowers provide visual stimulation and inspiration on this slog.

The effort is worth it for the marvelous views from the top. Included in the panorama is the summit of Mt. Assiniboine to the northwest, and most colourfully the tropical shades of Leman Lake below to the southwest. Parts of Tent Ridge (#80) and Wind Ridge (#77) can even be picked out to the north. Mt. Birdwood rises nearby to the northeast, while to the east is the valley of Burstall Creek with its lakes and beyond The Fortress and Mt. Chester. Glaciated Mt. Sir Douglas is the high peak to the southeast. Immediately below to the south are Burstall Pass and the ridge running south from it: the second option in this description.

In order to check that out, first descend from Snow Peak back to Burstall Pass. Then veer southwest over rolling terrain to gain the north end of the ridge, and head up from there over easy ground with one bit of scrambling. Several small subpeaks mark the crest, whose high point is at about gr 146231. Views from this vantage include Palliser Pass with attendant lakes far below to the southwest, and sharp Mt. Williams to the south. Descent southeast off the ridge leads toward the gap known as South Burstall Pass, from which head north down the wide draw to rejoin the Burstall Pass trail in the trees. If desired, an entertaining little extension can be made by detouring onto the knoll to the east. Keep in mind that its north end is quite steep, requiring scrambling and routefinding as it is bypassed on the west side.

The return to the trailhead completes a full, rewarding day.

Henry E. Burstall was a Canadian military officer in World War I.

Section 5 Banff National Park

Northwest along Mt. Rundle Southeast Ridge; Sulphur Mountain [#86] below skyline on left.

84 Mt. Rundle Southeast Ridge

Map p. 275
Photo p. 302

Distance: 12 km out-and-back

Trail/off-trail: 4—8 hr

Elevation gain: 1025 m (3360 ft)

Maximum elevation: 2700 m (8855 ft)

Maps: Gem Trek 1:50,000 Canmore and Kananaskis Village and 1:100,000 Banff & Mt. Assiniboine, and NTS 1:50,000 Canmore 82-O/3

Trailhead: Park off Highway 742 (Smith-Dorrien/Spray Trail) to the east near the edge of Whitemans Pond and off the right-of-way, 5.0 km (3.1 mi) south of the Canmore Nordic Centre entrance and 57.1 km (35.4 mi) north of the junction with the spur road to Kananaskis Lakes. {This trailhead is 0.6 km (0.4 mi) north of the Goat Creek trailhead parking area.}

The approach to the southeast ridge of Mt. Rundle takes the descent route for climbers who have done routes on the cliffs known as EEOR (East End Of Rundle). It is basically a hike with a little bit of scrambling near the top; once on the ridge, the undulating crest invites exploration.

Although the start is mainly a hike, it is one involving some 900 metres of elevation gain. Pick up the trail on the opposite (west) side of the road from the parking area, about 20 metres north of a sign for the Bow-Crow Forest and 100 metres north of the trailhead. This leads onto the ridge, treed at first, and then heads north: follow the well-beaten path. Near the top, either keep east on the crest or veer left on a trail up scree to a ledge system that goes right to get through a cliffband.

The end of this grunt is a narrow plateau, about 400 metres along, that sports two small peaks. The ridgewalk proper begins from the western one [gr 104597], and starts easily with a descent northwest into a saddle.

Although it appears inconsequential on the topo, this dip represents the crux of the route. For suddenly a sharp rocky crest looms up, and unless comfortable with exposed scrambling and tricky moves, the best bet is to turn it to the west. Sheep trail, slabs, and a small rockband lead to a higher rockband, at the base of which a scree gully leads up to the ridge once more. (The east side will go too but is more complicated.)

After this diversion, which results in an advance of only 200 metres or so, there is easy ground ahead. The first high point, at gr 100602, marks where the Banff National Park boundary comes in; it can also make for a nice lunch stop. Trundling {in this case it could be called Rundling} along, the second high point at gr 096611 brandishes some communication gizmos.

Shortly before the third high point [gr 090616], there is a cliff that is skirted by veering left to a cairn on the skyline. A short, easy chimney leads to (cont. p. 160)

(Cont. from p. 159) the top. The fourth high point [gr 083629] requires a bit of work, too, in the form of descending a notch {some exposure} just past an initial rockband. (In August, 2000, there was an inukshuk-style cairn just before the notch.) At the bottom of the notch, traverse along the base of the cliff for about 50 m, then scramble up to the ridge again.

This is the highest point of the day, and grants good views. Landmark Mt. Assiniboine rises to the southwest, while the less frequently seen Royal Group is further off to the south. Many iconic Rockies peaks fill the horizon to the west, while to the northeast is Carrot Creek (now reverting to a wildlife corridor). The town of Canmore fills much of the Bow Valley below, while nearer at hand are the several dramatic buttresses that 'fly' off at intervals from the ridge.

Of course, the long massif of Mt. Rundle continues ahead but clearly soon becomes more than a ridgewalk. One could push on to the base of the technical section but there doesn't seem a lot of point, plus the descent from this high point looks a bit gnarly. So the author did not go any further; it's a fair distance back, after all,

Return the same way, with the option of using a sheep trail on the west side to pass below the second high point. On covering this ground again, enjoy the different views and also savour such hardy wildflowers as alpine hawksbeard, alpine spring beauty, sawwort, roseroot, purple saxifrage, and mist maiden.

Mt. Rundle's name was given by James Hector in honour of Rev. Robert Rundle (1811-1896), a missionary to the Native people of the region in the 1840s.

Down Mt. Aylmer South Ridge to Lake Minnewanka; Fairholme Range on right skyline.

85 Mt. Aylmer South Ridge

Map p. 276

Distance: 34 km out-and-back

Trail/off-trail: 8—12 hr

Elevation gain: 1683 m (5520 ft)

Maximum elevation: 3163 m (10,375 ft)

Maps: Gem Trek 1:100,000 Banff & Mt. Assiniboine, and NTS 1:50,000 Canmore 82-O/3 and Lake Minnewanka 82-O/6

Trailhead: Lake Minnewanka parking area off Lake Minnewanka Road, 5.5 km (3.4 mi) from the Trans-Canada Highway interchange, north of the dam at the west end of the lake.

This long outing leads to the highest elevation of any ridgewalk in this book; as such, it gives extraordinary views. Note also that this trip has the most elevation gain of the 141 described.

From the trailhead, walk through the picnic area to pick up the trail, which crosses the bridge over Stewart Canyon in 1.5 km. Go up left at the far end of the bridge, then turn right to contour around a spur before dropping to the lakeshore. Head left at the junction in 7.8 km (to the right is a backcountry campground that can serve as an optional overnight base). Note that mountain biking to this point will shave off quite a bit of time if that is a concern.

Leave the shore of Lake Minnewanka to climb toward Aylmer Pass, but after 2.3 km take the right-hand trail. This ends in a further 1.7 km at the site of a former fire lookout, which as expected grants panoramic views.

But for the real McCoy, head off-trail up the ridge to the northwest. Simply keep on the well-defined crest, soon breaking out of a band of trees above the small open meadow where the lookout was situated. Keep in mind that bighorn ewes retreat to this high, remote location to have their lambs, so don't go too early in the season (there's likely to be too much snow higher up anyway) and don't disturb the sheep at any time.

Blue grouse like this habitat. Other highlights of the ridge come in the form of wildflowers, among them alpine forget-me-not, stonecrop, silky scorpionweed, rock jasmine, alumroot, and valerian.

The final approach to the summit of Mt. Aylmer bends to the northeast; to avoid a couple of rockbands on the ridge proper, it's advisable (even though a grovel) to skirt below them to the east on scree. Regain the ridge at a prominent notch; above this point [gr 087862], a switchbacking trail beaten into scree leads toward the lofty summit pyramid.

On top—thanks to a location isolated from other peaks—is a (cont. p. 162)

(Cont. from p. 161) 360 degree view with a veritable sea of summits, among them Mt. Assiniboine. Of course Lake Minnewanka spreads out in a long arc below. Ridgewalks in view include Sulphur Mountain (#86) and Sundance Range Northeast End (#87).

After soaking up the surroundings—a large scale map is recommended for identifying landmarks—descend to the notch. Either return the same way or if an inveterate explorer drop steeply west to Aylmer Pass and then turn south down the trail to Lake Minnewanka. **N.B.** There have been cougar sightings in the Aylmer Pass area.

The name of Mt. Aylmer comes from the Quebec hometown of J.J. McArthur, a pioneer surveyor who made the first ascent in 1889. This landmark, which serves as a barometer of alpine conditions for locals, is the highest peak within a 30 km radius of Banff townsite.

North on traverse of Sulphur Mountain ; Cascade Mountain on right with Tunnel Mountain and town of Banff below.

Sundance Range Northeast End [#87] with late-lying snow; on the skyline (l to r) Mt. Bourgeau, Mt. Brett, Pilot Mountain, and Mt. Temple.

86 Sulphur Mountain

Map p. 277

Distance: 7 km out-and-back (or 16 km linear)

Trail/off-trail: up to 4 hr

Elevation gain: 200 m (655 ft)

Maximum elevation: 2460 m (8070 ft)

Maps: Gem Trek 1:35,000 Banff Up-Close and 1:100,000 Banff & Mt. Assiniboine, and NTS 1:50,000 Banff 82-O/4

Trailhead: Upper terminal of the Sulphur Mountain gondola, whose lower terminal is at the top of Mountain Avenue {turn left at the bridge over the Bow River at the south end of Banff Avenue, then right at the lights in just 0.2 km (0.1 mi)}.

This well-known peak above Banff townsite can be traversed, making for an interesting outing with fine views.

Most will take the gondola to get an easy start on this outing, though purists can toil up the 5.5 km long Sulphur Mountain trail. (Truly dedicated ridgewalkers can do a complete traverse by starting from the Cave & Basin National Historic Site on the Sundance Canyon trail, then leaving the pavement after 600 metres to go up to the saddle south of "Philosopher's Knoll" [gr 972687]. Head up southeast from here {some easy slabby sections}, initially through a fireguard created to protect the town of Banff. Contrary to the indication on the government topo, there are some meadows along the west side of the lower portion of this route, so are views to be enjoyed too.)

From the gondola's upper terminal, escape the crowds and the mooching bighorn sheep to head southeast along the ridge, on a well-defined trail at first. This fades just at a narrow ledge which gives some sensation of exposure; an option is to scramble up before it on granite-like boulders. Either way, gain the crest and begin the passage of an undulating series of subpeaks. The two at gr 012644 and gr 018633 are of about equal elevation and represent the high points of the day. Mt. Rundle fills the view to the east, while the long Sundance Range runs above the valley to the west. [It's possible to suss out the ridgewalk at its northeast end (#87).]

Sheep will probably be sighted along the way; their trails make for good travel. A few subalpine larches grace the ridge, as well as other typical alpine inhabitants such as Clark's nutcrackers, hoary marmots, and pikas. The flora includes purple saxifrage, forget-me-not, and even prairie crocus. A highlight of this jaunt is the presence of excellently preserved fossils, the white remains in grey rock surrounded by bright orange lichens.

From gr 018633, there are two choices: either go back the same way, in which case a ride down the gondola awaits [free if hiked up]. Or—provided the seasonal closure of the Spray Valley for wildlife is not in effect—continue southeast (cont. p. 164)

(Cont. from p. 163) to the saddle [gr 024625] before the final subpeak. At this juncture, drop steeply south to hit the trail southeast of Sundance Pass. Now there's a long haul ahead: down to the Spray, parallel to it through the gap between Sulphur Mountain and the Goat Range, and on toward the townsite.

A connector runs up to the trailhead from the old fire road on the west side of the river, starting about 2 km past the footbridge that leads to the east side trail.

Alpine wallflower growing among rocks on Wawa Ridge [#88].

The author at cairn at south end of Twin Cairns [#89]; Monarch Ramparts [#91] below skyline on left, and Mt. Ball on centrte skyline.

87 Sundance Range Northeast End

Map p. 278
Photo p. 162

Distance: 18 km out-and-back with loop

Trail/off-trail: 8—12 hr

Elevation gain: 1300 m (4265 ft)

Maximum elevation: 2695 m (8840 ft)

Maps: Gem Trek 1:35,000 Banff Up-Close and 1:100,000 Banff & Mt. Assiniboine, and NTS 1:50,000 Banff 82-O/4

Trailhead: The large parking area at the Cave & Basin National Historic Site, at the east end of Cave Avenue, reached by turning right after the bridge over the Bow River at the south end of Banff Avenue.

This ridgewalk along a portion of the extensive Sundance Range requires a fair bit of bushwhacking but is rewarding nonetheless.

From the trailhead, take the wide paved trail past the Cave & Basin to the Sundance picnic area. A bicycle could be brought into play on this first 3.7 km. Now take the hiking trail up beside the waterfalls of brief Sundance Canyon, and where it leaves the creek after about 1 km, leave it to forge an off-trail route to the southwest.

The going is gentle at first, then becomes steeper, and the shrubbery is quite thick. Perseverance will be rewarded by breaking out in the open on the northeast arm of the range. Subalpine larches are a bonus of reaching this elevation, truly appreciated when they're found the hard way. Ditto for purple saxifrage.

Proceed over a series of knolls to a subpeak at gr 954645. Then veer southeast along a level stretch before a short dip prior to climbing on a good animal path to the high point of the day at gr 957631. There are views southeast along the rugged continuation of the range, and east to Sulphur Mountain and Mt. Rundle. The Bow River and Vermilion Lakes lie below. Among the encircling peaks are those to the north, including Mt. Cory, Mt. Edith with its three peaks, Mt. Norquay, and Cascade Mountain. Mt. Assiniboine comes into view too. Mt. Temple, another icon, lies to the northwest, as do Castle Mountain and Helena Ridge (Ridgewalks 95, 96, and 97).

There are possibilities of continuing south along the ridge, but the descent described here involves retracing steps to the saddle at gr 959637. Then drop east to a basin with three small-to-medium-sized lakes, and follow down the drainage from the largest one. It is feasible to hike right in the creek bed in dry conditions, all the way to the confluence with Sundance Creek (boggy area). Pick up the trail on the far side of the creek and turn left to follow it back to the pavement 300 metres down from the picnic area. Head east to the trailhead.

The names of the range and the creek come from the Native ceremony, which was performed in the vicinity.

88 Wawa Ridge

Map p. 279
Photo p. 164

Distance: 6 km out-and-back

Trail/off-trail: up to 4 hr

Elevation gain: 285 m (935 ft)

Maximum elevation: 2480 m (8135 ft)

Maps: Gem Trek 1:100,000 Banff & Mt. Assiniboine and NTS 1:50,000 Banff 82-O/4

Trailhead: Take the 9.0 km (5.6 mi) spur road to the parking area at the gondola terminal for the Sunshine Village downhill ski area. This starts at the Sunshine interchange on the Trans-Canada Highway, 9.0 km (5.6 mi) west of the Norquay interchange near Banff townsite and 21.0 km (13.0 mi) south of Castle Junction. Get to the Sunshine Village base complex by shuttle bus [call White Mountain Adventures (403) 678-4099]; or, if a diehard, hike 6.5 km up the access road.

This short outing in the Sunshine Meadows leads to a knoll with fine views.

From the end of the road at the centre of facilities for the downhill ski area, take the "Meadow Park" trail leading up north in a ski run. This veers west after about 600 metres and climbs to a high point with rest benches on the trail leading to Simpson Pass.

Leave the trail and head north, hiking on rocks or bare ground as much as possible to avoid trampling vegetation. Leave the last trees behind after some 400 m and climb gradually along the wide, open crest. Here can be found the purple, four-petalled blossoms of alpine wallflower, a rare member of the mustard family.

A short steeper section at the end leads to the top of the knoll, crowned with several tall cairns. Here are granted sweeping views south over the Sunshine Meadows area, including Twin Cairns (#89) and the twin peaks of Quartz Hill (#90). To the west lie Healy Pass and the Monarch Ramparts (#91), while to the north the route between Harvey Pass and Healy Pass (#93) can be checked out.

It's recommended to combine this short jaunt with a visit to Twin Cairns.

89 Twin Cairns

Map p. 279
Photo p. 164

Distance: 9 km loop

Trail/off-trail: up to 4 hr

Elevation gain: 352 m (1155 ft)

Maximum elevation: 2547 m (8354 ft)

Maps: Gem Trek 1:100,000 Banff & Mt. Assiniboine and NTS 1:50,000 Banff 82-O/4

Trailhead: As for Ridgewalk 88, Wawa Ridge.

The crest of this enjoyable short ridgewalk in the Sunshine Meadows area lies on the Alberta/British Columbia boundary, which here also represents the demarcation between Banff National Park and Mount Assiniboine Provincial Park.

The approach is as for Wawa Ridge (#88), and it is worthwhile taking that jaunt in before embarking on this outing. From the Monarch Viewpoint on the Simpson Pass trail, head south and then southeast. Pass an ephemeral pond in a small dip before beginning the steeper ascent to the north end of the summit ridge. As the name suggests, cairns proliferate on this route.

Wildflowers are abundant too, including moss campion and mountain meadow cinquefoil in unusual proximity. Another rewarding sighting can be the rare species mist maiden, also known as cliff romanzoffia. Aristocratic sounding, eh? Well, rightly so, since it comes from a Russian count of that name (1754-1826), sponsor of a botany expedition to the Pacific Northwest.

Twin Cairns also sports larger denizens in the shape of grizzly bears. The author saw diggings right beside the cairn at the south end of the ridge in July, 2000. Keep alert and don't assume that because you are up high a bear won't be as well.

Highlights of the views from Twin Cairns are—to the west—The Monarch with Eohippus Lake beneath its east face and the enticing Monarch Ramparts (#91) running off to the north {parts of Hawk Ridge (#134 and #135) are in view too}. To the southeast, the alluring Sunshine Meadows roll along beyond Grizzly, Larix, and Rock Isle lakes, with the summit of Mt. Assiniboine towering over all on the horizon.

On descent to the south, be careful not to continue onto the narrowing ridge that drops into the deep hole of the valley of North Simpson River. Instead, enjoy the gentle grassy ridge for a while, then bail southeast to Grizzly Lake. A small pond high on the slope serves as a landmark for the point at which to head down through meadows and open subalpine larch forest. (This ramp is north of a large rockslide.)

Pick up the trail at the northeast corner of Grizzly Lake and head east to Rock Isle Lake. Here either return to the trailhead or extend the ridgewalk by taking in Quartz Hill (#90).

90 Quartz Hill North and South Summits

Map p. 279

Distance: 10 km loop

Trail/off-trail: 4—8 hr

Elevation gain: 385 m (1265 ft)

Maximum elevation: 2580 m (8464 ft)

Maps: Gem Trek 1:100,000 Banff & Mt. Assiniboine and NTS 1:50,000 Banff 82-O/4

Trailhead: As for Ridgewalk 88, Wawa Ridge.

The two summits of this low peak make for a fine ridgewalk. They can be tackled in either order: this description suggests going for the north summit first via a gentler approach, then descending steeply from the south summit.

From the base of the downhill ski area, take the trail south to Rock Isle Lake. The most interesting variation for this outing gains the ridge south of the lake; it undulates at first, but the going is very pleasant and scenic.

After a kilometre or so, the angle becomes a bit greater as the north summit draws near. To continue to the south summit, drop into the intervening saddle and push on up the ridge. It appears to loom steeply but goes rather easily...there's even a bit of a path in places.

This higher south summit grants new views southeast beyond Howard Douglas Lake (mistakenly marked Sundown Lake on some maps) over extensive meadows to Citadel Peak and Citadel Pass. The summit of Mt. Shanks in Kootenay National Park, south end of the ridgewalk on the southern section of Hawk Ridge (#134), lies about 10 km to the southwest. Of course Mt. Assiniboine is the eyecatcher in the whole panorama.

Although the author hasn't done so yet, it looks feasible if desired to continue southeast on the ridge for about another kilometre before a precipitous drop into the valley of Simpson River, at which point veer northeast to join the trail near Howard Douglas Lake (which features a backcountry campground) and back over Quartz Ridge.

If not up for this longer option, descend steeply to the east from the south summit directly to Quartz Ridge (snow lingers here late into the season so an ice axe would not be amiss). Pick up the well-defined trail back to the start to end this ramble: inspiring on a fine summer day, though not much fun if the weather's bad since so much is in the open, even off the ridge.

South summit of Quartz Hill from saddle to north; Mt. Assiniboine on skyline to right.

North along Monarch Ramparts [#91] to Healy Pass and small peak (on right) near west end of Harvey Pass to Healy Pass ridgewalk [#93].

91 Monarch Ramparts

Map p. 280
Photo p. 169

Distance: 23 km out-and-back with loop

Trail/off-trail: 8—12 hr

Elevation gain: 760 m (2495 ft)

Maximum elevation: 2435 m (7985 ft)

Maps: Gem Trek 1:100,000 Banff & Mt. Assiniboine and NTS 1:50,000 Banff 82-O/4

Trailhead: Take the 9.0 km (5.6 mi) spur road to the parking area at the gondola terminal for the Sunshine Village downhill ski area. This starts at the Sunshine interchange on the Trans-Canada Highway, 9.0 km (5.6 mi) west of the Norquay interchange near Banff townsite and 21.0 km (13.0 mi) south of Castle Junction.

This route at the head of Healy Creek is a classic ridgewalk with great views, easy terrain, unusual wildflowers, the possibility of sighting wildlife, and a little-visited area of wilderness.

Take the Healy Creek trail from the parking area, which starts behind (west of) the gondola building {not on the main access road to Sunshine Village, but on an old road that runs below and parallel to it}. At 5.5 km, pass a backcountry campground that could be used as a base for this outing; 400 metres later, keep right at the junction but note the trail over the footbridge to the left: this is point where the loop closes on the return.

Climb more steeply, breaking out into vast meadows interspersed with subalpine larch trees in less than 2 km further. Healy Pass lies 9.2 km from the start—here the trail is left behind. Turn southeasterly (on a bit of path at first) to roller-coaster over a few bumps before gaining the long, broad, level stretch of Monarch Ramparts. And a wonderfully long stretch it is, the ridge running for over two kilometres.

It's a scenic route too, with numerous tarns below to the east and views farther in that direction to Cascade Mountain and the Fairholme Range. The panorama to the west isn't bad either, including Egypt Lake and Natalko Lake beneath steep rockwalls. Mt. Assiniboine of course is a prominent landmark to the southeast.

It is an open route, exposed in blustery conditions. [The prevailing westerly wind results in pronounced cornices on the leeward side of the ridge.] But even in such a habitat, the wildflowers are outstanding. They include spotted saxifrage, golden fleabane, white mountain avens, and moss campion, all of which are certainly welcome but not unexpected. The contenders in the unusual category are Sibbaldia and alpine lousewort: the later actually very attractive despite its unprepossessing name.

Wildlife to be seen along this jaunt includes golden-mantled ground squirrels and such bird species as horned lark, white-tailed ptarmigan, and even bald eagle and osprey. Keep in mind that grizzly bears are a possibility too, especially after dropping off the ridge to Eohippus Lake.

That is the way to go: where the Ramparts veer south and make a slight dip (some trees) before the steep north ridge of the imposing peak known eloquently as The Monarch, scoot down to the southeast on easy ground toward the large lake. This is a quiet corner of Mount Assiniboine Provincial Park in British Columbia, a pleasant place to relax a while.

The trail north to Simpson Pass is tricky to locate, but soon becomes well-defined and passes beside several shallow lakes on its way back into Banff National Park. Keep northerly from the pass on the trail that drops to the above-mentioned junction, from which the way is known.

The author on summit of unnamed peak in Massive Range [#92]; view west includes Mt. Ball on left.

East over route of Harvey Pass to Healy Pass ridgewalk [#93]; unnamed peak in Massive Range [#92] on left and Mt. Bourgeau on right.

92 Unnamed Peak in Massive Range

Map p. 281
Photo p. 171

Distance: 25 km out-and-back, or 24 km out-and-back with loop

Trail/off-trail: 8—12 hr

Elevation gain: 1460 m (4790 ft)

Maximum elevation: 2905 m (9530 ft)

Maps: Gem Trek 1:100,000 Banff & Mt. Assiniboine and NTS 1:50,000 Banff 82 O-4

Trailhead: The Bourgeau Lake parking area, on the west side of the Trans-Canada Highway 2.8 km (1.7 km) north of the Sunshine interchange and 0.5 km (0.3 mi) south of the bridge over Wolverine Creek.

This prominence in the Massive Range west of Banff townsite gives a superb vista down the Bow Valley.

Take the Bourgeau Lake trail to just before the lake, at which point keep to a trail through the forest north of the lake. The best route is to keep north of the draw that leads up to a short canyon. Arrive at more level going beside a small lake, then angle around and above it south to Harvey Pass. Now get on the ridgewalk: first west, then northwest to the knoll at gr 828654. Next head north, to a dip and up again, then veer northeast above the large cirque below. Skirt a bump on the ridge by passing below on the right, and arrive at the base of the summit block.

The final approach is up a gully, where all of a sudden the east face of this mountain falls dramatically away. Here there is a sweeping view east over Wolverine Creek to the Bow Valley and Banff townsite. Cascade Mountain and Mt. Rundle define the skyline in that direction; below those landmarks are Sulphur Mountain (Ridgewalk 86) and the Sundance Range (Ridgewalk 87). There is of course a 360-degree panorama: take a map to figure out the landmarks.

Descend the same way, or as an alternative, drop northwest from the base of the summit block via a gully, then contour/climb north to the saddle at gr 830673. There is a fine sheep trail to the northeast that gets through the cliffband below with their usual navigational panache. (Speaking of sheep, it is likely that wild bighorns—as opposed to their habituated cousins around Banff townsite—will be seen on this jaunt.)

Once through the cliffband, bend southeast down into a lush meadow area. Next stay above the trees to round the southeast ridge of the peak just scaled. The Bourgeau Lake trail is down to the south (don't go southeast as there are cliffs below).

93 Harvey Pass to Healy Pass

Distance: 27 km linear

Trail/off-trail: 8—12 hr

Elevation gain: 1155 m (3790 ft)

Maximum elevation: 2600 m (8530 ft)

Maps: Gem Trek 1:100,000 Banff & Mt. Assiniboine and NTS 1:50,000 Banff 82-O/4

Trailhead: As for Ridgewalk 92, Unnamed Peak in Massive Range.

This long but rewarding day surveys a vast territory from high atop the gentle ridge stretching between Harvey Pass and Healy Pass.

Start as for Ridgewalk 92, Unnamed Peak in Massive Range, then once above Harvey Pass, keep west, skirting below the first bump on the above route. Aim for the high point of the day at gr 821649. Here is as good as anywhere on this ridgewalk to stop and savour the views. To the west are peaks on the Continental Divide, prominent among them glaciated Mt. Ball. Northwest and north are many more landmark Main Ranges mountains, while to the south are the rolling alplands of the Sunshine Meadows. Mt. Assiniboine marks the culmination of the view in that direction.

Parts of this route follow well-defined animal paths, with bighorn sheep and mountain goats the prime movers in their development. Pikas also thrive in this alpine area. There are many subalpine larches in the meadows at the head of Lost Horse Creek, presenting a golden glow in autumn.

Among the wildflowers to be found on this outing are such survivors as moss campion, white mountain avens, forget-me-not, purple saxifrage, and alpine wallflower.

From the high point, drop southwest to a saddle, then go south over a small knoll and up to a prominence [gr 813627]. Below to the southwest is a broad saddle that connects with a high point [gr 806618]. It's possible to head down south to the Healy Pass trail from here. But the full deal calls for continuation northwest and west to a saddle, then the final ascent of the day up to gr 797622.

This is a fitting spot to have a breather. The views to take in include sparkling lakes below to the west: Egypt, Pharaoh, and Scarab among them [revealing a certain geographical inclination on the part of the Interprovincial Boundary Survey]. Then descend south to Healy Pass and take the trail east down the creek to the Bourgeau parking area at the end of the Sunshine road.

Harvey Pass is named after Nova Scotia-born Ralph L. Harvey, a pioneer skier who made the first winter crossing of the pass. Healy Pass is after Capt. John Healy, a man of many talents, including as a prospector in this area. The name of Lost Horse Creek recalls a wayward equine that belonged to outfitter F.O. "Pat" Brewster.

94 "Muleshoe Ridge"

Map p. 278

Distance: 7 km out-and-back

Trail/off-trail: up to 4 hr

Elevation gain: 880 m (2885 ft)

Maximum elevation: 2280 m (7480 ft)

Maps: Gem Trek 1:100,000 Banff & Mt. Assiniboine and NTS 1:50,000 Banff 82-O/4

Trailhead: Picnic area parking on the west side of the Bow Valley Parkway, 5.5 km (3.4 mi) north of its southern start off the Trans-Canada Highway and 12.0 km (7.4 mi) south of the Johnston Canyon parking area. **N.B.** There is a use restriction in effect on the Bow Valley Parkway between the Trans-Canada Highway and Johnston Canyon from March 1st to June 25th, under which traffic is requested to not travel from 6 p.m. to 9 a.m. daily.

This short but steep ridgewalk rewards with fine views.

Cross the road from the trailhead to pick up the Muleshoe trail, which runs through an area regenerating after a prescribed burn. The established trail ends after just over 1 km, at the base of a steep grassy slope. Take the faint path which climbs on up, then veer left to ascend north up the ridge that culminates at gr 899724.

Surprisingly, mountain goats frequent this western outlier of Mt. Cory. (A steep gendarme precludes access to the summit from this direction.) Wildflowers such as paintbrush, common harebell, shrubby cinquefoil, golden rattle, and wild gaillardia (brown-eyed Susan) add splashes of colour to the meadows. Higher up occur low larkspur, forget-me-not, and spotted saxifrage.

The ridgetop grants a panorama to the northwest, taking in nearby Mount Finger, named by Lawrence Grassi, the stalwart climber and guide who led the first ascent of the pinnacle. More distant features in that direction include Helena Ridge, Stuart Knob, and Castle Mountain, the venues for ridgewalks 95, 96, and 97.

Far below is the ox-bow lake, a former channel of the Bow River, which is the origin of the name Muleshoe due to the similar shape. To the southeast is another outlier of Mt. Cory, sporting a prominent vertical groove in the smooth cliff. Mt. Assiniboine is visible off in distance to the south.

Return the same way.

The author on "Muleshoe Ridge," looking north to (l to r) Mt. Temple (behind branches), Castle Mountain [#95], Stuart Knob [#95], TV Peak [#99], and Helena Ridge [#95, #96, and #97].

Southeast from the true summit of Castle Mountain [#95]; Helena Ridge in mid-distance to right.

95 Helena Ridge North Summit, Stuart Knob, and Castle Mountain True Summit

Map p. 281
Photo p. 175

Distance: 27 km out-and-back with loop

Trail/off-trail: 8—12 hr

Elevation gain: 1430 m (4690 ft)

Maximum elevation: 2880 m (9445 ft)

Maps: Gem Trek 1:100,000 Banff & Mt. Assiniboine and NTS 1:50,000 Castle Mountain 82-O/5

Trailhead: Parking area for Rockbound Lake trail on north side of Highway 1A (Bow Valley Parkway), 6.5 km (4.0 mi) west of Johnston Canyon and 0.2 km (0.1 mi) east of the intersection of connector from Trans-Canada Highway with Highway 1A at Castle Junction.

This long outing takes in three landmarks above Rockbound Lake: the north summit of Helena Ridge, Stuart Knob, and the true summit of Castle Mountain.

To begin, take the steady grind on the trail up to Rockbound Lake, reaching that cliff-girt body of water in around two hours of steady going. Continue around its eastern shores past the outlet, which rarely flows. Then get through the cliffband by taking the gully closest to the rounded knoll above, which has a well-defined section of trail.

From the knoll, head north up to the saddle at gr 747863. (In the groove below the saddle, there is a pronounced demarcation between brown scree on the left and bigger grey rocks on the right: the latter make for better progress.) Now turn left up its southeast ridge to the north summit of Helena Ridge at gr 746865. This symmetrical cone gives a close vantage upon an unusual dome formation below on Castle Mountain.

Continuing this ridgewalk, descend west (with a little bit of scrambling) to the long, wide, gentle ridge sweeping toward Stuart Knob. Bladder locoweed and bladder campion (an exotic species) thrive on the scree here despite the frequent strong winds.

The isolated peak of Stuart Knob is easily ascended from the north; one approach is to pass at the base of the south face to reach the ridge to the west, then double back east to the summit. The long narrow surface of Luellen Lake lies over 800 m below to the east.

From Stuart Knob, proceed southwest to the true summit of Castle Mountain at gr 719864 (elevation 2850 metres). This is almost 100 metres higher than the highest point toward its southeastern end, which is commonly thought of as the top of Castle Mountain. The final ridge to the cairn can be dangerously corniced: stay well back from the edge.

This spot grants a heart-pounding appreciation of the virtually vertical west face of Castle Mountain, and takes in a veritable sea of peaks. An interesting aspect of the panorama is the angle of view upon the hanging glacier on Bident Mountain and Quadra Mountain west across the Bow Valley through Taylor Pass.

Osprey may be sighted flying above the ridges of this walk, and fishing in Rockbound Lake, although the recently-discovered presence of toxaphene and other persistent organic pollutants in high alpine lakes and their fish does not bode well for these avian predators at the top of a food web. (And it was thought they were mostly "out of the woods" once the use of DDT was banned in North America...)

Return to the knoll above Rockbound Lake by backtracking to the dip toward Stuart Knob, then dropping (possible late-lying snow) into the wide rocky basin and heading southeast. Pick up the inbound route to finish the day.

An optional extension can be made to the south summit of Helena Ridge (#96) from the saddle at gr 747863, with return to that point before continuing on this ridgewalk.

Helena Ridge was named by geologist Charles D. Walcott for his second wife, who actively participated in his field work. Stuart Knob is named after their son. The renowned landmark of Castle Mountain was first given its descriptive name by explorer James Hector in 1858.

South from Helena Ridge South Summit [#96] over the route of Ridgewalk #97 and to the Sawback Range.

96 Helena Ridge South Summit

Map p. 281
Photo p. 177

Distance: 22 km out-and-back with loop

Trail/off-trail: 8—12 km

Elevation gain: 1440 m (4725 ft)

Maximum elevation: 2890 m (9480 ft)

Maps: Gem Trek 1:100,000 Banff & Mt. Assiniboine and NTS 1:50,000 Castle Mountain 82-O/5

Trailhead: As for Ridgewalk 95, Helena Ridge North Summit, etc.

This south summit of Helena Ridge is slightly higher than the north summit and is a more dramatic peak, as well as being higher than any part of better-known Castle Mountain. Maybe they should be called Helena Mountain and Castle Ridge?

Hike to the saddle at gr 747863 as described in Ridgewalk 95, Helena Ridge North Summit, etc. On this route, turn right over gentler slopes to the middle summit of Helena Peak [gr 755863]. This reveals the high cliffs below to the east, with an impressive waterfall leaping down from the saddle.

Reaching the south summit from here requires about 45 minutes, and entails some scrambling. The most intriguing views from the south summit are of the Sawback Range to the east, from the Bonnet Peaks to Mt. Ishbel. The east end of Luellen Lake is in sight, as are three smaller turquoise, larch-surrounded lakes immediately below.

A whole panoply of peaks fills the gaze to the west, from Mt. Assiniboine in the south to Mt. Forbes in the north. It is not feasible to directly continue the ridgewalk to the southeast, so descent can be made by backtracking to the second gully from the top and then dropping all the way down. This leads to Silverton Creek very close to Tower Lake, where the inbound trail is picked up. [Although the author has not done so, it appears feasible if desired to link with Helena Ridge Southeast End (#97) by descending about 300 metres vertical from the south summit and then traversing into the saddle at gr 767847.]

As an option instead of descending from the south summit, this ridgewalk could be combined with that to the north summit of Helena Ridge, Stuart Knob, and the true summit of Castle Mountain by returning to the saddle, then following the directions for Ridgewalk 95.

97 Helena Ridge Southeast End

Map p. 282

Distance: 24 km linear

Trail/off-trail: 8—12 hr

Elevation gain: 1240 m (4065 ft)

Maximum elevation: 2690 m (8825 ft)

Maps: Gem Trek 1:100,000 Banff & Mt. Assiniboine and NTS 1:50,000 Castle Mountain 82-O/5

Trailhead: As for Ridgewalk 95, Helena Ridge North Summit, etc.

The southeast end of Helena Ridge is an energetic outing that could be combined with the ridgewalk ascent of the south summit (#96), but for most folks it will provide enjoyment enough for one day by itself.

Take the Rockbound Lake trail steadily up to not far before Tower Lake, then strike off northeast for the saddle situated at gr 767847. A landmark on the lower portion of this steep off-trail ascent is a large area of reddish rocks, on whose south side the route passes. The high point of this route is at gr 770846. The most spectacular view from this spot is the sheer east face of the south summit. The long (cont. p. 180)

South Summit Helena Ridge [#96] from the south; Mt. Temple on centre skyline with Castle Mountain and Stuart Knob [#95] to right and Rockbound Lake below.

(Cont. from p. 179) serrated chain of the Sawback Range runs to the east, while to the southwest the Bugaboos can be picked out above Wolverine Pass. Of course nearby Castle Mountain and Rockbound Lake are impressive sights too.

Be aware, if choose to visit the adjacent, slightly lower feature to the east, that there is a deep, narrow hole as approach it from the intervening dip. On leaving this highest elevation of the day, it is perhaps preferable to drop straight south down to a gully in the next rockband. The author kept southeast along the ridgecrest, but then a cliff forces one southwest and he took a line down (before the gully mentioned above) that entailed steep scrambling and routefinding on a series of ledges.

Once safely below this rockband, use a grassy ramp to work back up to the ridge at a saddle (gr 774844). Now a gentle slope over light brown rock leads to the top of a knoll [gr 778845]. On leaving this, go south on the ridge for 500 metres, then drop east—there's a good vegetated slope that avoids the cliffs. A well-defined animal path crosses through the saddle at gr 783838, but the route continues northeast over easy ground to the top of another knoll before dropping southeast into a treed dip.

A gradual gain of about 75 metres leads to the final high point at gr 799839. Hereabouts there are extensive glades of subalpine larch with lots of wildflowers in the meadows. Species that stand out on this trip are purple saxifrage, mist maiden, and the rare moss gentian.

The descent route heads southeast and passes through trees for about 1 km, traversing slightly downhill, before connecting with the top of a large grassy slide path. To get onto those easier slopes may involve some tricky scrambling...it's probably better to contour above any cliffbands to find an easier way down.

Now drop steadily {slippery when wet} to the large meadow on the west side of Johnston Creek opposite a cutbank below where the Mystic Pass trail comes in. Pick up the trail at the footbridge over the creek above the Inkpots and head out to the Bow Valley Parkway via the trail to Moose Meadows or that through Johnston Canyon (scenic but may be crowded).

TV Peak [#99] (left) and Castle Mountain [#95] from the south end of Bell Ridge.

180

98 Bell Ridge

Map p. 282

Distance: 19 km out-and-back with loop

Trail/off-trail: 8—12 km

Elevation gain: 995 m (3265 ft)

Maximum elevation: 2720 m (8920 ft)

Maps: Gem Trek 1:100,000 Banff & Mt. Assiniboine, and NTS 1:50,000 Mount Goodsir 82 N/1 and Lake Louise 82 N/8

Trailhead: Parking area for Boom Lake trail on north side of Highway 93 South, 7.1 km (4.4 mi) west of Castle Junction and 3.0 km (1.9 mi) east of the Alberta/ British Columbia border in Vermilion Pass.

This ridgewalk gives the feeling of "being out there" thanks to the intricate route. **N.B.** An ice axe is necessary in one spot.

First take the trail toward Boom Lake, then go right at the junction with the O'Brien Lake trail. Climb steadily, then leave the trail after it has gone level for a while on a spur of Bell Ridge.

Scramble up reasonably stable boulders to gain the crest of the ridge. A little southerly detour gives the best view of Boom Lake spread out below, the cliffs of Boom Mountain rising above. The route continues over the gentle knoll at the east end of the ridge, then drops into a slight dip.

The character of the route now changes, requiring a balancing act on steeper rock as making way toward the high point at gr 646806. There is a second dip before a steeper-still scramble up to the greatest height of the day at gr 638807. This gives an impressive vista, the extent of which is well suggested by the fact that Mt. Sir Douglas is visible way off to the southeast.

Wildflowers along the ridge include spotted saxifrage, golden fleabane, creeping beardtongue, yellow mountain heather, sawwort, spring beauty, mist maiden, white mountain avens, even bronze bells. Pikas thrive in this natural salad bar; Clark's nutcrackers also frequent the ridge, particularly the lower portion.

A final saddle at gr 633805 represents the end of the ridgewalking on this outing. The descent north toward O'Brien Lake calls for caution—and a mandatory ice axe—on steep snow in the gully. {An alternative is to drop south to Boom Lake and exit on that trail.} From O'Brien Lake, the undulating trail leads back to the jumping off point for Bell Ridge and so back to the trailhead.

99 Protection Mountain to Rockbound Lake Map p. 283

Distance: 27 km linear

Trail/off-trail: 8—12 hr

Elevation gain: 1485 m (4870 ft)

Maximum elevation: 2970 m (9740 ft)

Maps: Gem Trek 1:100,000 Banff & Mt. Assiniboine, and NTS 1:50,000 Lake Louise 82 N/8 and Castle Mountain 82-O/5

Trailhead: Parking area for Protection Mountain trail on west side of Highway 1A (Bow Valley Parkway), 12.4 km (7.7 mi) north of Castle Junction and 14.1 km (8.7 mi) south of the Highway 1A junction with the Lake Louise downhill ski area access road.

A little-known old trail climbs to a former minesite above the forest (there are subalpine larches at treelimit) on the western aspect of Protection Mountain. From the end of the trail, it is possible to scramble up onto the ridge and enjoy a full day of rambling.

Once on the long crest of Protection Mountain, head southeast over easy ground. There is a dip at gr 697907, after which the ridge narrows and becomes more demanding as it approaches TV Peak (it is possible to contour below the peak to the north). This high point at the southeastern end of the mountain gets its unofficial name because of the various telecommunication sheds and towers on its summit. Highlights of the view include Mt. Temple and satellites to the west, Mt. Assiniboine to the south, Mt. Hector to the north, and rugged Front Ranges topography to the east.

From TV Peak, drop northeast to the saddle at gr 716903, then join the wide, gentle ridge heading south (perhaps traversing below the bump at gr 721903). This broad avenue in the sky is a classic ridgewalk, giving panoramic vistas and a sense of wide open spaces. Wildflowers that eke out an existence on these windswept, rocky heights include alpine hawksbeard, alpine bistort, golden fleabane, and yellow mountain saxifrage.

Undulating over a knoll en route, this enticing ridge joins Stuart Knob, which can be bypassed on the east with a bit of sidehill gouging (or ascended if energetic enough). Then drop into the austere basin to the south and descend to Rockbound Lake. The long—and anticlimactic in this case—grind down the trail to Castle Junction completes the journey.

The author on Protection Mountain; panorama includes Mt. Hector on centre skyline.

View to Hidden Lake beneath Ptarmigan Peak from ridge southwest of Mt. Richardson [#100]; Baker Lake and Mt. St. Bride to east.

100 "Whitehorn—Richardson Ridge"

Map p. 283
Photo p. 183

Distance: 14 km linear

Trail/off-trail/road: 4—8 hr

Elevation gain: 570 m (1870 ft)

Maximum elevation: 2630 m (8625 ft)

Maps: Gem Trek 1:50,000 Lake Louise & Yoho and 1:100,000 Banff & Mt. Assiniboine, and NTS 1:50,000 Lake Louise 82 N/8

Trailhead: Park at the Lake Louise downhill ski area and take the summer sightseeing lift (if operating; check at (403) 522-3555).

This ridgewalk uses the Lake Louise downhill ski area summer sightseeing lift (if in operation) for the approach—no hiking is permitted on the front runs because of a high concentration of grizzly bears attracted by artificially-created habitat. {An alternate approach is possible by hiking 3.9 km up the Temple fire road from the Fish Creek parking area and keeping left of Temple Lodge on a service road that bends northwest into the basin east of Whitehorn. Climb up to the saddle at gr 601014 to connect with the approach described below.}

From the upper terminal of the gondola, either head steeply up Grizzly Gully {the name is an appropriate reminder to take proper precautions} or take the more gradual road starting further to the left. **N.B.** Do not disturb any avalanche control projectiles that might be noticed on this outing; do report them to the ski area or park wardens.

Gain the ridge in the dip at about gr 601014 and proceed northwest to the summit of Whitehorn [a ski lift ends nearly at the top]. Continue by descending in the same direction for some 300 metres, on a crest that is home to the uncommon alpine wallflower (*Erysimum pallasii*). Now veer north, first dropping to a dip, then traversing the subpeak at gr 598028. The next feature along the ridge is a steep gendarme that must be bypassed by heading with glee down scree to the right. (The elevation has to be lost anyway.)

Next is a grind of about 200 m vertical up to the high point at gr 606034, a slope best tackled to the right of the ridgeline. Pushing on, there follows the descent to the first low point on the ridge connecting to Mt. Richardson. If full of energy, the top of this peak is some 600 metres higher (only the summit dome is glaciated, contrary to the indication on older editions of the government topos).

A highlight of this ridgewalk is the view into the valley below to the left, lush green meadows with a tarn, which appears as a Shangri-la of sorts...and probably is for mountain goats and the like. Of course, the south aspect of Mt. Hector (locally renowned for its resemblance to Snoppy sleeping on top of his doghouse) is prominent to the northwest, as is the ridgewalk below "Hector South" (#106). Distant landmarks such as Mt. Assiniboine to the south and Mt. Chephren to the north can be recognized.

Whatever choice is made, this first gap is the best spot to drop northeast toward Hidden Lake: a beautiful mountain tarn not often seen from this vantage. Pick up the trail on the west side of the lake's outlet stream, and take it down to the junction with the Boulder Pass trail near the backcountry campground and Halfway Hut day shelter. Cross the stream from Hidden Lake on a footbridge near the shelter and head down the valley of Corral Creek.

An anticlimactic 4 km of service road walking leads to the Fish Creek parking area. {If there is no shuttle vehicle waiting here, a shortcut leads westerly back to the start in approx. 1 km.}

Northeast from "Purple Mound" [#101] to subpeak of Redoubt Mountain (left) and Mt. St. Bride (centre).

Pinnacles on Heather Ridge [#102]; Mt. Richardson on centre skyline and Ptarmigan Peak on right.

101 Lipalian Mountain and Wolverine Ridge

Map p. 283
Photo p. 185

Distance: 15 km out-and-back with loop

Road/off-trail: 4—8 hr

Elevation gain: 1040 m (3410 ft)

Maximum elevation: 2730 m (8955 ft)

Maps: Gem Trek 1:50,000 Lake Louise & Yoho and 1:100,000 Banff & Mt. Assiniboine, and NTS 1:50,000 Lake Louise 82 N/8

Trailhead: The Fish Creek parking area, reached by travelling 2.0 km (1.2 mi) up the Lake Louise ski area access road [passing the Bow Valley Parkway turnoff], turning right onto a gravel road, and continuing 1.1 km (0.7 mi) to the parking area. There is no public vehicular access up the Temple fire road.

This makes for an enjoyable loop from the vicinity of Temple Lodge at the Lake Louise downhill ski area, though there are mundane parts on the approach and up ski runs.

From the parking area, it's a grind of almost 4 km up the fire road. Then there's 1 km more of slogging about 300 vertical metres up a ski lift maintenance track to the upper terminal of the Larch runs. Now the fun begins with a scramble up the northwest ridge of Mt. Lipalian. There's slippery scree at first, but more secure rock higher up.

The north peak of the mountain sports an antenna; the true summit is an easy 10 minutes south. This vantage point takes in the three highest peaks in Banff National Park: Mt. Assiniboine to the south, Mt. Forbes to the north, and of course nearby Mt. Temple to the west. Ridgewalks in view include "Hector South" and south (#106), "Whitehorn—Richardson Ridge" (#100), Protection Mountain (#99), Mt. St. Piran (#103), "Little Temple" (#104), Panorama Ridge (#105), and Bell Ridge (#98).

To continue the ridgewalk, backtrack toward the north peak, then descend east to a saddle and up to gr 637980, which the author calls "Purple Mound" for obvious reasons. Mountain goats, or at least their crisscrossing trails, will be seen in this area. Complete the circuit by descending north, then northwest, onto Wolverine Ridge [gr 629994]. Follow it to its northwest end, than bail off west down scree and through a few trees to an access track that leads down to the fire road.

Lipalian is an archaic geological term for rocks that occur on this mountain. Wolverine is a much less obscure name, referring to the largest member of the weasel family: a keystone species in the Canadian Rockies.

102 Heather Ridge

Map p. 284
Photo p. 185

Distance: 23 km out-and-back with loop

Road/trail/off-trail: 4—8 hr

Elevation gain: 975 m (3200 ft)

Maximum elevation: 2665 m (8740 ft)

Maps: Gem Trek 1:50,000 Lake Louise & Yoho and 1:100,000 Banff & Mt. Assiniboine, and NTS 1:50,000 Lake Louise 82 N/8

Trailhead: The Fish Creek parking area, reached by travelling 2.0 km (1.2 mi) up the Lake Louise ski area access road [passing the Bow Valley Parkway turnoff], turning right onto a gravel road, and continuing 1.1 km (0.7 mi) to the parking area. There is no public vehicular access up the Temple fire road.

Heather Ridge has an appealing name and indeed is an appealing destination. From the trailhead there is a less-than-inspiring 3.9 km trudge up the ski area service road, keeping straight at the two junctions encountered. (As alternatives, mountain bikes are allowed on this stretch or a passing service vehicle might stop to give a lift.) However it is reached, at the end of the road past Temple Lodge, head right up a short steep incline at the edge of a ski run, then pick up the hiking trail heading north.

Climb gradually up the valley of Corral Creek, breaking into open meadows shortly before the Halfway Hut day-use shelter. Veer right (northeast) for Boulder Pass at the Hidden Lake junction. Ptarmigan Lake and the country beyond are suddenly revealed at the pass; for this outing, leave the main trail that heads toward Deception Pass and Baker Lake to travel over rocky ground along the south side of the lake.

Then bend south and go up a draw to the north end of long, narrow Redoubt Lake. From here, ascend due east up the slopes of Heather Ridge. Once on the crest, follow along as it curves gently east. A highlight of this section is an abrupt cluster of sharp pinnacles, unusual formations that make for great photographic subjects.

The high point of Heather Ridge is at its east end [gr 660025]. This gives good views over several large lakes (Redoubt, Ptarmigan, Baker), as well as of Redoubt Mountain, Ptarmigan Peak, Fossil Mountain, and Brachiopod and Anthozoan mountains. Distant landmarks include Mt. Temple, Hungabee Mountain, and Mt. Balfour.

Wildflowers in the area include of course the mountain heathers, which come in three colours: pink, white, and yellow. Pikas frequent the rocky slopes where there is nearby vegetation to feed upon. Mountain goats also occur here.

Return the same way, or drop east to the saddle [gr 664029] between Heather Ridge and Brachiopod Mountain, then north down a drainage leading to the west end of Baker Lake. Keep north until intersect the Baker Lake trail below Deception Pass, then go left on it to Boulder Pass and out.

103 Mt. St. Piran

Map p. 284

Distance: 11 km out-and-back with loop

Trail/off-trail: 4—8 hr

Elevation gain: 920 m (3020 ft)

Maximum elevation: 2650 m (8690 ft)

Maps: Gem Trek 1:35,000 Guide to Lake Louise Day Hikes and 1:50,000 Lake Louise & Yoho, and NTS 1:50,000 Lake Louise 82 N/8

Trailhead: The northeast corner of Lake Louise; pass in front of the Chateau Lake Louise after crossing from the large public parking areas using either of two footbridges over Louise Creek.

The summit of Mt. St. Piran can be reached by gently graded switchbacks—the Swiss guides who established them in the early 1900s knew a thing or two about trail building! Famed English alpinist Edward Whymper even suggested that a teahouse be built there. Although that never happened, the view is impressive and the descent via Goat Pass makes for an interesting circuit.

Take the main trail toward Lake Agnes, turning right at Mirror Lake. Here appear the first subalpine larches, whose needles turn gold in the autumn before falling off. The most direct route for Mt. St. Piran is to turn right 500 metres past Mirror Lake on a connector leading up to the Little Beehive trail (this shortcut bypasses the Lake Agnes teahouse).

Turn right again, and in 300 metres pick up a path that goes left off the main trail that leads to the site of a former fire lookout on the Little Beehive. (There was a sign at this junction in August, 2000, although a short initial section of the path was covered with debris, apparently in an effort to avoid confusion with the main trail.)

This path is the start of an established route toward the summit of Mt. St. Piran that was built by the Swiss guides about a century ago. It shows their careful selection of grade as it zigzags up to a gap in the northeast ridge. The path becomes less well-defined here, but the way to the summit is clear.

The well-known signature peaks of the Lake Louise area present themselves at the top, as may a pika eking out life here—and perhaps squeaking out its high-pitched call. One cause for alarm for these small creatures known colloquially as rock rabbits (they are related to hares) is golden eagles, which soar on wind currents generated by the surrounding cliffs.

The pikas are attracted by a proliferation of vegetation at this modest elevation; among the wildflowers that can be seen in the alpine zone are valerian, golden fleabane, stonecrop, two species of saxifrage (spotted and purple), the three species of mountain heather (white, pink, and yellow), white mountain avens, mist maiden, saw-

Summit of Mt. St. Piran from descent to Goat Pass; Mt. Hector on left.

wort, creeping beardtongue, moss campion, and inconspicuous Sibbaldia with five tiny yellow petals.

Upon leaving, rather than going back down the trail, it's an easy matter to traverse this small peak by descending the broad southwest ridge. There's even a rough path leading through the last rocky bit down to the saddle known as Goat Pass at gr 516963, where mountain goats indeed disport themselves.

From the pass, a path has been etched in on the descent of the steep slopes to the basin above Lake Agnes and so to the maintained trail curving around its west end. Now's the chance to hit the teahouse, then return via the approach trail. Or, if so inclined, zigzag up to the Big Beehive for a view back to Mt. St. Piran.

St. Piran was the home town in Cornwall, England, of Willoughby Astley, first manager of the original Lake Louise Chalet.

"Little Temple" [#104] above Lake Annette, from the west; Ptarmigan Peak and Redoubt Mountain in distance.

104 "Little Temple"

Map p. 284
Photo p. 189

Distance: 12 km linear

Trail/off-trail: 4—8 hr

Elevation gain: 940 m (3085 ft)

Maximum elevation: 2660 m (8725 ft)

Maps: Gem Trek 1:50,000 Lake Louise & Yoho and 1:100,000 Banff & Mt. Assiniboine, and NTS 1:50,000 Lake Louise 82 N/8

Trailhead: Paradise Creek parking area on the west side of the Moraine Lake Road, 2.5 km (1.6 mi) from its start off Lake Louise Drive.

This ridgewalk on a subsidiary peak of mighty Mt. Temple gives a goat's-eye view of Paradise Valley.

Start by hiking just over 5 km up the Paradise Valley trail to the Lake Annette junction, where turn left and climb to the lake. Now leave the trail to go around the southwest corner of the lake, then start climbing east. Take either the ridge to the left (scrambling required) or the major gully, which is not glaciated despite the indication on the topo map {1980 edition}. Whichever way taken, the goal is the col [gr 566904] above Temple Lake and at the base of Anderson Couloir on Mt. Temple.

It's not possible to continue east due to cliffs, so veer north, then northeast, as scrambling to the twin summits of "Little Temple." The first (southwest) peak, at gr 566910, is slightly higher. Here the elevation seems insignificant, dwarfed by Mt. Temple soaring almost 900 metres higher, but in most places this would be considered a respectable height. Mountain goats certainly like this vicinity, so it's possible to get an inkling of their perspective on the surroundings, including both pristine Paradise Valley and heavily developed Bow Valley.

Such landmarks as Saddle Mountain, Fairview Mountain, and Sheol Mountain lie northwest across Paradise Creek, while to the southwest is imposing Hungabee Mountain at the head of the valley. Panorama Ridge (#105) rises not far away to the southeast; further off to the north are the ridges south of Mt. Hector (#106).

Descent is steeply down open slopes to the southeast to reach the east end of Temple Lake, a little gem that often has bergy bits floating in it late into summer. A rough path beside the outlet stream crosses the Moraine Lake to Paradise Valley trail and continues down to Moraine Lake Road, hitting it about 6 km from its start. (There is a small parking area nearby on the east side of the road.)

105 Panorama Ridge

Map p. 285

Distance: 15 km out-and-back with loop

Trail/off-trail: 4—8 hr

Elevation gain: 940 m (3085 ft)

Maximum elevation: 2825 m (9266 ft)

Maps: Gem Trek 1:50,000 Lake Louise & Yoho and 1:100,000 Banff & Mt. Assiniboine, and NTS 1:50,000 Lake Louise 82 N/8

Trailhead: Southeast corner of Moraine Lake parking lot.

With a name like this, who can resist getting up on it for a walk? It takes effort, but is well worthwhile since there is indeed a panorama from the ridge.

There is a route onto the ridge from the west, up a gully from Lower Consolation Lake (as described in the author's book **Hiking Lake Louise**, **Third Edition**, Luminous Compositions, 1999). But to "get the most value" out of the day, approach the ridge from the north.

Take the Consolation Lakes trail, then after 1.7 km turn left onto the trail toward Taylor Lake. A small shallow lake 400 metres on provides fine reflections: a short detour to its north side is recommended if it is a calm day. Almost a kilometre past the lake, turn left downhill at a sharp junction (don't continue straight). Go level (some vague, boggy stretches) for a while, then start climbing.

There is a long, larch-covered arm that can provide a way onto the ridge; however, the quickest means to get up to open terrain is to push on. Pass a drainage that the trail dips into, reach a level section, then leave the trail where it (cont. p. 192)

The Consolation Lakes—Upper (left) and Lower—from Panorama Ridge.

(Cont. from p. 191) climbs a little. The forest is open, with some subalpine larches; a nice little draw leads to a steeper slope, which in turn issues onto the northeast arm just at treelimit.

Big thin plates of shaly rock lie on the ridge above, which is taken south and southwest over scrambly terrain. Just before the summit ridge is a sort of moraine, running parallel to it on the east, which cradles a meltpool. The ridgetop permits the first views of Bident Mountain, Quadra Mountain, and the Consolation Valley with its two clear turquoise lakes and a pass at its head.

The names of the mountains derive from the numbers of summits they sport, while that of the valley was given by Walter Wilcox in 1899 in contrast with the austere reaches above Moraine Lake, originally known as Desolation Valley.

Other landmarks in the vista include Mt. Temple with its southeast face rising in tier upon tier, only slightly less imposing than its north face; and Mt. Hector, the Slate Range, and Protection Mountain and Castle Mountain in an arc from north to southeast. To the west above Mt. Babel are such members of the chain of summits that give the Valley of Ten Peaks its name as Mt. Fay, Deltaform Mountain, Neptuak Mountain, and Wenkchemna Peak.

The high point at the north end of Panorama Ridge lies about 10 minutes away, then after descending gradually there is a sharper drop to the dip at gr 607848. Beyond this dip, any attempt to reach the cairn visible ahead on the higher south end of the ridge will likely be stymied by a blank wall [approx. gr 609845]. (This is after an earlier tricky section that can be rather precariously turned on the left.)

Descent from the ridge is accomplished by means of a chimney a few paces back from the aforementioned wall (small cairn of three rocks at its top). Farther down a major gully sweeps all the way down to the south end of Upper Consolation Lake, from which the most direct and easiest way lies along the eastern shores of the two bodies of water. Then cross Babel Creek near the outlet of Lower Consolation Lake to connect with the established trail and return to Moraine Lake to complete the loop.

West from "Hector South," including Hector Lake and glaciated Mt. Balfour on centre skyline.

106 "Hector South" and South

Map p. 286
Photo p. 16

Distance: 10 km linear

Off-trail: 4—8 hr

Elevation gain: 1140 m (3740 ft)

Maximum elevation: 2970 m (9742 ft)

Map: NTS 1:50,000 Hector Lake 82 N/9

Trailhead: Park as far as possible off the Icefields Parkway on the east side, 13.7 km (8.5 mi) north of the junction with the Trans-Canada Highway and 10.3 km (6.4 mi) south of the Mosquito Creek bridge. (The cliffs of the crux section of this ridgewalk can be seen through the trees from the west side of the highway at this point.)

The high open terrain south of Mt. Hector makes for rewarding ridgewalking once on the crest. That feat isn't as simple as it sounds in this case, since there's no trail, but pushing up through the forest to above the trees isn't too bad. (The author on a first reconnaissance began too far north and ended up on the southwest ridge of Mt. Hector itself [gr 505123], then went to the saddle at gr 515124 and up to the south over steep broken ground to join the described route.)

Head up northeasterly from the trailhead; the way is shrubby at first but becomes more open. Look to join a slide path (be aware of the possibility of avalanches). This provides good going; when the young subalpine firs get thick, move to the north edge. It's advisable to stay in the gully to its top so as to avoid loose scree.

Some 500 metres of elevation gain leads to the zone of subalpine larches (these are the northernmost stands of those trees in Banff National Park). Marmots and pikas will express their consternation at unaccustomed human visitors. Mountain goats are much more sanguine, merely moving away at a deceptively easy gait.

At the top of the slide path, continue over easy rocky ground toward the obvious crux beyond a short level rib. This section of blocky boulders and small cliffbands requires scrambling and routefinding...if it looks intimidating, the option exists to traverse right and negotiate less exposed terrain with scree above.

Although dwarfed by nearby Mt. Hector [which has an incongruous communication shed on a flat section below the summit], "Hector South" attains a respectable height. The outstanding panorama, first reported by surveyor J.J. McArthur and outfitter Tom Wilson in 1891, takes in the mountains on the continental divide and peaks farther west including the Goodsirs and The President and Vice-President.

To the south lies an unusual view of the steep towers of Pika Peak and Ptarmigan Peak in the compact Slate Range, with the glacier between them. The distinctive wedge of Mt. Assiniboine breaks the horizon farther off, while (cont. p. 194)

(Cont. from p. 193) Mt. Temple with its renowned north face soars high into the sky in the Lake Louise region. Other ridgewalks that can be seen from this lofty position include Panorama Ridge (#105) and Bow Peak (#111).

The most unusual view from "Hector South" is east into the seldom-seen valley immediately to the north, featuring a good-sized turquoise lake. Beyond are Molar Mountain and Cataract Peak with its shoulder cape of ice. The east ridge of "Hector South" has a narrow technical section, but continuing south is an attractive proposition. Arrive at a saddle [gr 529104], then climb to a three-way hub [gr 532097].

Although it appears enticing to go east on a higher ridge from here, time and distance will probably conspire to suggest a turn south. Descend to a small dip before veering southeast along a gently undulating arm with appeal of its own. It embraces an attractive alpine valley cradling a small lake, and also sports eye-catching cushions of moss campion: always an uplifting sight.

The arm rises at its end to a cairn-topped knoll [gr 540073], which sadly represents the end of the ridgewalking on this route. Before leaving, enjoy the view south over the Pipestone River where it carves a deep notch through forest before flowing into the Bow.

This good thing coming to an end, drop southwest, first to a small lake-in-the-larches, then steadily down through trees (some shrubs and deadfall) to hit the highway.

Pinnacle on ridge between Molar Pass and North Molar Pass; route of Ridge Northwest of North Molar Pass - Part 2 [#109] right of centre.

107 Molar Pass to North Molar Pass

Map p. 287
Photo p. 14

Distance: 25 km out-and-back with loop

Trail/off-trail: 4—8 hr

Elevation gain: 940 m (3085 ft)

Maximum elevation: 2770 m (9085 ft)

Maps: Gem Trek 1:70,000 Bow Lake and Saskatchewan Crossing, and NTS 1:50,000 Hector Lake 82 N/9

Trailhead: Parking area for Mosquito Creek trail on the west side of the Icefields Parkway, south of the Mosquito Creek bridge (via entrance road to Mosquito Creek youth hostel). This is 24.0 km (14.9 mi) north of the Trans-Canada Highway and 9.0 km (5.6 mi) south of the Crowfoot Glacier viewpoint.

This outing makes for an enjoyable circuit at the headwaters of Mosquito Creek, incorporating a visit to a summit that is unusually sharp for the Rockies.

Getting to Molar Pass takes two hours or so, the last part of the trail passing through attractive upper subalpine meadows. From the pass, head northeast up moderately inclined slopes with a cliffband to the left. At the top of the knoll, lose a little elevation as heading east, then turn northeast again over rockier ground toward the pinnacle at gr 529225.

Ascent of this narrow tapering peak, slightly overhanging to the north, is more in the nature of scrambling than ridgewalking, yet is not overly demanding. From here, Mt. Hector stands dominant, a permanent robe of white draped over its northern expanse. Also outstanding from this perspective is Molar Mountain with the sheer, dark walls of its twin summits. Among the many landmarks discernible to the west, Mt. Balfour is particularly impressive due to the cascading glaciers on its east face.

The ridge continues northwest from the pinnacle, passing a group of bright red towers (see photo p. 14) that are easily turned, and descending mostly easy slopes to North Molar Pass. Pick up the trail here, turning left to descend past shallow Mosquito Lake and connect with the inbound approach.

As an option rather than going to Molar Pass, it is possible to traverse the pinnacle from the west. Take the trail toward North Molar Pass, then veer off (optimally at the high point before the dip to Mosquito Lake) to get onto the rounded level stretch at the base of the pinnacle. Next are some jumbled boulders and a rising line below a cliff to get to its right side, which has a gully permitting access back to the ridge.

108 Ridge Northwest of North Molar Pass - Part 1

Map p. 287

Distance: 27 km out-and-back with loop

Trail/off-trail: 8—12 hr

Elevation gain: 1045 m (3430 ft)

Maximum elevation: 2875 m (9430 ft)

Maps: Gem Trek 1:70,000 Bow Lake and Saskatchewan Crossing, and NTS 1:50,000 Hector Lake 82 N/9

Trailhead: As for Ridgewalk 107, Molar Pass to North Molar Pass.

This is the middle in the series of three ridgewalks accessible via the Mosquito Creek trail.

Take the established trail to North Molar Pass: at 2590 m in elevation, it is just 20 metres lower than Sentinel Pass above Moraine Lake, the highest point reached by maintained trail in Banff National Park. From the pass, grovel up the steep slope to the northeast—careful, don't knock stuff down below!

The summit at gr 541233 is the high point on this outing, and makes for a nice breather to take in the surroundings. Mt. Hector with its glaciated north face stands out, as does Cataract Peak (over 3300 m high) almost due east. There is an expansive panorama over the Pipestone Valley, and even a surprising glimpse—through a saddle to the north—of a lake at the head of a tributary of the Clearwater River.

Wildflowers clinging to the rocky terrain include such alpine specialties as alpine wallflower, purple saxifrage, and mist maiden.

The ridge to the northwest is not as level as it appears from below, and includes some gendarmes—but they can be easily turned on the east side. The ridge veers north before dropping northwest again to the saddle at gr 525254, the last part over easy ground. From the saddle, drop southwest to the north end of a fair-sized lake.

A goat path leads along the west side of the lake. After following its drainage beside a mini-canyon for about 500 metres, cut south to intersect the inbound trail near shallow Mosquito Lake. As angling across the meadows, glance back toward the ridge just travelled to see a group of pinnacles on its southern slopes, as well as the eye-catching bulk of what appears to be a rock glacier {a large lobe of slowly-moving boulders}. [Also be aware that grizzly bears frequent this area; their diggings can be seen.]

Tramp back down the Mosquito Creek trail to finishs a satisfying sojourn in the mountains.

Ridgewalker John Blum in front of pinnacle on Ridge Northwest of North Molar Pass - Part 1; note remnant snow patches from winter cornice.

Northwest from high point of Ridge Northwest of North Molar Pass - Part 2 [#109]; Siffleur Valley on right.

109 Ridge Northwest of North Molar Pass - Part 2

Map p. 287
Photo p. 197

Distance: 23 km out-and-back with loop

Trail/off-trail: 4—8 hr

Elevation gain: 1145 m (3755 ft)

Maximum elevation: 2975 m (9760 ft)

Map: NTS 1:50,000 Hector Lake 82 N/9

Trailhead: As for Ridgewalk 107, Molar Pass to North Molar Pass.

This is the continuation north of the series of ridgewalks beginning at Molar Pass. It is the most difficult, and also reaches the highest elevation of the three.

Take the Mosquito Creek trail as per the previous description. Climb into vast subalpine meadows, going as far as boulders just beyond shallow Mosquito Lake. Rather than taking the trail up the grade toward North Molar Pass, veer north. Traverse gradually, dropping into and climbing out of a few dips, including the drainage of the lake described in Ridgewalk 108. Head up to a subpeak via the south-trending ridge (slabs at its base). Then continue west, moving left off the crest in order to get up through a rockband: this is the crux of the route. The true high point is not right after the crux, but farther west and separated from the first point by a small chasm.

This unnamed peak [gr 505262] is ascended most often via its southwest ridge by participants in the Skyline Hikers camps periodically held in the area. But it is not frequently visited, as testified to by the entries dating back some 20 years in the summit register. The most intriguing views from this top are those down to Pipestone Pass, almost due north and less than a kilometre away but over 500 metres lower, and those over the huge meadows in the upper valley of the Siffleur River.

Descent is via the aforementioned southwest ridge, which features interesting pillars on its north side. Climb a short chimney at about midpoint so as to stay on the crest. Near the bottom, edge westerly to drop into the notch of the north tributary of Mosquito Creek. A rough path materializes on its northwest bank, leading to the main trail at the footbridge over the side stream.

An option is to combine this ridgewalk with Part 1 (#108) or even with that and #107, if time and energy allow. Although this book describes individual routes that can be done as daytrips, such extensions would be facilitated by setting up an overnight base at the Mosquito Creek backcountry campground.

One caveat the author must issue is that the 'true' continuation from the saddle at the base of Part 1 to the subpeak at gr 514258 remains unknown ground; though it appears feasible, this southeast ridge does steepen near the top.

110 Dolomite Peak Southeast Ridge

Map p. 287

Distance: 6 km out-and-back

Off-trail: up to 4 hr

Elevation gain: 875 m (2870 ft)

Maximum elevation: 2730 m (8955 ft)

Maps: Gem Trek 1:70,000 Bow Lake and Saskatchewan Crossing, and NTS 1:50,000 Hector Lake 82 N/9

Trailhead: Park off the shoulder on the east side of the Icefields Parkway at a small clearing with grey soil, 1.1 km (0.7 mi) north of the Mosquito Creek bridge. See trailhead information for Ridgewalk 107, Molar Pass to North Molar Pass, for distances to Mosquito Creek.

This short trip gets high quickly and allows unusual views into the valley of Mosquito Creek, among other scenic delights.

Head due north up through open forest from the start, reaching treelimit after about 250 metres of elevation gain. Then simply follow the open ridge as it curves northwest, reaching the first of two knolls after some 600 metres more of ascent. The next knoll can be readily gained, but going further is beyond the scope of this book since it ventures into the realm of technical climbing.

An excellent and unique perspective over the Mosquito Creek (cont. p. 200)

The author on Dolomite Peak Southeast Ridge; Ridge Northwest of North Molar Pass - Part 1 [#108] to his left below skyline peaks.

(Cont. from p. 199) environs, including the ridgewalks from Molar Pass to North Molar Pass and northwest of North Molar Pass (#107—#109), spreads out as if from the air. Landmark peaks such as Bow Peak, Mt. Balfour, Mt. Hector, Mt. Lefroy, and Mt. Temple can also be recognized.

Such subalpine and alpine specialties as glacier lily, spring beauty, valerian, white mountain avens, and purple saxifrage adorn the surroundings on this outing. Pikas, as expected, occur in the vicinity, harvesting the vegetation for their year-round activities.

Backtrack to return to the trailhead, possibly getting in some glissading on late-lying snow (have ice axe at the ready to self-arrest if necessary).

Ridgewalker John Blum ascending northwest ridge of Bow Peak; view north over Bow Lake to peaks including Mt. Chephren right of centre.

111 Bow Peak

Map p. 286

Distance: 15 km linear

Trail/off-trail: 4—8 hr

Elevation gain: 930 m (3050 ft)

Maximum elevation: 2869 m (9409 ft)

Maps: Gem Trek 1:70,000 Bow Lake and Saskatchewan Crossing, and NTS 1:50,000 Hector Lake 82 N/9

Trailhead: Park off the right-of-way on the south side of the Icefields Parkway, 7.5 km (4.7 mi) north of the Mosquito Creek bridge and 1.3 km (0.8 mi) south of the Crowfoot Glacier viewpoint.

This challenging ridgewalk above the Icefields Parkway involves some scrambling and has a horrible ending, but yields an unforgettable day.

Start off on the Crowfoot Pass trail, which is vague at first: head south from the trailhead to hit the faint path leading to the outlet of Bow Lake [gr 403223]. **Caution:** The ford here is difficult in times of high water. Now follow the good trail that parallels the Bow River for a kilometre before crossing a stream and climbing up a draw in a steady ascent. The path tops out in the high saddle of Crowfoot Pass, just after passing between two small lakes.

Veer east from the pass in a steep scramble to the summit ridge of Bow Peak; plugging upward over the big, mostly solid rocks eventually reels it in. Several hundred metres of more level going sees arrival at the large cairn with summit register. The view from the top is stunning: a veritable sea of peaks, highlighted by Mt. Assiniboine to the southeast, to the southwest Mt. Balfour with cascades of ice on its east face, and to the east Mt. Hector with its immense north glacier. Below to the south stretches out the full extent of large Hector Lake, which represents the finish of this adventure.

The continuation of the traverse is straightforward at first, with the horizontal strata providing easy flat bits like sidewalks. But it soon throws down the gauntlet with the need for routefinding and downclimbing to negotiate a series of sudden drop-offs. Chimneys and ledges will be employed, packs will be relayed if in a group, and leaps across a gap may be taken. All in all, enough to lend spice to the outing before forging on to the southeast end of the summit ridge. (Getting around the first of three bumps at this end, which looks tricky from the summit, is no problem.)

The descent takes the obvious southeast spur to an open knoll. Below, however, there is a price to pay for the glorious alpine experience: a purgatory of bushwhacking on steep slopes with fallen trees. Give thanks upon reaching the shore of Hector Lake, then turn left toward the backcountry campground. An established trail, with another ford of the Bow included for good measure, leads to the highway.

112 Ridge West of Helen Lake

Map p. 288
Photos Front and Back Covers

Distance: 11 km linear

Off-trail/trail: 4—8 hr

Elevation gain: 840 m (2755 ft)

Maximum elevation: 2820 m (9250 ft)

Maps: Gem Trek 1:70,000 Bow Lake and Saskatchewan Crossing, and NTS 1:50,000 Hector Lake 82 N/9

Trailhead: Park on the east side of the Icefields Parkway about 1 km (0.6 mi) north of the junction for Num-Ti-Jah Lodge on Bow Lake, on the first level section after an uphill grade.

This is an adventurous outing along an undulating ridge that gives superb vistas of lakes, glaciers, and mountains.

Head up from the highway on a bearing slightly north of east, breaking out above the trees in half an hour or so. The high point of the day is a subpeak west of Cirque Peak [gr 394277], which surprisingly allows a view of part of Isabella Lake on Dolomite Creek to the north.

More to be expected, there is a sweeping panorama over the full extent of Bow Lake to the southwest, and a whole gamut of peaks including Mt. Temple, the tops of the Goodsirs, the summit of Mt. Balfour, and Mt. Chephren. Dolomite Peak with its many towers is less than 5 km to the southeast, while glaciated Mt. Hector is further off in that direction. Bow Peak, whose traverse constitutes Ridgewalk 111, stands out nicely too. If it is clear, distant landmarks will be recognizable, including Mt. Assiniboine to the south and Sunwapta Peak to the north.

It is well worth switching from the well-nigh mesmerizing mountain scenery to take notice of the many wildflowers along the way. These include western spring beauty, glacier lily, and golden fleabane in the alpine zone; and false hellebore, yellow violet, and red paintbrush lower down.

From the high point, the route goes south along the dipping, curving ridge, with cliffs to the east above the basin in which nestles Helen Lake (which stays icebound well into the season). Be alert to the sudden drop-off at the end of the ridge not far above the established trail: this cliff at gr 409243 is skirted below its west side. Once on the trail, it's clear sailing to the parking area opposite the Crowfoot Glacier viewpoint {about 4 km from the start if a car shuttle isn't set up}.

Snow lies late on this ridge (certainly into July) so ice axe and gaiters may be needed; the corollary is that there might be glissading to enjoy!

Ridgewalker John Blum below high point of Ridge West of Helen Lake; north spur of Cirque Peak to right.

Large split boulder on Ridge South of Observation Peak [#113]; Bow Lake, Crowfoot Glacier, and Crowfoot Mountain on right.

113 Ridge South of Observation Peak

Map p. 288
Photo p. 203

Distance: 9 km linear

Off-trail/trail: 4—8 hr

Elevation gain: 900 m (2950 ft)

Maximum elevation: 2970 m (9740 ft)

Maps: Gem Trek 1:70,000 Bow Lake and Saskatchewan Crossing, and NTS 1:50,000 Hector Lake 82 N/9

Trailhead: Park at a short section of old road to the east of the Bow Summit turn-off, 5.0 km (3.1) mi north of the Num-Ti-Jah Lodge turn-off and 16.5 km (10.2 mi) south of Waterfowl Lakes campground.

This is a relatively short ridgewalk that requires a fair bit of elevation gain, but despite the short time on top it is well worthwhile for the amazing views.

From the trailhead, head up the steep slopes below Observation Peak, taking a line slightly north of east. Rather than tackling Observation Peak itself (although that could be an option if time and energy allow), aim for the saddle at gr 373306. Whatever approach taken, there will be scree to churn up, although yellow clusters of alpine hawksbeard can relieve the "trudgery." The ridge proper represents a welcome respite.

Proceed southeast to the first peak [gr 382302], then down to a dip and up to the second peak [386300]. These vantage points give superb panoramas, including of a lot of lakes: among them Bow, Bow Glacier, Caldron, Peyto, Isabella, and Alice. A highlight is the glimpse into the upper reaches of Dolomite Creek.

Descend southeast toward Cirque Peak past a small rockband to the saddle at gr 395292, then veer southwest down an unnamed drainage. Eventually pick up a well-defined (though muddy at times) horse trail on the south side of the creek. This bends to the south as it travels through forest, hitting the Icefields Parkway just 800 metres north of the Num-Ti-Jah Lodge turnoff and 4.0 km south of Bow Summit.

The author on Mt. Sarbach Northeast Ridge; Howse (on left) and North Saskatchewan rivers below.

114 Mt. Sarbach Northeast Ridge

Map p. 289

Distance: 17 km out-and-back

Trail/off-trail: 4—8 hr

Elevation gain: 1140 m (3740 ft)

Maximum elevation: 2660 m (8725 ft)

Maps: Gem Trek 1:70,000 Bow Lake and Saskatchewan Crossing, and NTS 1:50,000 Mistaya Lake 82 N/15

Trailhead: Parking area for Mistaya Canyon on west side of Icefields Parkway, 14.5 km (9.0 mi) north of Waterfowl Lakes campground and 4.0 km (2.5 mi) south of the bridge over the North Saskatchewan River.

This ridgewalk grants great views without the hazardous scramble to the summit of Mt. Sarbach.

From the trailhead, make the short downhill walk to the bridge over the Mistaya River...it's well worth checking out the canyon here. Then tackle the steep hike up to the site of the former Sarbach fire lookout: get on this trail by taking the trail to the right at the west end of the bridge, then turning left at the junction in 200 metres.

From the lookout site, head up the slope behind the clearing, passing through a zone of whitebark pines. Rather than heading for the ridgecrest here, traverse west to get on the other side of the ridge, then head up to the gap at gr 166514. {This approach avoids unnecessary and tricky scrambling up and down a series of notches.}

Now on the ridge, climb south to the reward of all the elevation gain: a wide, level ridge over 1 km long—it feels like a sports field in the sky. Follow southwest along this walkway with glorious views all round, including Glacier Lake to the west.

Other landmarks include Mt. Murchison to the east, Mt. Wilson to the north, and ahead to the south the triangular face of the north peak of Mt. Sarbach. {Beyond the scope of this ridgewalk, that point can be reached by scrambling up over 300 metres vertical on the west side—ice axe likely required. Reaching the true summit of the south peak involves travel across a seriously exposed section and is best left for roped parties.}

Return the same way to complete this energetic excursion.

Mt. Sarbach is named after Peter Sarbach (1844-1930), the first Swiss climbing guide to work in Canada and leader of first ascents of a number of notable peaks including Mt. Lefroy, Mt. Victoria, and this mountain.

115 Parker Ridge

Map p. 289
Photo p. 8

Distance: 10 km out-and-back

Trail/off-trail: 4—8 hr

Elevation gain: 625 m (2050 ft)

Maximum elevation: 2636 m (8645 ft)

Maps: Gem Trek 1:75,000 Columbia Icefield, and NTS 1:50,000 Columbia Icefield 83 C/3 and Parks Canada 1:50,000 Columbia Icefield (1981)

Trailhead: Parking area on the south side of the Icefields Parkway, 4.3 km (2.7 mi) north of the Nigel Creek trailhead and 4.2 km (2.6 mi) south of the Banff/Jasper national parks boundary at Sunwapta Pass.

The well-known trail onto Parker Ridge in the far northern part of Banff National Park is worthwhile, but venturing west along the ridge is even more rewarding. **Caution:** Be careful of snow conditions; avalanches don't just happen in winter.

Take the established trail, sticking to the maintained path to avoid the trampling and erosion that were problems in the past. It is recommended to first continue over the broad ridgecrest and east along the contouring defined path to its end, which gives the best view of the full extent of the Saskatchewan Glacier. Once back at the high point of the trail, strike off up the knoll to the west. Be as careful as possible not to walk on any vegetation struggling to survive in this exposed alpine zone.

Wildflowers that cling to life up here include moss campion, alpine hawksbeard, purple saxifrage, golden and mountain fleabanes, white mountain avens, sawwort, alpine cinquefoil, white and yellow mountain heathers, bladder locoweed, and purple hedysarum. **N.B.** The last-named plant is a favourite food of grizzly bears, which frequent Parker Ridge.

From the knoll, drop southwest to a dip, then begin the steady climb up the sharper ridge. This tops out at a short level section before a brief loss of elevation preceding the final scramble up to the sharp point at gr 904808. This is a fine spot to soak up the panorama, the most wonderful aspect of which is nearby Mt. Athabasca with its ice cap and the subsidiary pinnacle known as Hilda Peak. Also in view are Mt. Wilcox, Wilcox Pass, and Nigel Peak (Ridgewalk 116 visits a spur of the southeast ridge of Nigel Peak). Below to the south is the wide valley of the North Saskatchewan River, whose waters originate in the Columbia Icefield and flow through the city of Edmonton, ultimately to empty into Hudson Bay. Return the same way.

The ridge is named for Herschel C. Parker, a member of the Appalachian Mountain Club. What does someone from New England have to do with the Rockies? Well, Mr. Parker was one of the pioneer mountaineers in the area, including as a member of the party that made the first ascent of Mt. Lefroy in 1897.

Southwest from Parker Ridge including Mt. Bryce (centre) and Castleguard Mountain (right).

The author on Nigel Peak Spur of Southeast Ridge [#116]; Cirrus Mountain (left) and part of Parker Ridge [#115] (centre and right mid-distance).

Cairn at gr 290823 on Ridgewalk 117; view north to valley of Coral Creek and surrounding peaks.

116 Nigel Peak Spur of Southeast Ridge

Map p. 289
Photo p. 207

Distance: 7 km out-and-back

Off-trail: up to 4 hr

Elevation gain: 585 m (1920 ft)

Maximum elevation: 2595 m (8510 ft)

Maps: Gem Trek 1:75,000 Columbia Icefield, and NTS 1:50,000 Columbia Icefield 83 C/3 and Parks Canada 1:50,000 Columbia Icefield (1981)

Trailhead: As for Ridgewalk 115, Parker Ridge.

Parker Ridge is highly recommended, and while in the area it's worthwhile to check out this ridgewalk, which sees far fewer visits.

From the trailhead, walk about 100 metres east on the Icefields Parkway to connect with the old road (known as the "Wonder Trail") on the north side of the highway. Take this gradually revegetating right-of-way for some 400 metres, to where it bends east. Now head off-trail, dropping north to cross a tributary of Nigel Creek.

Gain the ridge by aiming for a ramp, harbouring a few trees (including whitebark pines), which provides access otherwise blocked by cliffs. It's a steep haul up over rocky ground but once on the crest the going is straightforward. Simply head northwest, always keeping in mind the precipitous drop on the west side—which becomes more apparent near the top. (Take care if doing this ridgewalk early in the season, when snow lingers on the edge.)

Bighorn sheep frequent this ridge; if the animals themselves are not sighted, there is evidence in the form of droppings, trails, and possibly tracks in snow. Wildflowers include a profusion of purple saxifrage in early summer, and alpine wallflower: an uncommon denizen of the high country.

The views are rewarding, including Hilda Peak and the Hilda Glacier below the eastern aspect of Mt. Athabasca. Colourful Boundary Lake and the Boundary Glacier come into sight later, tucked beneath the ridge northeast of Mt. Athabasca (#118). The top of Dome Glacier and Mt. Kitchener reveal themselves to the west, while to the northwest are Wilcox Peak, Wilcox Pass, and Nigel Peak (with a prominent pinnacle on the skyline). To the south are Parker Ridge (#115), Mt. Saskatchewan, Cirrus Mountain, Mt. Coleman with its glaciated northeast aspect, Mt. Wilson with its extensive icefield, and other landmarks all the way to Mt. Hector.

There are various cairns along the ridge; the end of the line for this ridgewalk is at gr 905847, where the terrain now also abruptly descends to the northwest. To conclude this outing, reverse the route...making sure to go down the ramp used on the way up to avoid the cliff at the end of the spur. {Going down this bit is more fun than climbing up it: there is even some scree jumping to be had.}

117 Ridges West of Coral Creek

Map p. 290
Photo p. 207

Distance: 30 km out-and-back with loop

Trail/off-trail: over 12 hr

Elevation gain: 1250 ft (4100 ft)

Maximum elevation: 2605 m (8545 ft)

Maps: NTS 1:50,000 Whiterabbit Creek 83 C/1 and Cline River 83 C/2

Trailhead: The parking area for the Coral Creek trail, on the north side of the bridge over the Cline River on the David Thompson Highway (Highway 11), 47 km (29 mi) west of the Nordegg turnoff and 36 km (22 mi) east of the Banff National Park boundary. [Note: This is not to be confused with the parking area on the south side of the bridge, which is the main trailhead for Pinto Lake.]

This foray into the White Goat Wilderness Area is a demanding trip, with the rewards of travelling in wild country where no hunting, motorized vehicles, or even horses are permitted.

The outing starts easily, with a level stretch of about 2 km along an old road parallel to the Cline River. Then bear right (dead end ahead) on the horse trail and climb gradually. Break out into the open with views of steep-walled Coral Creek Canyon to the left. Coral Creek was named by illustrious Canadian geologist, explorer, and mountaineer A.P. Coleman "after the many fossil corals among its gravels."

The start of this ridgewalk is also now visible across the valley. Don't, however, be tempted by an apparent trail on the opposite bank into taking a side trail to the left. There is no magic arch here; instead, after climbing just a little further, the main trail takes a steady grade down to the flats of Coral Creek above the canyon.

The main trail, which continues north to Job Lake, is left here. A large cairn of white rocks marks the point where the trail continues on the far bank of Coral Creek. **Caution:** Don't necessarily wade Coral Creek opposite the cairn...this crossing is difficult in high water, and a better spot may be found upstream where the current is divided into several smaller channels. Take all precautions on this ford, and be prepared to abandon this trip for a safer time if the water level is too high and fast. Also, be aware that the level of the creek may rise during a hot or a rainy day.

Once safely over Coral Creek, pick up the narrow trail that climbs out of the valley. It levels out in less than 1 km, but avoid the temptation to cut up right for the ridge too soon: signs at the otherwise unmarked Wilderness Area boundary represent a good place to do so. The going is easy through open forest with buffaloberry shrubs (bear food!). Eventually break into grassy meadows and a steepening climb to the knoll at gr 305803. Continuing north, there is a slight dip; the most straightforward route stays west of undulating bumps and veers northwest on the main ridge. (cont. p. 210)

(Cont. from p. 209)

The high point at gr 297814 gives fine views of Coral Creek and steep limestone peaks to the east including Mt. Stelfox. There is also a magnificent panorama to the southwest over the Cline River of Mt. Cline, Resolute Mountain with its north glacier, and the precipices of the Whitegoat Peaks. This section of ridge runs further: drop west down to a saddle, then head north. The next knoll can be bypassed to the east en route to a knoll with a tall cairn [gr 290823]. Returning from here makes for a rewarding trip; if elect to press on as below, be prepared for a long day.

Go north before bailing west on open slopes. Ideally pick up a sheep path to the saddle at gr 285824. Another sheep path leads north, close to the edge of a cliff at first, before heading west over a gentle knoll (open despite the indication on some maps). A slight loss of elevation follows, and it's suggested to traverse below the knoll at gr 274827 on its southeast side, rather than going to its top only to descend.

This area was the location for lots of moss gentian, a tiny and rare wildflower. It looks like a solitary forgetmenot without the yellow centre; close inspection reveals that the petals (which only open in direct sunlight) are pointed rather than rounded.

Head along the ridge south of the aforementioned unvisited knoll, then switch to a southwest bearing. Ascend gradual, rocky terrain toward the prominent unnamed feature whose summit is at gr 257814. The final bit toward the top gets steeper, but there are large rocks rather than scree on the northeast ridge, which facilitates things (though the rocks can easily shift when weight is put on them).

Travelling this far west and this high has brought long, narrow Landslide Lake into view across the Cline Valley. Of the Abraham Lake reservoir there is not much seen, partly because the pronounced alluvial fan of Canyon Creek fills much of the vista. The remote site of the Cline fire lookout can be marvelled at; as can the steep summit of Mt. Michener—named after Canada's renowned Governor General from 1967 to 1974. (The name of the Cline River was given by explorer Norman Collie in honour of 19th Century fur trader Michael Cline.)

Descent southeast down the ridge is over large rocks at first, then over gentler ground. (A tall cairn of white rocks is situated partway along.) Toward the south end of the ridge, the option of dropping southwest to the flats of Boulder Creek (so-named unofficially but aptly) far below presents itself as a choice apparently preferable to dropping east and bushwhacking through forest. Be aware that this is an "out-of-the-frying-pan-into-the-fire" scenario, for things get tricky near the bottom.

It is possible with patience and some routefinding to negotiate a way through the steep reddish slabs; however, it is probably preferable to either go east higher up (as previously mentioned) or at least stay south where the going gets steeper, until the descent west to the creek is through forest. If either of the Boulder Creek alternatives is chosen, the flats aren't really a sidewalk stroll but they work, with a few detours necessary where the channel swings against a steep bank.

The trail back along the north side of the Cline River is found upstream of some incipient hoodoos. These are on the opposite, west side of Boulder Creek, above its confluence with the Cline (there's a campsite where the trail meets the creek). The return is easy except for a fair bit of windfall, and is long and rather anticlimactic apart from the potentially hazardous ford of Coral Creek.

All in all, a challenging and stimulating ridgewalk.

Section 6 Jasper National Park

Mt. Athabasca from summit of "Boundary Peak."

118 Ridge Northeast of Mt. Athabasca

Map p. 291
Photo p. 211

Distance: 8 km linear

Trail/off-trail: 4—8 hr

Elevation gain: 950 m (3115 ft)

Maximum elevation: 2879 m (9445 ft)

Maps: Gem Trek 1:75,000 Columbia Icefield, NTS 1:50,000 Columbia Icefield 83 C/3, and Parks Canada 1:50,000 Columbia Icefield (1981)

Trailhead: Parking area for the hiking trail to the toe of the Athabasca Glacier, situated just off the Icefields Parkway west of the Icefield Centre, between the road that runs down toward the toe and the road (open to shuttle buses only) to the Snocoach loading area.

This relatively short ridgewalk has an alpine character, situated as it is close to heavily glaciated Mt. Athabasca.

From the trailhead, hike about 500 metres up the service road leading to the Snocoach loading area. Then head southwest before the road begins to dip downhill to cross a drainage. A faint path leads to a collection of material including piles of lumber.

To gain the ridge, follow black tubing up a draw, then cut up left. Ascend steadily over broken ground. It is possible to contour east; however, the full-value ridgewalk veers right to go above a steep cliff. Surprisingly, the cliff has a gentle, spacious plateau at top [gr 862834]. This is an unusual vantage point upon the steep glaciated north aspect of Mt. Athabasca: it is possible to see the tracks of climbing parties heading for its summit via several routes; there may even be people on the mountain (most likely heading down after an early start).

Wildflowers at the lower elevations of this ridgewalk include moss campion, purple saxifrage, purple hedysarum, yellow mountain saxifrage, sawwort, bladder locoweed, white mountain avens, and alpine hawksbeard.

To continue the ridgewalk, proceed east, first into a small dip, then up the steep slope of the subsidiary feature unofficially known as "Boundary Peak" since it is on the line between Jasper and Banff national parks. If there is snow in a gully, it is preferable to go up it (ice axe necessary) rather than slogging up the slag-like rocks, even though any gully will likely be to the north and thus not go direct to the summit.

There is a superb panorama from the top [gr 867829], including of course Mt. Athabasca and the technical ridge connecting to it. The Boundary Glacier, little-known despite its proximity to the highway, lies in the valley immediately below to the south and east, with steep, rocky Hilda Peak rising above it on the other side.

Among other landmarks are: Tangle Ridge (#120) to the northwest, Nigel Peak to the north, Cirrus Mountain to the southeast, and to the west and northwest such biggies as Mt. Columbia, Snow Dome, and Mt. Alberta. Once it's time to leave, some routefinding is required to continue northeast down the ridge.

Detour left briefly to avoid a cliff at a small plateau with cairns; once below the cliff, head down scree to join the line of the alternate contouring route. Head easterly toward Boundary Lake, pausing en route at some excellently preserved spiral-shaped fossils (possibly of gastropods {snails}).

Not far beyond an oval "Banff Park Boundary" sign in a cairn about 1.5 m high, enter forest and engage in a stint of downhill bushwhacking to reach Boundary Lake. A faint path runs along its north shore and then down to an old road, where turn left. A path starting before boulders on the old road connects to a parking area on the Jasper/Banff boundary in Sunwapta Pass.

South from Mt. Wilcox North Peak [#119], including south peak (centre), Mt. Athabasca (right), and (on left) the wide, level terrain of Wilcox Pass and, beyond it, Nigel Peak Spur of Southeast Ridge [#116].

119 Mt. Wilcox North Peak

Map p. 291
Photos p. 5 (Contents), p. 10
(Acknowledgements), and p. 213

Distance: 11 km out-and-back

Trail/off-trail: 4—8 hr

Elevation gain: 940 m (3085 ft)

Maximum elevation: 2779 m (9115 ft)

Maps: Gem Trek 1:75,000 Columbia Icefield, NTS 1:50,000 Sunwapta Peak 83 C/6, and Parks Canada 1:50,000 Columbia Icefield (1981)

Trailhead: Tangle Falls parking area on west side of Icefields Parkway, 7.3 km (4.5 mi) north of the Icefield Centre opposite the toe of the Athabasca Glacier.

This straightforward route leads to the lower north peak of Mt. Wilcox, allowing fine views of the Athabasca Glacier region.

Cross the road from the parking area to pick up the trail toward Wilcox Pass that starts just south of Tangle Falls. Go up a section of old road, then turn left into forest. Climb to join Tangle Creek above the falls, passing the remains of an old cabin en route. Once in the long, wide, almost level expanse of Wilcox Pass, leave the trail heading west for the obvious ridge leading to the north peak of Mt. Wilcox.

Wildflowers along the way include white mountain heather, white mountain avens, Jacob's ladder, alpine hawksbeard, purple saxifrage, moss campion, and bladder locoweed. Pikas will chide passers-by for disturbing their alpine idyll.

The crest is not particularly narrow but it is well defined and leads up at a steady angle. The summit [gr 832887] gives good views over the Athabasca Glacier and to Mt. Athabasca, as well as of the Dome Glacier. To the northwest is Tangle Ridge (#120) with its massive, squat profile; the ridge northeast of Mt. Athabasca (#118) lies to the southeast. To the east is a feature not readily observed: a good-sized lake in the basin below Nigel Peak.

Return the same way, possibly dropping east down a scree chute near the point where joined the ridge on the way up. **N.B.** Don't try either to descend to the west or to traverse to the south peak...the author has done both and on both occasions nearly met his nemesis. A peril of accessibility can be the temptation to try something beyond the feasible.

The names of Mt. Wilcox and Wilcox Pass honour pioneer explorer and mountaineer Walter Wilcox, whose writing and photography encouraged and inspired many early visitors to the Rockies.

120 Tangle Ridge

Distance: 13 km loop

Trail/off-trail: 4—8 hr

Elevation gain: 1160 m (3805 ft)

Maximum elevation: 3020 m (9905 ft)

Maps: Gem Trek 1:75,000 Columbia Icefield and NTS 1:50,000 Sunwapta Peak 83 C/6

Trailhead: As for Ridgewalk 119, Mt. Wilcox North Peak.

Tangle Ridge rewards the effort of reaching it with superlative views.

Take the trail from Tangle Falls as for Ridgewalk 119, but after about forty minutes, leave the trail at approx. gr 820911. Drop north to cross the creek and head northeast along the terrace above the north bank of a tributary in a V-shaped notch.

As break out above the trees, head northerly, either to an unnamed pass [gr 833926] or directly up to the southeast end of Tangle Ridge. The going is over small dark rocks often forming small hillocks, which are surprisingly stable. Once on the more gradual summit ridge, simply head for the top [gr 805941]. {A small circular shed and other gizmos reside there.}

The prominence of this feature makes it a superb place to check out the surroundings. To the southwest is the summit of Mt. Columbia, second-highest peak in the Rockies after Mt. Robson, and almost due west is Mt. Alberta with its precipitous black east face. To the north, pyramidal Sunwapta Peak sweeps up from the valley of the same name.

Nigel Peak presents an aspect not usually seen—its glaciated, horn-shaped north face—in the view southeast. Meanwhile, to the south, the well-known profile of Mt. Athabasca is easily recognized; in front of and below it is the sharp-pointed north peak of Mt. Wilcox, whose north ridge makes for an enjoyable outing (#119). Of course, there are many other features to be identified: it is well worthwhile bringing up binoculars and a map (such as the one of Jasper National Park at a scale of 1:200,000) to figure things out. Even Mt. Hector can be picked out over 100 km away!

For the descent, head down the obvious rib slightly east of south. Bits of faint path occur toward the bottom, on the west side of the major gully leading to Tangle Creek. Bighorn sheep frequent this area.

The going gets vague in rocks carried down the gully in high water: keep south to connect with the trail on the other side of Tangle Creek above the gorge that funnels down to the falls. Return to the trailhead to complete a satisfying day's efforts.

The name of the creek, subsequently applied to the falls and the ridge, was given by explorer Mary Schäffer, who mentions "a fierce scrimmage" in getting through the valley in 1907.

Southeast from Tangle Ridge [#120] to Nigel Peak (centre) and Mt. Athabasca (right), with "Boundary Peak" [#118] below it to left.

Lake on route of Ridges Northeast of Mt. Edith Cavell; view north including knoll at gr 306396 (left) and Mt. Tekarra (centre skyline).

121 Ridges Northeast of Mt. Edith Cavell

Map p. 292

Distance: 16 km out-and-back with loop

Trail/off-trail: 4—8 hr

Elevation gain: 655 m (2150 ft)

Maximum elevation: 2420 m (7940 ft)

Maps: Gem Trek 1:100,000 Jasper and Maligne Lake, and NTS 1:50,000 Amethyst Lakes 83 D/9 and Athabasca Falls 83 C/12

Trailhead: Take the Icefields Parkway (Hwy. 93) south from Jasper townsite for 7.5 km (4.7 mi) and turn right onto Hwy. 93A. Turn right again at 13.0 km (8.1 mi) onto the Mount Edith Cavell Road (steep, narrow, winding, and rough; no trailers) and follow it to the parking area at the end after a total of 27.5 km (17.1 mi).

These high, rolling ridges stand in marked contrast to the angular topography surrounding them, and make for a most enjoyable ramble. **N.B.** Avoid contributing to trampling and erosion by keeping to well-defined paths, even though late-lying snow may cover parts of them (the snow is actually preferable for travel).

Take the Cavell Meadows trail at the start, branching off from the interpretive trail at a switchback to travel through rocky moraine for a brief spell. Then climb steadily up, at first in a trough beside the moraine wall, with the enjoyable distractions of wildflowers including partridgefoot, and wildlife including pikas and marmots.

Once near the top of the loop through the meadows, branch off onto a defined path that leads up to a knoll at approx. gr 308370. This popular spot grants fine views of Angel Glacier and is a nice place for a breather before beginning the off-trail portion of this ridgewalk.

From the knoll, traverse east and north onto a slightly higher ridge that leads down to a gap where a small lake drains out. Continue north up a gradual incline to the knoll at gr 306396. The trees that do grow hereabouts are small, low specimens that have been sheared off by wind and ice in their exposed location. The knoll gives good views west over the valley of the Astoria River toward the Ramparts. From here, drop east into a valley (boggy bits), then climb again to reach the knoll at gr 323390.

The next stage is an easy stroll southeast over open terrain to a final knoll [gr 326377]. Mt. Kerkeslin with its distinctive tiered strata lies to the east across the valley of the Athabasca Valley. Mt. Christie and steep-sided Brussels Peak rise further off to the southeast. Mt. Tekarra and the grey slabby peaks of the Colin Range are recognizable to the north.

Such characteristic (and delicate!) alpine flora as moss campion, purple saxifrage, and alpine harebell grow here, so be careful where tread. Also take care not to disturb any caribou that might be sighted in this area. Golden-crowned (cont. p. 218)

(Cont. from p. 217) sparrow and white-tailed ptarmigan are examples of the birdlife that can be seen in the vicinity.

Complete a circuit by returning to the small lake and rejoining the beaten track at the first knoll of the day. If energetic, it is possible to scramble up to the peak at gr 316366 (which has cliffs on the north aspect that preclude a more direct ascent from the ridgewalk described). It is also feasible, with more difficult scrambling, to forge on to the lower peak to the south [gr 316355]. If returning via the saddle at the base of the east ridge of Mt. Edith Cavell [gr 308356], be aware that there are very steep snow slopes on its north side.

Whatever choice is made, return via the Cavell Meadows trail to finish a rewarding day.

Cloud rolls over knoll between Indian Pass and Whistlers Pass, southwest of Indian Ridge.

South over route of Bald Hills and Beyond [#123]; distant vista includes (l to r) Sunwapta Peak, Mt. Athabasca, Mt. Alberta, and Mt. Columbia.

122 Indian Ridge

Distance: 12 km out-and-back with loop

Trail/off-trail: 4—8 hr

Elevation gain: 480 m (1575 ft)

Maximum elevation: 2730 m (8955 ft)

Maps: Gem Trek 1:35,000 Jasper Up-Close and 1:100,000 Jasper and Maligne Lake, and NTS 1:50,000 Jasper 83 D/16

Trailhead: Upper terminal of Whistlers Tramway near Jasper townsite (diehards can reach here by hiking up the trail from near Whistlers youth hostel).

This ridge makes for an energetic extension beyond the crowded stroll to the top of The Whistlers.

From the tram terminal, take the easy trail for just over 1 km to the summit of The Whistlers, named for marmots with their loud, high-pitched alarm calls. Now leave the trail, and the masses, behind, and strike off down southwest to the saddle at gr 229528. From here, the author's recommendation is to drop into the large basin to the southwest, thereby ensuring the least climbing back up at the end of the day.

Angle down gradually toward the creek: a good landmark is a clump of trees whose bark has been girdled by porcupines. From that point on the west side of the creek, traverse up to the north (right) to gain the ridge at gr 214534. Now proceed southwest and south, with sections of hands-on scrambling, to gain the northwest peak of Indian Ridge [gr 206524].

Shortly after leaving this peak for the higher summit to the southeast, the most demanding part of the outing appears in the form of a notch with steep walls. Avoid the dropoff by descending on the west side and contouring along to easy ground again. Now cruise to the high point of the day [gr 220516], savouring such alpine specialties in the wildflowers department as arctic poppy, alpine harebell, moss campion, alpine lousewort, purple saxifrage, and alpine wallflower. Pikas love this sort of country.

The views from the top include Mt. Edith Cavell, Mt. Robson if it's clear, Roche Noire and satellites to the west, and closer at hand the convoluted terrain of the Trident Range. Terminal Mountain to the south stands out, the tarns and meadows at its base contrasting with steep red cliffs above.

Descent is down the northeast ridge back to the aforementioned saddle, with sections of trail including across (rather than over) the northwest aspect of the knoll [gr 226525] above the pass. The last bit is the haul back up to The Whistlers, then down to the terminal and finally down to the valley, either by tram or on foot. (Note that there is no free ride down for those who hike up.)

123 Bald Hills and Beyond

Map p. 293
Photo p. 218

Distance: 28 km loop

Trail/off-trail: over 12 hr

Elevation gain: 960 m (3150 ft)

Maximum elevation: 2650 m (8690 ft)

Maps: Gem Trek 1:100,000 Jasper and Maligne Lake, and NTS 1:50,000 Athabasca Falls 83 C/12

Trailhead: Parking area at the very end of the Maligne Lake Road west of the bridge at the lake outlet, 45 km (28 mi) from its start at the junction with Highway 16 (Yellowhead Highway) east of Jasper townsite.

As the name suggests, the Bald Hills are an area of open rolling terrain—as such, they provide for excellent ridgewalking.

Start up the old road to the former fire lookout. The site of the cabin, at an elevation of 2170 metres, lies 5.2 km from the trailhead via the old road, or 4.0 km from the start if the steeper shortcut at 2.6 km is taken. (The more direct approach rejoins the old road just 50 metres south of the lookout site.)

Go south on the old road, which veers west and climbs the slope before coming to an end. A trail has been established up to a large level area at gr 534400. The ridgewalk continues southwest into a dip before gaining a knoll at gr 533396. Next follows an undulating course, first southeast, then south, over a series of bumps small and large to reach a subpeak at gr 539377.

To push on to the high point of the Bald Hills, descend south from the subpeak, then bend west on an obvious ramp. The final approach to the summit is up through a rock band. A large cairn stands on top [gr 529367]; the elevation of over 2600 metres, plus the central location, combine to afford superlative views.

Long, narrow Maligne Lake, largest natural body of water in the Rockies, lies to the east. Beyond it rise steep, grey peaks of the Queen Elizabeth Range including Leah Peak and Samson Peak (their names honour the Native couple who gave explorer Mary Schäffer directions to the lake). Maligne Mountain with its large glaciers lies farther south, while to the southeast are mounts Charlton and Unwin (also connected with Schäffer). Sunwapta Peak shows a pyramidal shape from this angle; other distant landmarks even further south include mounts Athabasca, Andromeda, and Alberta. Indian Ridge (#122) is visible to the northwest, while closer at hand—for those who are ambitious, though the outing to this point is certainly a satisfying accomplishment—is the route for the extension of this ridgewalk.

N.B. Keep in mind that committing to this extension makes for a very long day with lots more elevation loss and gain, and that the crux comes in its final hours. If determined to press on, descend from the summit, first northwest, then west where cliffs at the bottom force the route that way. Skirt a large talus pile, then drop through the open corridor of a small drainage to reach Evelyn Creek. Cross it and commence a bushwhack (it was for the author at least) up through forest and shintangle to the continuation of the ridge.

The grade levels off above treelimit, leading to a long enjoyable stretch of ridge rambling. By the way, caribou enjoy the same thing in this area, so keep eyes open. Falcons, possible peregrines, also frequent the vicinity, and may even nest among rocky pinnacles. Other pleasures of this outing include myriad wildflowers, among them such treasurers as arctic poppy, alpine harebell, moss campion, moss gentian, alpine lousewort, alpine hawksbeard, alpine wallflower, and forget-me-not.

Although the author has not confirmed this, it appears that if time or energy suggest, it is feasible to drop northeast off the ridge at either of two well-defined spurs, eventually connecting with an established trail. Otherwise, push on, with a steeper grade leading to the high point at gr 481418. Taking a breather here allows for absorption of more fine views, including Mt. Edith Cavell and its attendant ridges (#121) to the west, and the sharp apex of Mt. Columbia—highest peak in Alberta—way off to the southeast.

Now unfolds the most demanding part of the day: the descent to the northeast. Big blocks call for exacting balance; the author found it preferable to drop off the ridge to the left temporarily. Then, when it looks like difficulties are at an end, a sheer dropoff bars the way, unless perhaps you're the accomplished solo climber Peter Croft.

The recommendation is to descend north from the ridge before this obstacle, carefully picking a way down to a steep, narrow gully that delivers to gentler terrain. Then contour north to pick up the Skyline Trail below Little Shovel Pass. From the pass, it is a steady two hours back to the trailhead to finish a long but rewarding day (take a flashlight or headlamp in case it gets dark).

Summit of Mt. Greenock [#124] from south ridge; note snow plastered on trees.

124 Mt. Greenock

Map p. 293
Photo p. 221

Distance: 6 km loop

Off-trail: 4—8 hr

Elevation gain: 1080 m (3540 ft)

Maximum elevation: 2085 m (6840 ft)

Maps: Gem Trek 1:100,000 Jasper and Maligne Lake, and NTS 1:50,000 Snaring River 83 E/1

Trailhead: Turn north off the Yellowhead Highway (No. 16) onto the Celestine Lake Road, some 9.0 km (5.6 mi) north of the east exit into Jasper townsite. The pavement ends in 6.2 km, past the Snaring campground and Snaring River bridge. Continuing a further 7.7 km sees arrival at the start of one-way travel (although government vehicles can be on the road at any time). Public traffic eastbound is in the intervals 0800-0900, 1100-1200, 1400-1500, and 1700-1800; westbound 0930-1030, 1230-1330, 1530-1630, and 1830-1930 [no trailers allowed]. For this ridgewalk, drive 3.9 km (2.4 mi) from the start of the one-way section and pull off on the track to the right {do not drive along this track}. **N.B.** The one-way is narrow (very narrow in one place with a dropoff) and has steep and rough sections, especially near the trailhead. There is also an unbridged crossing of Corral Creek, near the beginning of the one-way section, that could be hazardous to small vehicles in high water.

It's surprising that Mt. Greenock is even named, given that is it merely a bump on the long ridge of Roche de Smet; nevertheless, its excellent vantage point makes this a rewarding outing.

From the parking spot, join the rocky, open east rib leading to the summit. Soon reach a pipeline right-of-way and pick up a sheep trail that angles up right to stay on the rib. Note: this rib has many sections of steep rock...although routefinding will avoid most, there is still a lot of scrambling required. Most of the grey, slabby limestone is at a nice angle for simple friction climbing; water erosion has created miniature sharp-peaked ridges, called *rillenkarren*, that give good grip.

The first smooth cliff can be turned on the left. The second steep bit can be breached via a bit of a chimney that has good holds. A dip follows, then a steep section. Further on is another dip, this one treed and with holes in the ground that gave rise to the author's nickname "Squirrel Midden Hollow." A third cliff can be bypassed on the left, leading to a grovel up a scree gully. It is preferable to soon get onto slabby edges to the right to traverse up to level ground again, briefly.

At this stage, the east rib peters out and some steep—but treed—ground must be covered to get onto the west rib. After it is gained, there is a gradual stretch, then steeper (but straightforward) terrain to the summit. Despite its minor status, there is a register in the small cairn. Perusal reveals few entries since it was placed in 1987, and mentions that Mt. Greenock served as a photographic survey station in 1915. This is appropriate, as there are fine views: across Jasper Lake to Talbot and Edna lakes, and southeast to the Colin Range. Distinctive Roche Miette forms the northwest end of the Miette Range, with Ridgewalk 125 below. Gargoyle Mountain rises above the valley of Vine Creek to the west. Signal Mountain, Mt. Tekarra, and Mt. Edith Cavell lie to the south; the ridges northeast of the latter (#121) can be easily discerned. Part of Indian Ridge (#122) can also be identified.

Bighorn sheep can be expected in this habitat; bird species that might be seen include common raven, Clark's nutcracker, spruce grouse, and Townsend's solitaire. Whitebark pine is recognizable by its five-needled growth form. Spotted saxifrage forms clumps of colour on rocky ground at higher elevations.

It is easy to descend via the treed west rib, taking the pipeline right-of-way near the bottom to return to the start.

Mt. Greenock was named, possibly after a town in Scotland, by surveyor M.P. Bridgland.

Roche Miette (left of centre) from ridge to west [#125].

South up valley of Fiddle River from high point of Sulphur Skyline Ridge [#126].

125 Ridge West of Roche Miette

Map p. 294
Photo p. 223

Distance: 4 km out-and-back

Off-trail: up to 4 hr

Elevation gain: 475 m (1560 ft)

Maximum elevation: 1475 m (4840 ft)

Maps: Gem Trek 1:100,000 Jasper and Maligne Lake, and NTS 1:50,000 Miette 83 F/4

Trailhead: Pulloff on west side of Highway 16, approx. 5.5 km (3.4 mi) south of the junction for Miette Hotsprings at Pocahontas and just north of the northern of two bridges over branches of the Rocky River. There is an Historic Sites and Monuments Board plaque for Jasper House at this pulloff.

This is a short, easily accessible ridgewalk that provides a nice break and is feasible much of the year thanks to its low elevation and southerly orientation.

Cross the highway from the trailhead and pick up a rough path at the north end of a rock cutting. This brings you onto a terrace which is then followed above a rockband, often along sheep trails. (Stay to defined paths where possible so as to avoid trampling and erosion of the sandy soil here.)

Simply keep to the ridgeline and climb steadily. There are glimpses of the rocky tower of Roche Miette en route. The final bit veers east and entails a push through trees to get to the high point [gr 368902]. This gives fine views, including of the braided channels of the Rocky River before it joins the Athabasca, and of course of the Athabasca Valley itself, with Jasper Lake and Talbot Lake. The landmark of Pyramid Mountain is conspicuous to the southeast, and Mt. Greenock (#124) is easily identified.

A variety of wildflowers grow along this ridge, among them common harebell, brown-eyed Susan (wild gaillardia), kinnikinnik, and purple hedysarum. The last of these is a preferred food for bears, so it's a good idea to make noise on this outing.

Return the same way to complete this brief but enjoyable leg-stretcher.

126 Sulphur Skyline Ridge

Map p. 294
Photo p. 223

Distance: 7 km loop

Trail/off-trail: up to 4 hr

Elevation gain: 700 m (2295 ft)

Maximum elevation: 2070 m (6790 ft)

Maps: Gem Trek 1:100,000 Jasper and Maligne Lake, and NTS 1:50,000 Miette 83 F/4

Trailhead: Turn north off Highway 16 onto the Miette Hot Springs Road, 7.1 km (4.4 mi) west of the Jasper National Park east entrance or 41.1 km (25.5 mi) east of the eastern Jasper townsite turnoff. Follow the road 17.5 km (10.9 mi) to its end at the parking area for the hot springs complex.

This short ridgewalk features good access and pleasing views.

Start up the paved service road that runs east from just south of the pool to a water tank. Continue on the narrower trail, climbing steadily to Shuey Pass, reached in about 30 minutes. At the pass, take the right turn at the signed junction and commence climbing more steeply up a series of switchbacks.

The trail then traverses below a knoll to gain a dip before following close to the ridge to the summit [gr 503852]. This vantage point reveals a superb vista south toward distant Fiddle Pass: a scene of varied landforms, with a series of rocky ridges and hillocks sweeping down to the winding river that flows along the vegetated valley floor.

There are also fine views west and southwest over the valley of Sulphur Creek to peaks of the Miette Range including Utopia Mountain and Mt. O'Hagan. The latter feature is named after Dr. Thomas O'Hagan, who worked many years in Jasper and whose son Howard was a well-known writer.

To continue this outing, follow the ridge down from the summit as it first heads west and then bends northwest. A sheep trail is defined along much of the route; the author expected to see bighorns but instead had a sighting of a black bear. Small mammals such as pika, golden-mantled ground squirrel, and chipmunk thrive in the environs. The end of the ridge drops steeply through forest directly toward the hot springs pool.

The names of Sulphur Creek and the ridge, as with Sulphur Mountain near Banff townsite, derive from the minerals associated with the hotsprings.

127 "Fiddle—Sulphur Ridge"

Map p. 294

Distance: 6 km linear

Trail/off-trail: up to 4 hr

Elevation gain: 750 m (2460 ft)

Maximum elevation: 2120 m (6955 ft)

Maps: Gem Trek 1:100,000 Jasper and Maligne Lake, and NTS 1:50,000 Miette 83 F/4

Trailhead: As for Ridgewalk 126, Sulphur Skyline Ridge.

This ridgewalk is a more demanding alternative to Sulphur Skyline Ridge, involving more difficult off-trail travel and routefinding.

Hike to Shuey Pass as per the Sulphur Skyline Ridge description, then at the signed junction leave the trail, heading northwest. After a brief stint through trees, hit an open slope with scree and—much preferable—rocky ribs that make for enjoyable scrambling. Still, there is over 425 metres of elevation gain in about 1 km of horizontal travel. The rocky ribs peter out, leading to more slogging. Go left at the first cliff, and don't be deceived by a few cairns and false summits en route to the top [gr 502873]. Expect to take about an hour from the trail.

The rolling crest of Ashlar Ridge stands out to the northwest, the treed east aspect much different from the sheer west face. The mystery of Mystery Lake, at least as far as its location, is solved in the view east. Fiddle Peak and other summits of the Fiddle Range rise to the north, while Roche Miette is unmistakable to the west. The Miette pool is far below to the west.

The author cannot vouch for it firsthand, but it looks feasible to descend east, then southeast, before dropping south to join the trail that leads back up to Shuey Pass. The described route goes northwest from the summit to a subsidiary knoll; a little bump just before can be turned on the west side. Continue northwest (rather than north) down over open ground with cliffs on the left. Sheep trails exist in spots.

Among the wildflowers that can be seen are felwort and the related tiny, exquisite moss gentian, as well as yellow mountain saxifrage.

There is a small cliffband about three-quarters of the way down to the valley floor: it can easily be avoided by angling left. A well-defined path lies below it; the final descent is a steep one through trees and alders.

Hit the road about 1 km below the pool.

Northwest from "Fiddle—Sulphur Ridge;" Ashlar Ridge in centre mid-distance.

Woolly lousewort, photographed near Cardinal Divide [#128].

128 Ridge East of Cardinal Divide

Map p. 294
Photo p. 227

Distance: 8 km out-and-back

Trail: up to 4 hr

Elevation gain: 200 m (655 ft)

Maximum elevation: 2215 m (7265 ft)

Maps: NTS 1:50,000 Mountain Park 83 C/14

Trailhead: Cardinal Divide south of the community of Cadomin, reached via Highway 40 from just west of Hinton or via Highways 47 and 40 from west of Edson.

This easy saunter leads up to and then along the edge of the escarpment that runs east of the Cardinal Divide, which separates the headwaters of the Cardinal and McLeod rivers.

From the parking area on the pass, head northeast on an old Cat track—now bordered by rocks to mark the way and prevent trampling of the hardy but fragile vegetation. A trademark wildflower of this area is woolly lousewort with its deep purple, fern-like leaves; other species include purple saxifrage and moss campion.

At first dipping and weaving like Muhammad Ali as it climbs gently, the route makes a final steeper beeline to gain the edge of the long cliff. Simply turn east and follow along or near the crest (a faint quad track exists). All the while be entertained by the antics of many marmots (perhaps first being startled by their loud alarm whistles). Pikas inhabit the rocky northern slopes of the amphitheatre-like escarpment, and white-tailed ptarmigan find the arctic-style terrain to their liking.

The ridge veers northeast and climbs gently to the high point at gr 860621, indicated by several cairns and a survey marker. The escarpment turns east again and descends gradually into trees, but the 'summit' represents the boundary of the new Whitehorse Creek Wildland Provincial Park and gives fine views.

Of particular interest is the Mountain Park area below to the northwest: site of a once thriving community connected with coal mining. Also in sight is the pass leading into Jasper National Park, which—although given as Cardinal Pass on the 1996 edition of the topo map—is best known as Rocky Pass. (A trail leads through it and down to the South Boundary trail on the Medicine Tent River, a tributary of the Rocky River.)

Return the same way.

The Cardinal Divide marks the northwestern limit of the watershed of the Cardinal River, named after fur trader Jacques Cardinal.

Section 7 British Columbia

West from Akamina Ridge [#129], including Boundary Mountains in Glacier National Park (left) and start of Ridgewalk #130 on right below skyline.

129 Akamina Ridge

Map p. 295
Photos p. 11 and p. 229

Distance: 18 km out-and-back with loop

Trail/off-trail: 4—8 hr

Elevation gain: 890 m (2920 ft)

Maximum elevation: 2565 m (8415 ft)

Maps: Parks Canada 1:50,000 Waterton Lakes National Park (1988) and NTS 1:50,000 Sage Creek 82 G/1

Trailhead: Parking area for Akamina Pass trail, on east side of Akamina Parkway 15 km (9.3 mi) from its start near Waterton townsite.

This deservedly popular ridgewalk in Akamina—Kishinena Provincial Park features the distinctive purple-red argillite rock characteristic of much of this area of the southern Canadian Rockies. Although the park lies in the southeastern corner of B.C., access is difficult from the west; most parties enter from the east via Akamina Pass on the border with Alberta.

A 'pure' line can be made by following the rough cutline along the Alberta/B.C. boundary toward Forum Peak, but this goes through prime grizzly bear habitat and entails potentially hazardous scrambling near the end. The recommended route for this ridgewalk is to hike for about 1 km west from the pass, then take the signed trail for Forum Lake past the ranger station (the short side trip to Forum Falls is worthwhile).

The trail to the lake climbs steeply at first, then tapers off and passes through subalpine larches shortly before arriving at the body of water cupped in a rocky cirque. From the north shore, a sign indicates the trail for Akamina Ridge. This was recently cleared and flagged when visited in Sept., 2000, though the trail work ended at an open slope of mostly beargrass. Traverse up to gain the ridge at a saddle [gr 135332], then proceed south by scrambling over blocky terrain up to the top of a rounded knoll.

A short detour east from here leads to Forum Peak, which gives fine views not obtained on the main ridgewalk. The vistas include Cameron Lake, Mt. Custer, the valley of Boundary Creek down to part of Upper Waterton Lake, and to Upper Kintla Lake and the Glacier National Park peaks surrounding it.

The main Akamina Ridge route heads west, then southwest, from the rounded knoll, with patches of trail near the first high point [gr 125318]. The second high point, and true summit of Akamina Ridge, lies 1 km northwest over gentle terrain. The ridge continues northwest over a third knoll before bending north toward Bennett Pass. {A more direct descent to Wall Lake appears possible via a steep scree gully to the northeast from blue rocks at approx. gr 106332}.

Do not continue down to Bennett Pass unless combining the ridge to the west (#130) with this trip, which makes for a long day. Turn right at an inconspicuous T-junction to drop steadily down to the southeast before picking up a drainage leading east to Wall Lake. Before the lake is a meadow of wild chives that waves in the usual wind; around the lake are tall trees contrasting with the alpine environs less than 1 km away. Wall Lake is an appropriate name: looking from its shores, it seems implausible that there is a way to reach the heights above. The trail widens at Wall Lake, and leads across a bridge over the outlet creek to travel north and then east. It eventually connects with the old road leading over Akamina Pass near a backcountry campground some 500 metres west of the Forum Lake junction.

Akamina is a Native word that has been variously translated as "high benchland" and "mountain pass." The protected area became a provincial park in 1995, and joined the UNESCO Crown of the Continent World Heritage Site in 1998.

East from gr 073337 on Ridgewalk 130; Akamina Ridge [#129] in mid-distance.

Dolomite Lake from Wildhorse Ridge [#131]; view northeast including route of Ridgewalk #132 in mid-distance: Coyote Ridge (left) and The Sugarloaf (right of centre).

130 Ridge West of Akamina Ridge

Map p. 295
Photo p. 231

Distance: 8 km out-and-back

Trail/off-trail: 4—8 hr

Elevation gain: 180 m (590 ft)

Maximum elevation: 2430 m (7970 ft)

Maps: Parks Canada 1:50,000 Waterton Lakes National Park (1988) and NTS 1:50,000 Sage Creek 82 G/1

Trailhead: Point above Bennett Pass on Ridgewalk 129, Akamina Ridge.

This ridge west of Akamina Ridge can be done as an extension of that ridgewalk, or on its own with approach via Wall Lake. Either way, it's a long day but a rewarding one.

The ridgewalk starts at the junction above Bennett Pass, reached at the 10 km point on the Akamina Ridge route or by way of an 8 km hike via Wall Lake. Take the well-defined trail that switchbacks down to the pass. Leave the trail to climb over open ground, first heading northwest, then north to the summit of the symmetrical peak at gr 098344. From here, descend southwest to a rocky outlier before dropping quite steeply to a notch [gr 092336].

Climb steeply west from the notch, then top out on a gentle ridge that runs west almost 2 km, with a dip before the high point [gr 073337]. Subalpine larches grace part of this high crest, which has steep dropoffs especially to the northwest at the west end. There are glimpses of tiny Ashman Lake to the north, and over the aptly-named Grizzly Gulch (be alert for bears).

An unusual isolated, cliff-girt outcrop (possibly a nunatak: a feature whose summit was never glaciated) stands near the headwaters of Upper Kintla Creek. Waterfalls plunge over cliffs, and austere peaks fill the view to the south and west, including around the head of Grizzly Gulch.

Return by reversing the route. A bit of elevation gain can be avoided by traversing below the symmetrical peak before dropping to Bennett Pass, though it is advisable to go at least as high as the last trees on its southwest ridge before launching across the scree on a downward course.

131 Wildhorse Ridge

Map p. 296
Photo p. 231

Distance: 20 km out-and-back

Trail/off-trail: 4—8 hr

Elevation gain: 820 m (2690 ft)

Maximum elevation: 2480 m (8135 ft)

Map: NTS 1:50,000 Queen Creek 82 G/14

Trailhead: Turn east off Highway 93/95 onto Whiteswan Forest Service Road, 4.5 km (2.8 mi) south of the bridge over the Kootenay River south of the community of Canal Flats. **N.B.** There may be a one-way section due to washouts on this stretch. At 21.3 km (13.2 mi) from the highway, past the Lussier Hot Springs parking area and just before Alces Lake in Whiteswan Lake Provincial Park, turn right. This is a rough road but passable to 2WD vehicles in most conditions. Turn right at 29.6 km (18.4 mi) from the highway to cross Coyote Creek, keep straight at 30.7 km (19.0 mi), and reach the parking area for Top of the World Provincial Park at approx. 52 km (32 mi).

An established trail leads almost to Wildhorse Ridge in B.C.'s remote Top of the World Provincial Park. **N.B.** Be aware that grizzly bears frequent the environs, and that the trail may be closed due to bear activity.

From the trailhead, take the wide trail that leads along the Lussier River and to Fish Lake in 6 km. From this focal point of the park, go past the cabin and the tenting area and cross the outlet. Proceed along the west shore and up a series of switchbacks to the junction with the trail cutting across the slide path toward Sparkle Lake.

For Wildhorse Ridge, keep straight (trail overgrown in 1999) into a basin that sees avalanche activity. Subalpine larches grow here, and marmots gambol about. The trail climbs up the north side of the basin almost to its head, then cuts back into forest to gain the ridge above Dolomite Lake.

Head west on fainter trail, eventually non-existent, to gain the high point of Wildhorse Ridge [gr 096224]. This vantage looks west over the valley of the Wild Horse River (as it is correctly known), named for the wild horses that roamed the area from at least the early 1800s as recorded by explorer David Thompson.

The view also includes the valley of the Lussier River to the north, with many cutblocks (some for salvage purposes after a fire). To the east almost the entire extent of Fish Lake is in sight, as well as Mt. Morro: at 2912 m the highest elevation in the park. To the northeast lie The Sugarloaf and Coyote Ridge, described next (Ridgewalk 132). [These two ridgewalks can be combined in a long day of approx. 27 km.]

There is not much scope for exploring north or south along the ridge without soon getting into quasi-technical terrain, so return the same way.

132 Coyote Ridge

Map p. 296

Distance: 19 km loop

Trail/off-trail: 4—8 hr

Elevation gain: 765 m (2510 ft)

Maximum elevation: 2425 m (7955 ft)

Map: NTS 1:50,000 82 G/14 Queen Creek

Trailhead: As for Ridgewalk 131, Wildhorse Ridge.

This outing presents a classic opportunity to cruise along an undulating, mostly open ridge.

Access to Coyote Ridge is via the same Fish Lake trail as for Wildhorse Ridge (Ridgewalk 131) [these two can be combined in a long day of approx. 27 km]. Shortly before the lake, turn left for Coyote Creek and The Sugarloaf. The trail climbs up to a shoulder, then drops into a drainage (may be dry) and climbs again to run above an escarpment. Turn left at the junction in a small meadow (bear diggings) to head up The Sugarloaf on a trail marked with flagging tape and orange diamonds with a central white horizontal stripe. There may be windfall, and the trail is vague on a grassy slope where it first breaks into the open, but becomes better defined again on the ridge.

Leaving established trails beyond The Sugarloaf, head north for Coyote Ridge, first dropping into a treed saddle. There is a good path at first, marked with flagging tape; it fades, but there are numerous game tracks. These traverse below the crest on the east side, so eventually cut up to the open ridge. Now things are very enjoyable, enlivened by wildflowers such as glacier lily, Jacob's ladder, and wild blue flax, and by wildlife such as Clark's nutcrackers, golden-mantled ground squirrels, and chipmunks. Subalpine larches festoon the ridge in places.

There is a good game path north of the first knoll [gr 136264], in a grassy corridor east of the rocky west aspect and a narrow band of trees. A similar easy section occurs en route to the third knoll [gr 126277]. Mt. Morro appears to the southeast between the first and second knolls from the third.

Continuing on, now heading northwest, suddenly an old bulldozed track appears. However, leave it to head westerly down a well-defined ridge from approx. gr 123279 on the northern boundary of the park. There is a fine path at first; it disappears, but the steady descent is not as bad as might be anticipated. There is a juniper zone, then a zone of Douglas-fir trees with open ground beneath, then an area of many fallen trees {take care: slippery and rotting}.

The angle eases off near the valley bottom; a bias should be given slightly south in order not to end up too far downstream. An old cleared trail with flagging tape will be crossed not long before striking the current trail along the east side of the

View of south peak of Coyote Ridge from saddle to north; The Sugarloaf beyond and Mt. Morro on left.

Lussier River. The bridge saves a ford; it is downstream of both the signed side trail to some sink holes and a porcupine-chewed sign for cross-country skiing.

The bridge is just west of a junction with a post (no sign in '99); there is a picnic table nearby, then a second bridge and the main hiker trail leading back to the trailhead in a few hundred metres.

West to high point at gr 712176 on Ridgewalk 133; Kindersley Summit in centre mid-distance.

133 Ridges Beyond Kindersley Summit

Map p. 296
Photos p. 9 and p. 235

Distance: 16 km out-and-back with loop

Trail/off-trail: 8—12 hr

Elevation gain: 1240 m (4065 ft)

Maximum elevation: 2690 m (8825 ft)

Maps: Gem Trek 1:100,000 Kootenay National Park, and NTS 1:50,000 Tangle Peak 82 J/12 and Radium Hot Springs 82 K/9

Trailhead: Parking area on the north side of Highway 93 South and east of the crossing of Sinclair Creek, 10.5 km (6.5 mi) east of the west entrance to Kootenay National Park

This ridgewalk, some of which is quite ambitious, makes for an interesting day on the western edge of Kootenay National Park.

The most direct approach to Kindersley Summit is via Sinclair Creek; there is also a trail via Kindersley Pass but it is longer and involves more elevation gain. Another benefit of going by way of Sinclair Creek is that it gives a preview of the ridgewalk.

So head up the drainage from the trailhead, making lots of noise as this narrow valley with its noisy creek and slide paths is grizzly bear habitat. Kindersley Summit (the high point on the trail) lies 6.5 km from the start, with much of the elevation gain occurring in the final kilometre or so.

A short detour can be made southeast to the attractive subpeak at gr 721166 (there is a path leading up). The main ridgewalk goes northwest from Kindersley Summit up to the high point of the day [gr 712176]. A rock outcrop en route looks like an Easter Island statue. Other, more contemporary structures appear at the top.

The views encompass Mt. Assiniboine and neighbouring Aye and Eon mountains to the northeast, while the Bugaboos stand out to the west. The Royal Group and Mt. Joffre with its north glacier rise to the east.

Continue by descending east, over steep ground at first, then on grassy slopes. Bighorn sheep frequent the natural pastures, which have alpine hawksbeard adding splashes of yellow. The gentle going comes to an end at a saddle [gr 726178] between branches of Sinclair and Nixon creeks {old porcupine-chewed sign}. A faint path leads back to Kindersley Summit and could be taken if the day seems full enough already.

To push on, climb steeply to the peak at gr 730182. The ridge then turns southeast and becomes trickier. Shortly after leaving the above peak, a vertical drop requires a detour off the ridge to the right for a while. Once regained, the going is easier; however, it later gets quasi-technical and the author chose to backtrack without reaching gr 745164. A small cairn (1999) marked the descent gully: steep but otherwise fine. Rejoin the Sinclair Creek trail and head back to the start.

134 Hawk Ridge Southern Section to Mt. Shanks

Map p. 297

Distance: 24 km linear

Trail/off-trail: over 12 hr

Elevation gain: 1580 m (5180 ft)

Maximum elevation: 2850 m (9350 ft)

Maps: Gem Trek 1:100,000 Kootenay National Park and Banff & Mt. Assiniboine, and NTS 1:50,000 Banff 82-O/4 and Mount Assiniboine 82 J/13

Trailhead: Small parking area north of bridge over Vermilion River on east side of Highway 93 South, 63 km (39 mi) north of the west entrance to Kootenay National Park and 30.5 km (19 mi) south of the Alberta/British Columbia boundary at Vermilion Pass.

This southern section of Hawk Ridge provides for a long, challenging day. Note that it would be difficult to bail off this ridge to the right due to cliffs, so once about halfway along the committment is to continue to Mt. Shanks (cont. p. 238)

Northwest along Hawk Ridge Southern Section; Mt. Ball left of centre on skyline and Hawk Ridge Northern Section [#135] on left below skyline.

(Cont. from p. 237) (before that, backtracking would be feasible).

Begin with the steady series of switchbacks up through forest to Honeymoon Pass, reached in about 90 minutes. Where first reach the level meadow at the south end of the pass, turn right through open forest to the right side of a slide path. Look to connect with a narrow watercourse of slate rock to the left, leading up (with a bit of scrabbling at the top) to the ridge at treelimit.

Grind up an energy-sapping slope (loose slate in a clay-like base) to the ridge ahead to the left, then after some scrambling gain the first peak on this long outing [gr 743560]. The northern section of Hawk Ridge (#135) is in view, with the Goodsirs off to the northwest. Nearer at hand is the southern aspect of Mt. Ball, surprisingly heavily glaciated given its southerly orientation. To the east are the seldom-seen western profiles of peaks such as Pilot Mountain and Monarch Mountain; the Monarch Ramparts (#91) are also visible.

To the west are Mt. Verendrye and other peaks of the Vermilion Range, while to the southeast, in the direction headed, is Mt. Assiniboine—which later on this outing falls out of sight behind the bulk of Mt. Shanks. Immediately on leaving the first peak lose about 200 metres of elevation to a dip, then make that up and more to reach the second peak [gr 752549]. North from this spot, Mummy Lake and the southern of the two Pharaoh Peaks are briefly in view.

The route continues over two lower bumps, then up to a high point before descending (some fun scree) to the second major gap [gr 767526]. Next is a steep haul up to a subpeak of Mt. Shanks [gr 771523]. The ridge beyond this has a broken crest which is avoided by means of sidehill gouging to its right. There is a stretch of tricky going on narrow, slabby terrain where the ridge turns left below Mt. Shanks.

The summit has a more-or-less permanent icy expanse on its north side, as well as accommodating a couple of communication sheds and associated paraphernalia. Mt. Assiniboine is at last again in view, presenting a less well-known profile. The Simpson and Vermilion rivers wind through their valleys far below.

To return to that level, descent is via the wide scree gully a short distance back along the approach. Things go quickly, with a few small cliffbands to navigate through, then when the slope is about to become gentler a final cliffband looms ahead. Rather than attempting to downclimb, skirt it easily to the right to a recent burn and then rejoin the drainage.

Fortunately, there was (1998) pink flagging tape of a scientific study near a confluence. Follow this: no matter how rough the going is, how much slippery deadfall and annoying alder obstructs passage, and how long it seems to take, it is at least a semblance of a route. Eventually reach the old road just below the site of the former Mt. Shanks fire lookout, which serves as the final stretch out to the highway, an easy end to a big day.

135 Hawk Ridge Northern Section

Distance: 17 km linear

Trail/off-trail: 8—12 hr

Elevation gain: 1325 m (4345 ft)

Maximum elevation: 2595 m (8510 ft)

Maps: Gem Trek 1:100,000 Kootenay National Park and Banff & Mt. Assiniboine, and NTS 1:50,000 Banff 82-O/4 and Mount Goodsir 82 N/1

Trailhead: As for Ridgewalk 134, Hawk Ridge Southern Section to Mt. Shanks.

This is a gentler ridgewalk than that along the southern section of Hawk Ridge to Mt. Shanks, though it still requires a fair bit of effort.

To start with, there is the steady haul up the Honeymoon Pass trail. Then almost the same amount of elevation gain lies ahead, only this time over a much shorter distance. The most direct approach is to head up the talus slope to the left before the last stream crossing below the pass; though this is steep, a reconnaissance from the southern section suggests it is feasible. (The author took a line up the edge of the large avalanche path that comes down to the meadows in the pass, but this degenerates into a stiff push through dense growth and scrabbling up through small rockbands.)

The initial steep rocky scramble tapers off to stands of subalpine larch and later open meadows. The high point at gr 726574 grants expansive (cont. p. 240)

Southeast along Hawk Ridge Northern Section; Mt. Shanks at end of southern section [#134] on centre skyline and Mt. Assiniboine to its left.

(Cont. from p. 239) views, including of pyramidal Mt. Assiniboine to the southeast, and—closer at hand—the surprisingly heavily glaciated southern aspect of Mt. Ball. Among other landmarks are the pointed Goodsirs to the northwest, and (in one of those unexpected revelations that the mountains give) peaks to the east such as Mt. Bourgeau and Cascade Mountain close to Banff townsite.

The inviting ridge to the northwest beckons, further enhanced by wildflowers such as purple saxifrage and even the species known as river beauty or {more appropriate in this case} mountain fireweed (*Epilobium latifolium*). There are scattered trees in the dip at gr 715578. Mammals that inhabit the ridge include pika and mountain goat: if the latter aren't actually sighted, there is evidence in white fur and droppings. The name of the ridge suggests that hawks are among the avian members of this alpine community, at least as visitors.

An interesting rib between the next two high points along the way provides variety; there is a view of Castle Mountain through Ball Pass from the third 'peak' of the day. (This summit has cloth on the ground that apparently served for an aerial survey.) The ridge veers slightly left after this point at the source of one of the headwater branches of Verdant Creek, whose seldom-seen valley has been below to the right all the while.

The author chose to drop off to the west from the third peak for a little while, though did not descend to a green plateau but chose to keep to a rocky rib. {If a blue polka-dot handkerchief catches the eye, it was lost by yours truly.} The final saddle of the day has game trails passing through it. From the fourth peak [gr 696606] with its big cairn, don't "look a gift horse in the mouth." Go ahead and take the open gully that leads northwest all the way down to Hawk Creek, some 1000 metres below. In the right conditions, this route might even offer good glissading.

Once at the bottom of the valley, cross Hawk Creek (possibly on a fallen log) and climb up to hit the trail. Turn left and head down to the highway to finish a rewarding day.

North from saddle at gr 610603 to Numa Mountain (left) and Numa Pass (right).

136 Numa Mountain and North

Map p. 299

Distance: 23 km loop

Trail/off-trail: 8—12 hr

Elevation gain: 1310 m (4295 ft)

Maximum elevation: 2720 m (8920 ft)

Maps: Gem Trek 1:100,000 Kootenay National Park and NTS 1:50,000 Mount Goodsir 82 N/1

Trailhead: Parking area for the Numa Creek trail, on the west side of Highway 93 South 79.5 km (49 mi) from the west entrance to Kootenay National Park near Radium Hot Springs and 14 km (8.5 mi) from the Alberta/British Columbia boundary at Vermilion Pass.

This ridgewalk gives excellent views of the renowned Rockwall. Numa means "thunder," by the way; if there's any it's best not to head out on this trip.

Cross the footbridge over the Vermilion River near the start, then hike along the level for about 1.5 km to Numa Creek. Now follow up the north side of the valley 5 km further to a junction and a nearby backcountry campground. Next turn south toward Numa Pass. Getting there has already covered over 13.5 km and almost 950 m of elevation gain, yet the ridgewalk has only just begun. [Taking the trail up Floe Creek to Floe Lake (named for the ice that "floe-ats" in it) is only slightly shorter, involves more elevation gain, and calls for a vehicle shuttle or a lot of jarring pavement pounding at the end. The approach described completes a near-perfect loop.]

Climb northeast from the pass to a knoll. Descend slightly to another saddle, then commence the ascent of Numa Mountain. There's a false summit before the true top at gr 617594. This peak gives superlative views, notably west to Floe Lake and Foster Peak and the precipices of the Rockwall. The north end of Hawk Ridge (#135) is almost due east across the valley of the Vermilion River, while Mt. Assiniboine soars skyward to the southeast. The Wenkchemna Peaks stand out to the north, showing a different profile than from Moraine Lake. And the Bugaboos etch out a striking profile to the west.

Continue by turning down to the north, if preferred skirting a 'scrambly' bit to the west. A mountain goat path materializes in the saddle at gr 610603, which sports some trees including subalpine larches. Climb at a moderate grade for about 300 metres of gain to the outlier at gr 606614.

Next comes an almost level stretch of over 1 km to a high point. The author descended northwest down a small drainage from here, but it is more direct and should be feasible to continue further north along the ridge and then down a drainage that joins the Numa Creek trail a mere 1 km from the trailhead.

137 Mt. Hunter Southeast Ridge

Map p. 300

Distance: 20 km out-and-back

Trail/off-trail: 8—12 hr

Elevation gain: 1420 m (4660 ft)

Maximum elevation: 2535 m (8315 ft)

Maps: NTS 1:50,000 McMurdo 82 N/2 and Golden 82 N/7

Trailhead: Parking area just south of the Trans-Canada Highway at the Wapta Falls turnoff, 24.7 km (15.3 mi) west of the Field junction and 4.8 km (3.0 mi) east of the west entrance to Yoho National Park.

This ridgewalk continues beyond the site of the former Upper Mt. Hunter fire lookout, whose wooden tower is gone (footings still visible), although the log cabin residence survives. En route, the more recent steel tower and Panabode cabin of the Lower Mt. Hunter lookout can be visited with a slight detour.

The trail to the upper lookout site takes two hours or so; travel beyond is off-trail, though a semblance of path (with old blazes) exists in what appears to be an old cleared corridor continuing up the ridge a short distance. About an hour of ridgewalking leads above treelimit to the first subpeak at gr 249792.

In the dip after this first high point, there is a cairn marking the national park boundary (which comes up from the south and runs northwest along the ridge ahead); another cairn sits 10 minutes further on. Now, with a sheer drop-off to the east, the character of the outing has changed, though not such that there is exposure.

To gain the second subpeak {if summit fever dictates; otherwise enjoy the view}, leave the ridge at the last trees and traverse left. Don't go up from the first rib (dicey going); instead, cross the basin ahead, rising up to the right to hit the second rib at the top of a gully running below some almost horizontal strata. (This point on the second rib is above a sharp drop more-or-less level with where hit the first rib.)

Now continue into the next basin, perhaps having climbed a short way up the second rib before dropping into this basin, to go up to the summit "from behind." Views include big glaciated peaks to the west, among them the Howser Towers of the Bugaboos, and the steep-sided pyramid of Mt. Sir Donald near Rogers Pass.

The peaks around Porcupine Creek catch attention with their red colour, while to the east are landmark mountains on the continental divide such as Mt. Victoria and Hungabee Mountain. To the southeast rise in sharp profile Mt. Vaux and Chancellor Peak, with between them the distinctive summits of the Goodsirs. The Kicking Horse River courses in its valley far below, actually running on both sides of the ridge, with an abrupt change of direction at Wapta Falls. The true summit of Mt. Hunter, recognized by its wavy strata, lies a long way off (more than three kilometres

Southeast from Mt. Hunter Southeast Ridge to glaciated Mt. Vaux on left, The Goodsirs in distance, and Chancellor Peak in centre.

away over what looks to be difficult going); the author has not made it that far.

Grizzly bear diggings occur near the ridge between the two subpeaks, and the author had a close sighting of a black bear on the trail between the two fire lookouts—so be bear aware. Another possibility on this outing is sighting mountain goats (albeit probably at a distance); their presence is signalled by white hairs caught in vegetation. Unpleasant evidence of another kind of wildlife may come in the form of numerous spider webs across the trail.

Wildflowers along this outing include bunchberry, wild rose, nodding onion, alumroot, low larkspur, leather-leaved saxifrage, stonecrop, and moss campion.

Although we know that Mt. Hunter was named by James Hector, it's not certain who he had in mind.

Southeast from Mt. Carnarvon South Ridge [#138] including Mt. Stephen above Mt. Burgess.

138 Mt. Carnarvon South Ridge

Map p. 298
Photo p. 243

Distance: 15 km out-and-back with loop

Trail/off-trail: 4—8 hr

Elevation gain: 1275 m (4180 ft)

Maximum elevation: 2575 m (8445 ft)

Maps: Gem Trek 1:50,000 Lake Louise & Yoho and NTS 1:50,000 Golden 82 N/7

Trailhead: Turn south off the Trans-Canada Highway 2.6 km (1.6 mi) west of the Field junction and drive 8.0 km (5.0 mi) to the Emerald Lake parking area. The Hamilton Lake trail begins to the west at the south end of the parking area.

This short extension of the Hamilton Lake trail allows access to the south ridge of Mt. Carnarvon, which grants a rare sighting of the heavily glaciated southern aspects of the peaks of the Mummery Group. This ridgewalk also gives an overview of the beautiful turquoise waters of Hamilton Lake.

Reaching Hamilton Lake takes about two hours at a steady pace; the ascent through forest is varied with glimpses of the canyon of Hamilton Creek and a view of the ethereal cascades of Hamilton Falls dropping through a series of three plunge pools.

From the end of the trail at Hamilton Lake, cross the outlet rocks and head southwest on a traverse to the south ridge, aiming to hit it just above the trees. There is a path at first, which then fades out. Once almost done with steep sidehill gouging, and before a cliffband, a path materializes again to lead onto the end of the ridge.

Now turn north over easier terrain and gain almost 300 metres vertical to a level section more-or-less west of Hamilton Lake. En route there are views across the Blaeberry Valley to the Mummery Group, spectacularly ice-clad on this side despite facing the sun. Mt. Mummery was named by J.N. Collie in honour of A.F. Mummery, a renowned British climber of the late 19th century.

This ridge also permits views to the west that cannot be had from Hamilton Lake, over the Amiskwi Valley to the Van Horne Range and beyond. Otherwise the panorama is much the same as from the open area before the lake, taking in such highlights as Mt. Vaux, Chancellor Peak, and the Goodsirs.

A bonus of this outing for the author in summer, 1998, was the sighting of a cow moose and calf near the route above the lake, presumably up high to escape the heat of that season.

The area near the high point of this ridgewalk hosts unusual slivers of rock sticking up like fins, giving the impression of walking on water in a shark-infested sea. Descent is east to the lake via mostly vegetated slopes, then out on the trail.

139 Whaleback Mountain

Map p. 301
Photo p. 9

Distance: 24 km out-and-back with loop (or 25 km loop)

Trail/off-trail: 8—12 hr

Elevation gain: 1120 m (3675 ft)

Maximum elevation: 2630 m (8625 ft)

Maps: Gem Trek 1:50,000 Lake Louise & Yoho, and NTS 1:50,000 Lake Louise 82 N/8, Hector Lake 82 N/9, Blaeberry River 82 N/10, and Golden 82 N/7

Trailhead: Turn north off the Trans-Canada Highway 3.7 km (2.3 mi) east of the Field junction and follow the Yoho Valley Road 13 km (8 mi) to its end. The parking area for the Yoho Valley trail is past the larger areas for Takakkaw Falls, near the end of the one-way loop.

The traverse of Whaleback Mountain in Yoho National Park (distinct from Whaleback Ridge (#10) in southwestern Alberta) is easy and offers amazing views.

Starting at Takakkaw Falls, head up the Yoho Valley trail to Laughing Falls, where turn left up the Little Yoho Valley trail. After a couple of k's, turn right on the Whaleback trail. Climb up the steady switchbacks to the high point on the trail, reached after in two hours from the trailhead.

Now head west over hummocky terrain to the left-hand base of (cont. p. 246)

East over Whaleback Mountain to (l to r) Mt. Balfour, Mt. Daly, and Mt. Niles.

(Cont. from p. 245) slabs at the east end of Whaleback Mountain. Scramble up to easier ground running along the ridge, now above the slabs. A long, gentle ramble lasts for over 2 km, first heading west, then veering northwest above a textbook anticline. There is a significant drop to the north, which makes this outing feel more "out there" than it is.

The views on this section are exceptional, a highlight being the view northwest to pointed Mont des Poilus and the Glacier des Poilus below it. To the west is McArthur Peak, also sporting an expanse of ice on its eastern aspect. The dramatic pair of The President and The Vice President lie to the south, while to the north are Yoho Peak and Mt. Collie. To the northeast are Mt. Gordon and Mt. Rhondda above the Wapta Icefield. Not to be overlooked are Mt. Balfour, Mt. Daly, and Mt. Niles to the east, while to the southeast is a whole slew of trademark peaks. This is a superb panorama for such little effort.

Smaller in scale, but no less impressive, are the wildflowers to be found in the alpine setting. Among them are moss campion, silky scorpionweed, mountain fireweed, sawwort, golden fleabane, alpine hawksbeard, and purple saxifrage.

The ridge narrows shortly before Isolated Col between Whaleback Mountain and Isolated Peak. Pinnacles in the col make for intriguing photographic subjects. Descent south from the col is on a surprisingly well defined path that passes beneath a waterfall cascading from the now-unseen glacier above and drops into a vegetated basin [bear alert]. A steeper descent through forest leads right to the Stanley Mitchell Hut of the Alpine Club of Canada.

Return can be made over the approach by turning left here. Another option if feel energetic enough is to take the Iceline Trail back. Go straight south from the hut, turn left to cross the footbridge, then go right 200 m or so to pick up the scenic Iceline Trail. Keep in mind that it is a rocky, undulating trail that adds 1 km distance and considerable elevation gain and loss compared to the direct return. But it rewards with beauty, including an overview of the traverse just done and excellent views of thundering Takakkaw Falls.

Whaleback Mountain's name is a rather generic description of its shape; the origin of the many other placenames in the area can be discovered in **Central Rockies Placenames** (Mike Potter, Luminous Compositions, 1997).

South from Ridge North of Paget Peak, including Mt. Victoria, Mt. Huber, and Mt. Biddle on left, and Cathedral Mountain on right.

140 Ridge North of Paget Peak

Map p. 301

Distance: 12 km out-and-back

Trail/off-trail: 4—8 hr

Elevation gain: 1085 m (3560 ft)

Maximum elevation: 2700 m (8855 ft)

Maps: Gem Trek 1:50,000 Lake Louise & Yoho and NTS 1:50 000 Lake Louise 82 N/8

Trailhead: The Wapta Lake picnic area on the north side of the Trans-Canada Highway, 5.5 km (3.4 mi) west of the Alberta/B.C. boundary and 11 km (6.8 mi) east of the Field junction.

This ridgewalk continues beyond a well-known hike and scramble on an extension north to the continental divide, enabling unusual views.

Take the established trail to the Paget fire lookout, which for the time being serves as a shelter. Scramble up north on rocky slopes to the top of Paget Peak; although it is named, this minor summit does not represent the high point of the day.

Push on north, descending slightly and passing over an intervening knoll before commencing the steeper ascent to the highest elevation of this outing [gr 444023]. This point on the continental divide (and the B.C./Alberta boundary) grants a surprising view of the Bath Glacier on its high shelf. (The extent of glaciation is not as great as indicated on the 1980 edition of the government topo, so there is no ice to cross on this journey.)

Of course, there are many other features to take in, among them the curved summit of Mt. Niles to the northwest. Sherbrooke Lake lies below to the west, with the whole length of narrow Mt. Ogden above. Back to the south lie Narao Peak, Cathedral Mountain, and Mt. Victoria with white waves of snow and ice tumbling down its north face. Mt. Hector is prominent to the east, while peaks as far southeast as Mt. Cory near Banff can be identified.

Wildflowers that can be sighted on this ridgewalk include glacier lily, white mountain avens, valerian, fringed grass-of-Parnassus, western spring beauty, sawwort, alpine hawksbeard, moss campion, and purple saxifrage.

Paget Peak is named after the Rev. E.C. Paget (1857-1927), a Calgarian who made its first ascent in 1904 with 14-year-old Edward Wheeler, son of A.O. Wheeler, first president of the Alpine Club of Canada.

Most will return via the approach, but a circuit can be made by descending southwest from the high point. (Keep in mind that this is grizzly bear habitat.) Strike the established trail along the east shore of Sherbrooke Lake near the lake's north end, and take the trail out to the start.

141 Mt. Schäffer Southwest Ridge (Lower Section)

Map p. 301

Distance: 7 km out-and-back with loop

Trail/off-trail: up to 4 hr

Elevation gain: 450 m (1475 ft)

Maximum elevation: 2485 m (8150 ft)

Maps: Gem Trek 1:50,000 Lake Louise & Yoho and NTS 1:50,000 Lake Louise 82 N/8

Trailhead: Le Relais day-use shelter at Lake O'Hara, reached via shuttle bus (call (250) 343-6433) or by hiking 11.2 km up the road.

This is a short ridgewalk in the sublime Lake O'Hara region, where the number of visitors at one time is limited in order to retain its wild character.

From Lake O'Hara, take the Big Larches trail to Schäffer Lake. Then head for the higher (eastern) of the two trails leading to Lake McArthur—either via McArthur Pass or the more direct route from Schäffer Lake. From the cairn at the highest point of this trail, strike north up the moderately-angled slope, possibly keeping to the left below the top of the knoll but above a dropoff on the left.

Whatever approach taken, all choices lead to a rounded knoll with excellent views of almost the entire expanse of McArthur Lake. Dramatic glaciated Mt. Biddle rises at its south end, and Park Mountain on the west side of the lake.

Descent is down to the left from past the knoll, in a scree gully that sports a beaten path. Ascent to the summit of Mt. Schäffer is in the realm of quasi-technical scrambling, and unroped descent down its north ridge is not for the faint of heart.

Mountain goats are hardy denizens of these rugged environs: it's always a bonus to sight those solid creatures of the alpine. Pikas, whose toughness belies their cuteness, also frequent this habitat. See pages 215, 220, and 162 for background on names.

McArthur Lake from Mt. Schäffer Southwest Ridge.

The Maps

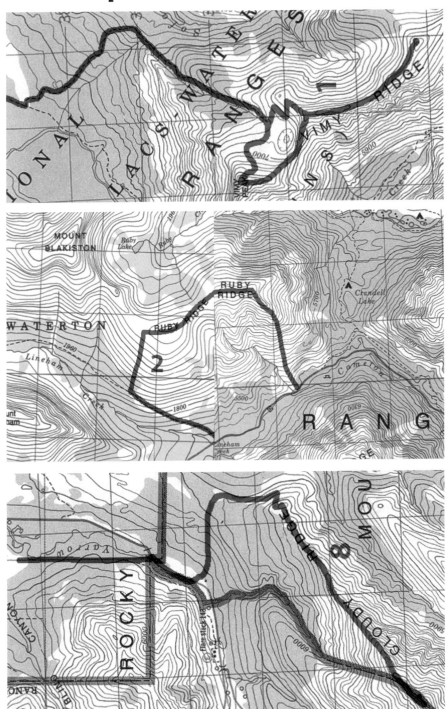

See note re. grid references on p. 14.

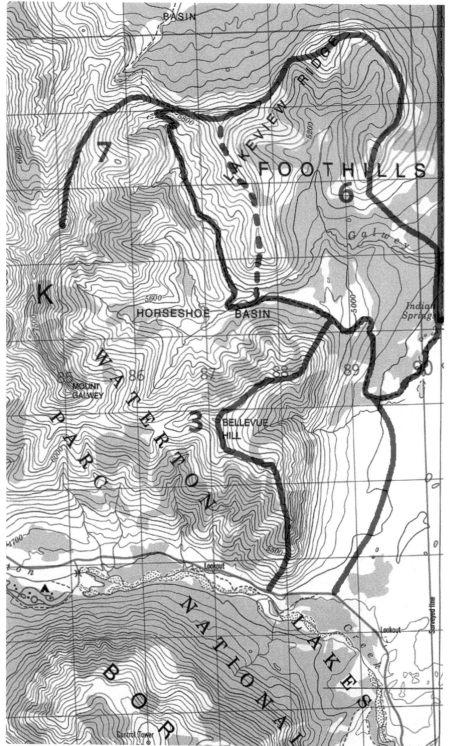

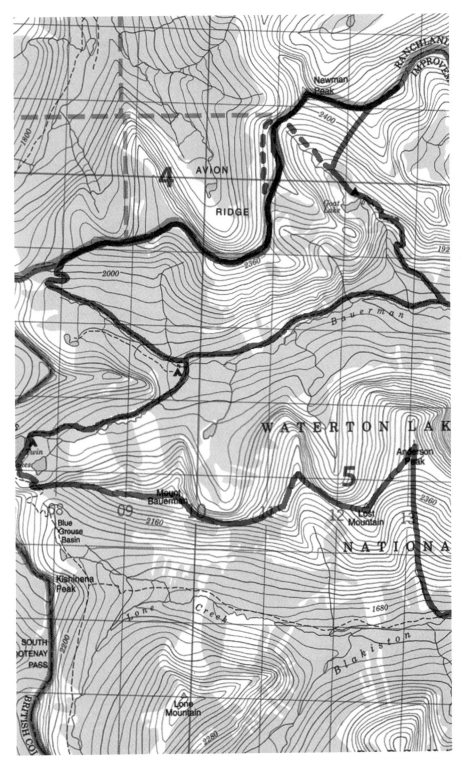

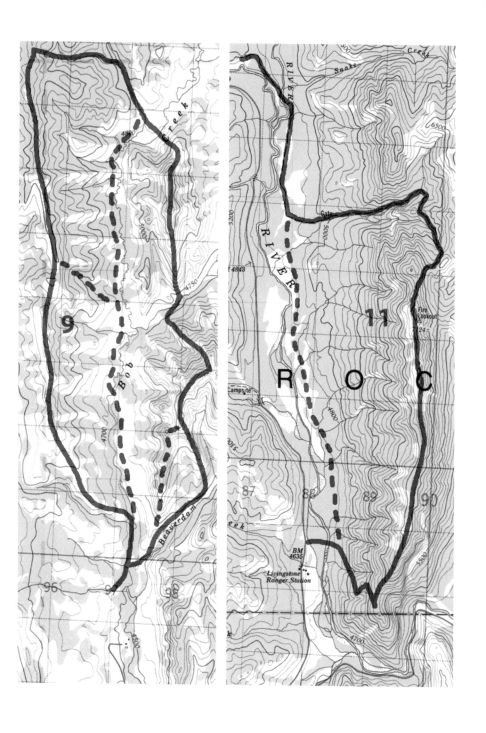

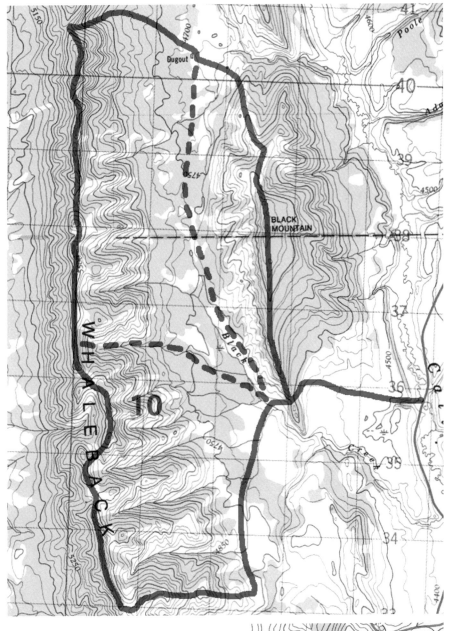

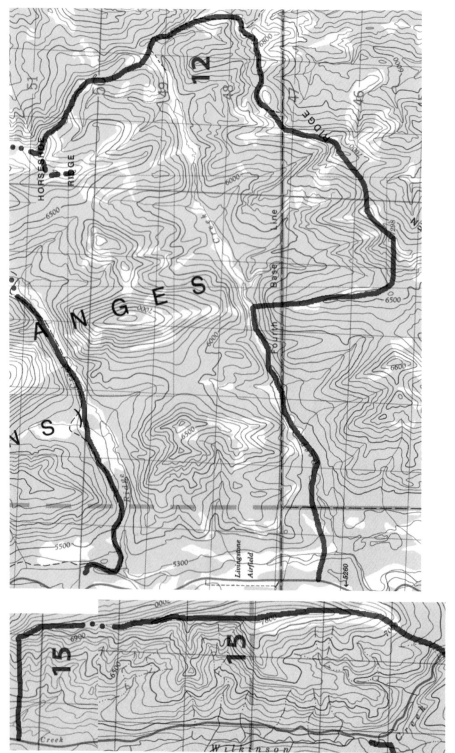

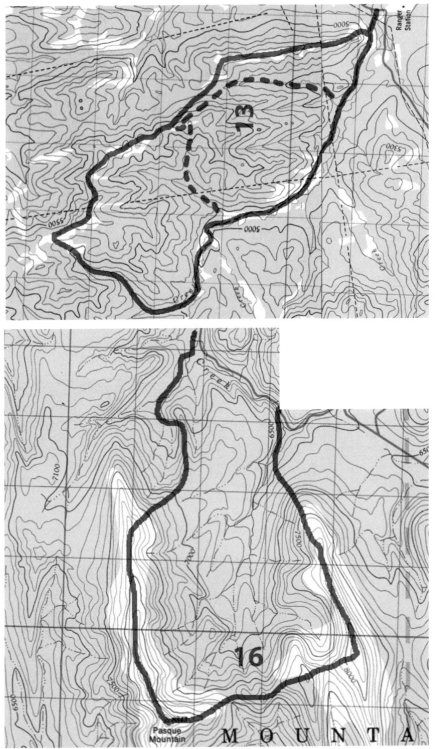

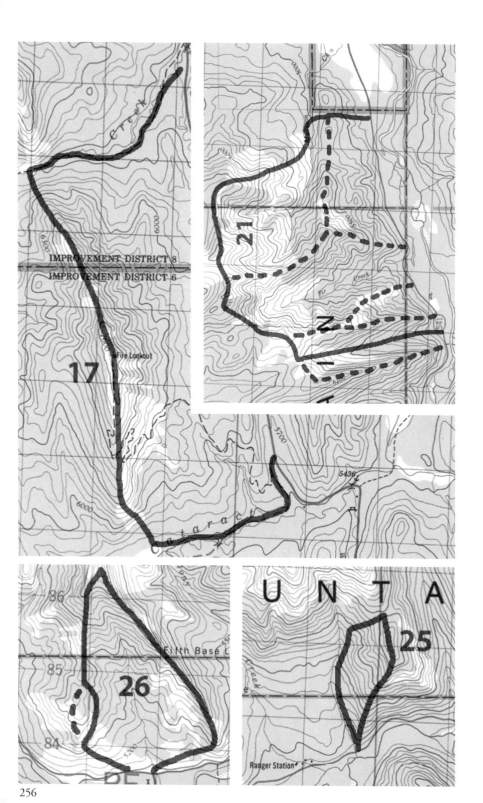

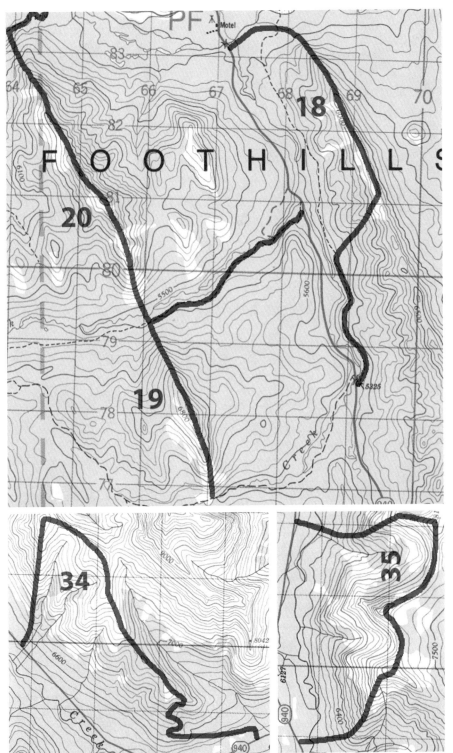

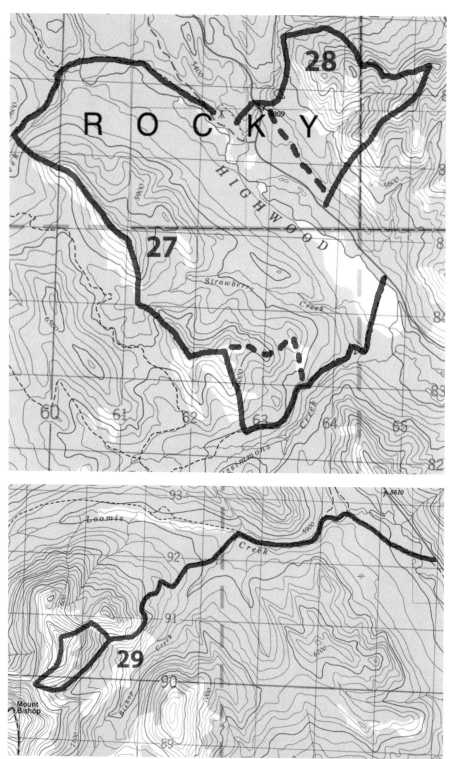

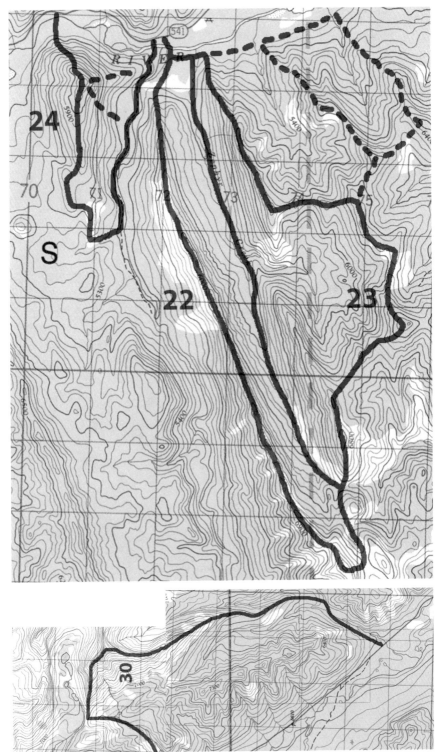

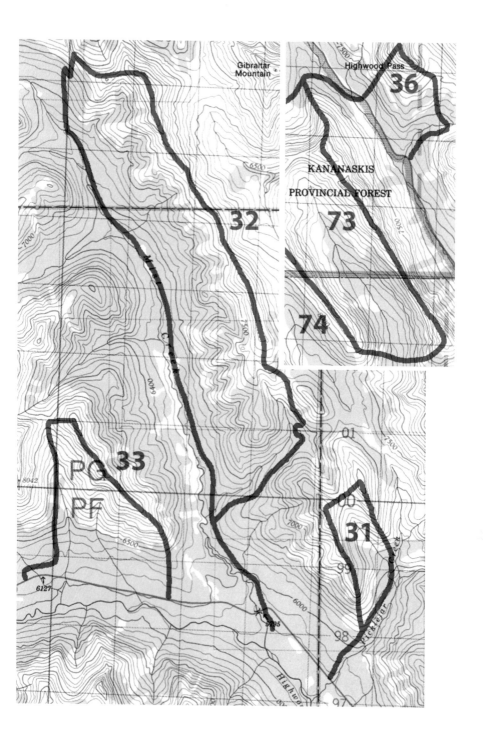

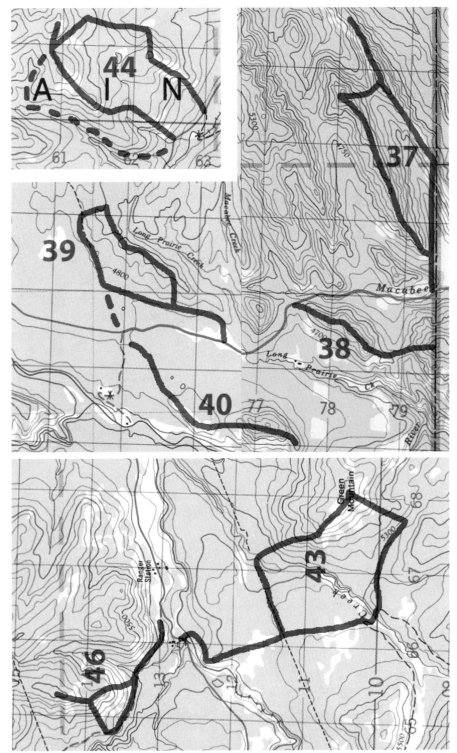

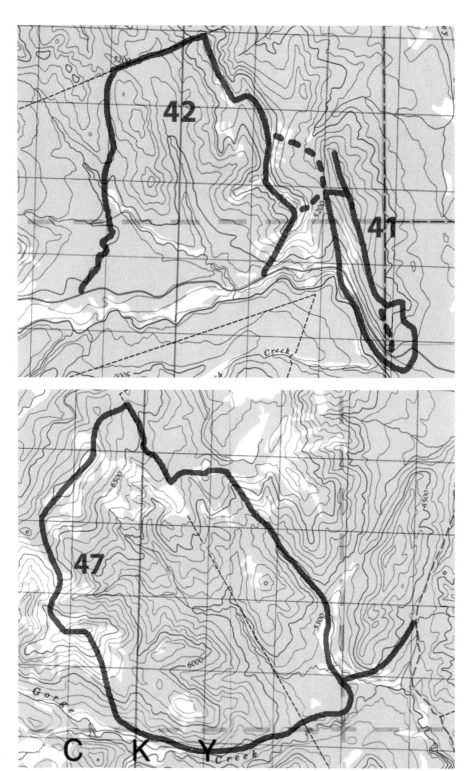

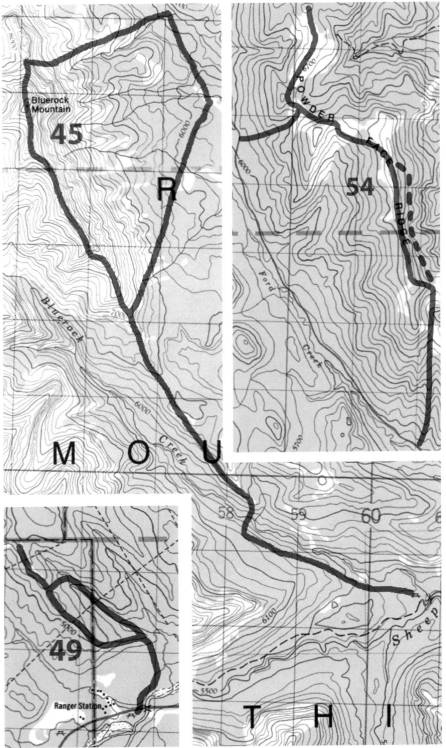

Bluerock
Mountain

45

R

Bluerock

Creek

M O U

POWDER

EAGE

RIDGE

54

Ford

Creek

58 59 60

49

Ranger Station

6100

Sheep

T H I

263

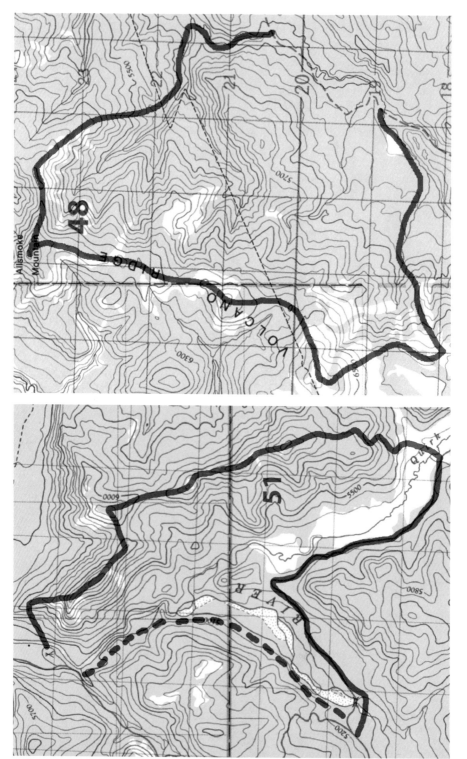

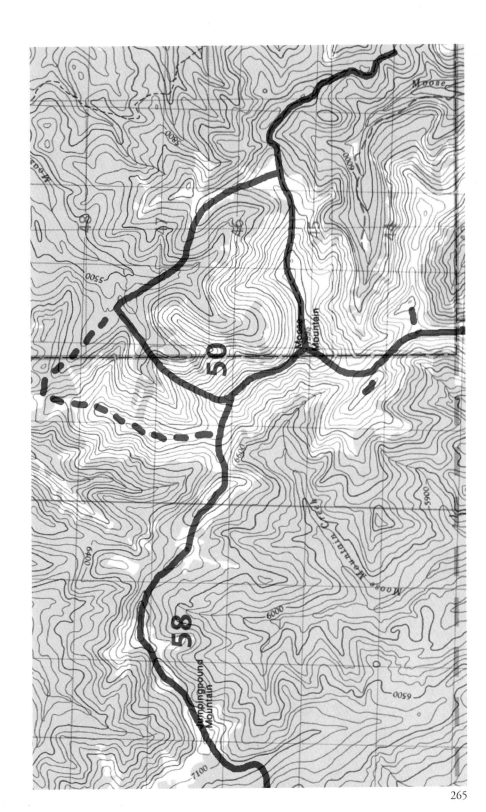

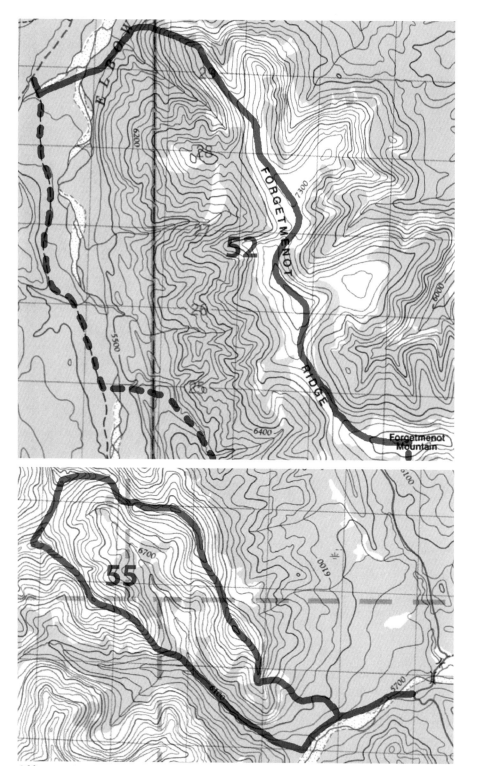

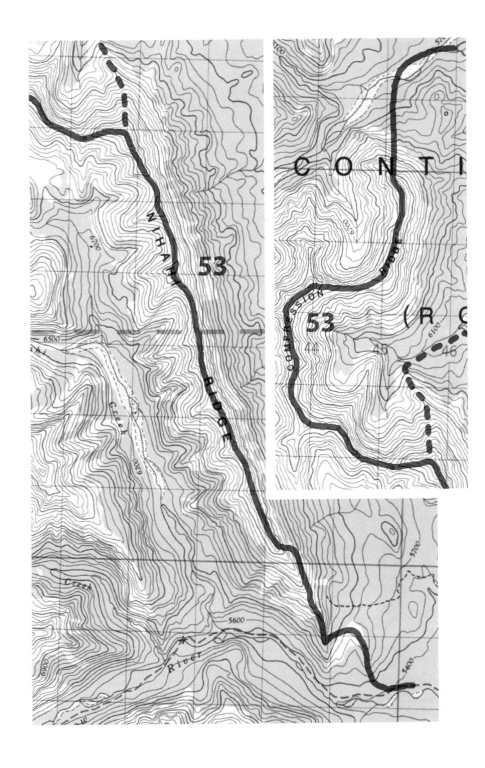

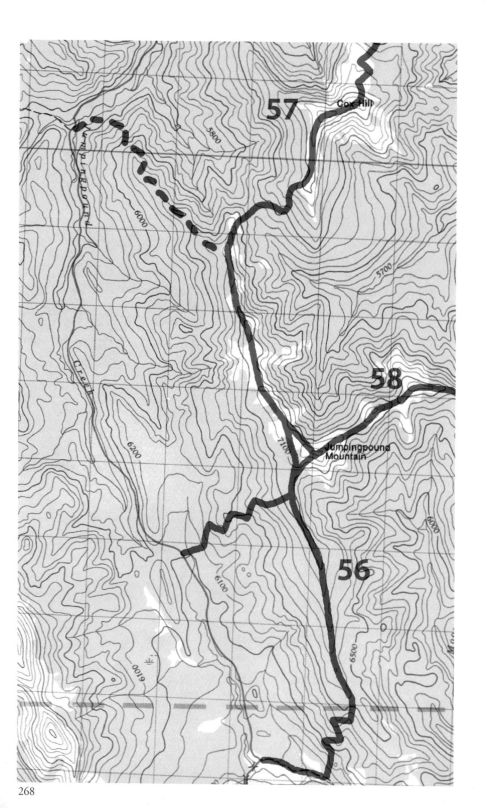

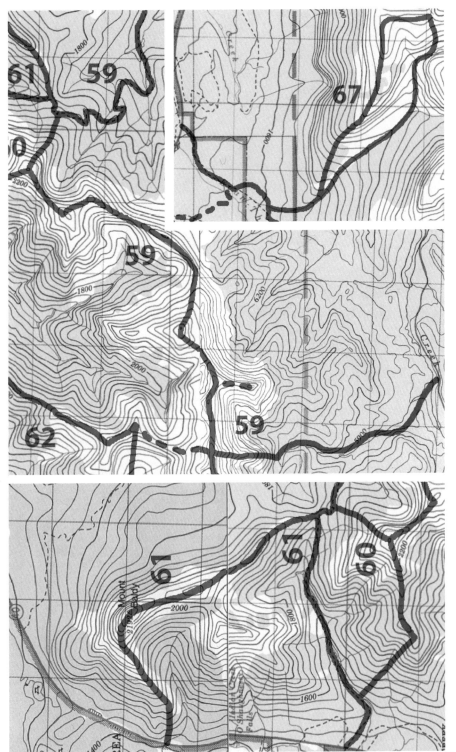

269

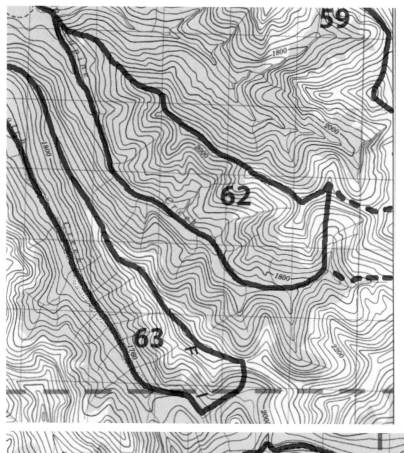

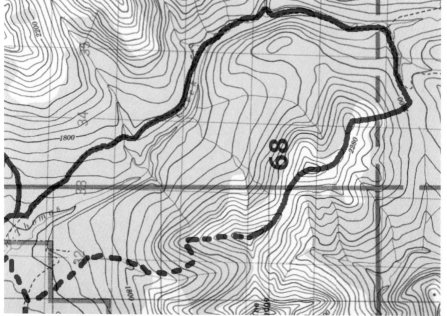

270

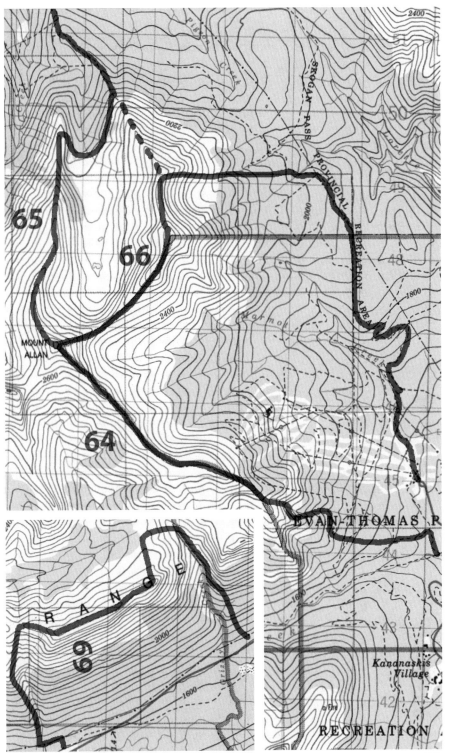

271

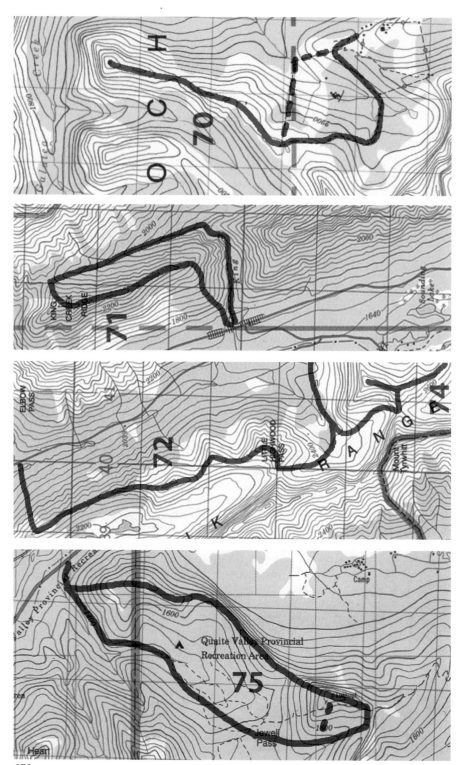

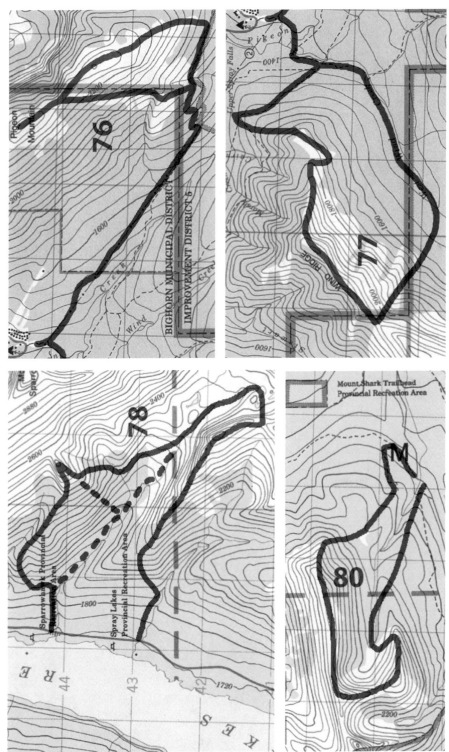

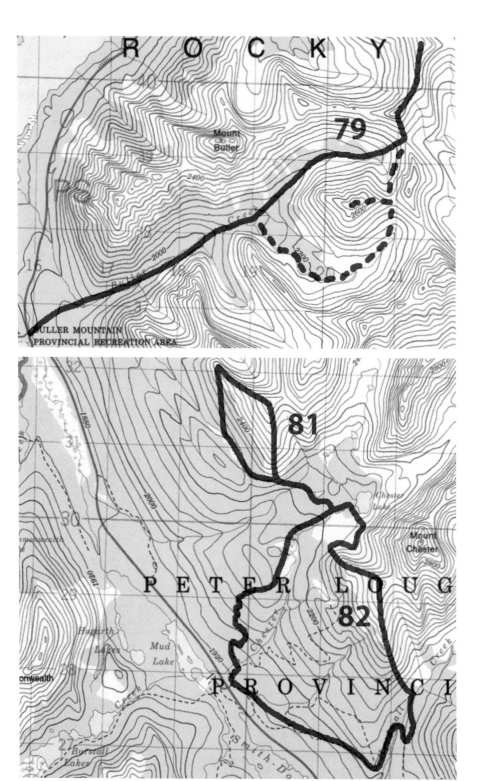

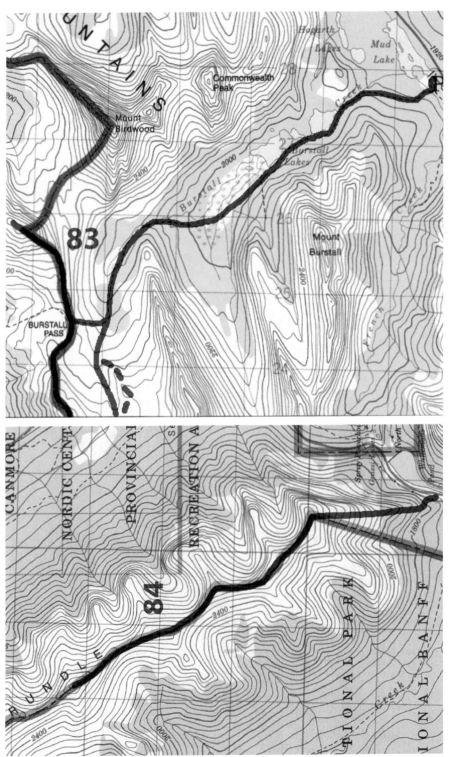

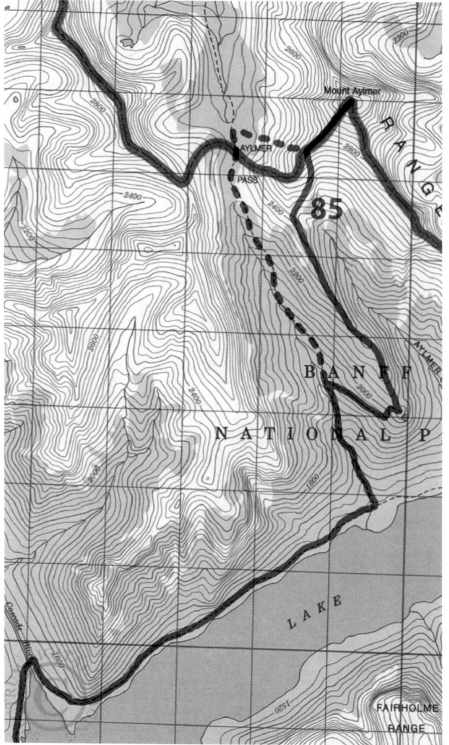

Mount Aylmer

AYLMER

PASS

85

RANGE

AYLMER

BANFF

NATIONAL P

LAKE

Cascade River

FAIRHOLME

RANGE

276

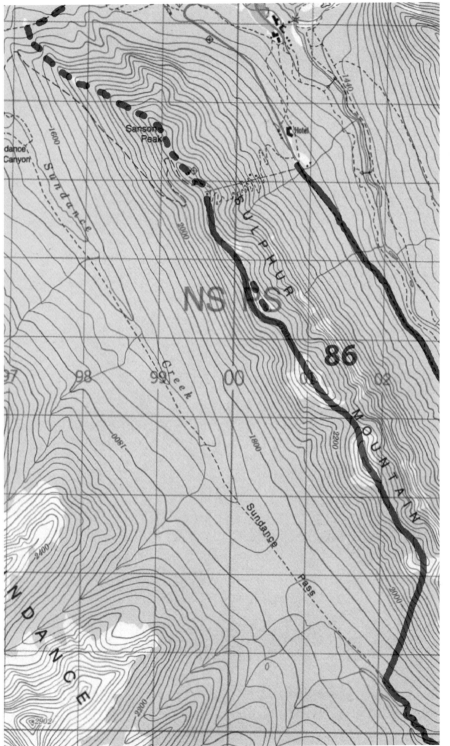

Sundance Canyon

dance
Canyon

Sundance

Sansone
Peak

Hotel

SULPHUR

NS RS

86

Creek

MOUNTAIN

Sundance

Pass

97   98   99   00   01   02

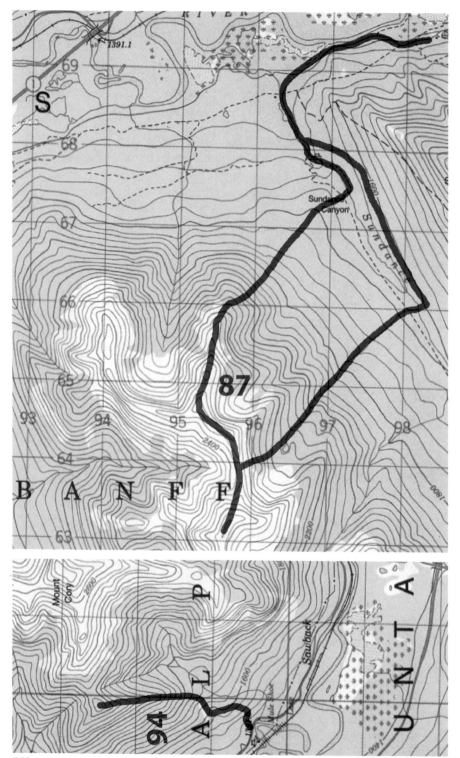

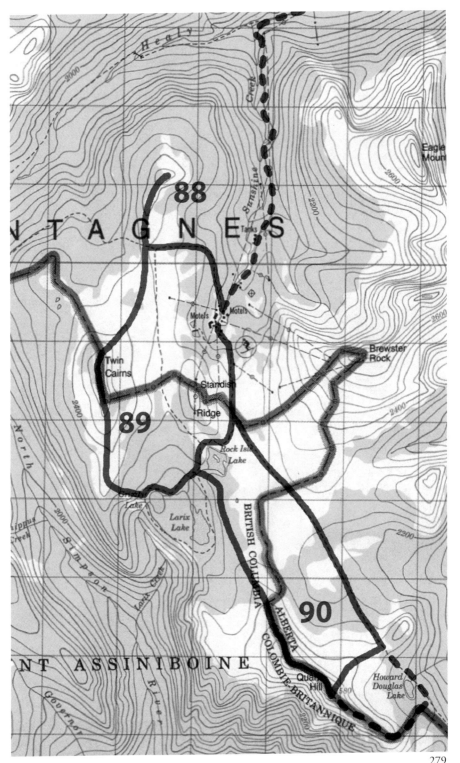

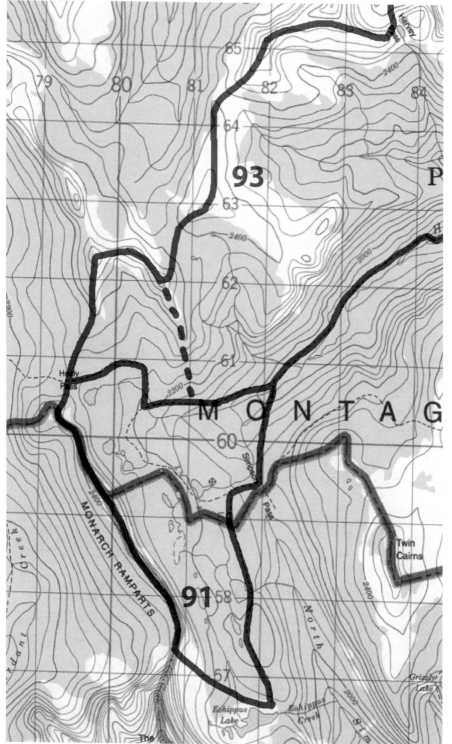

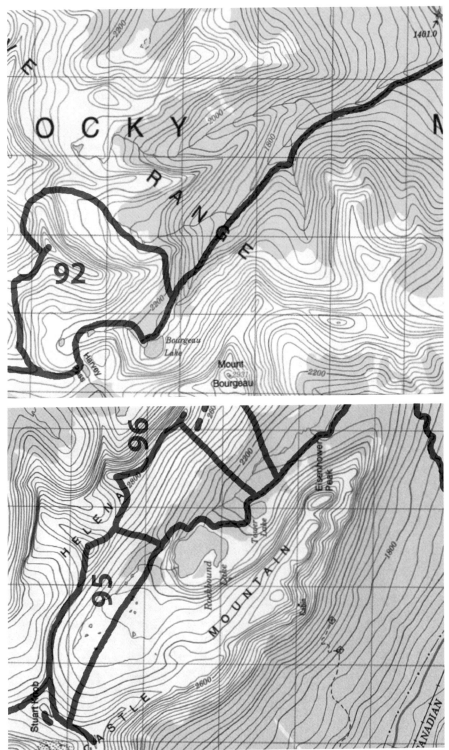

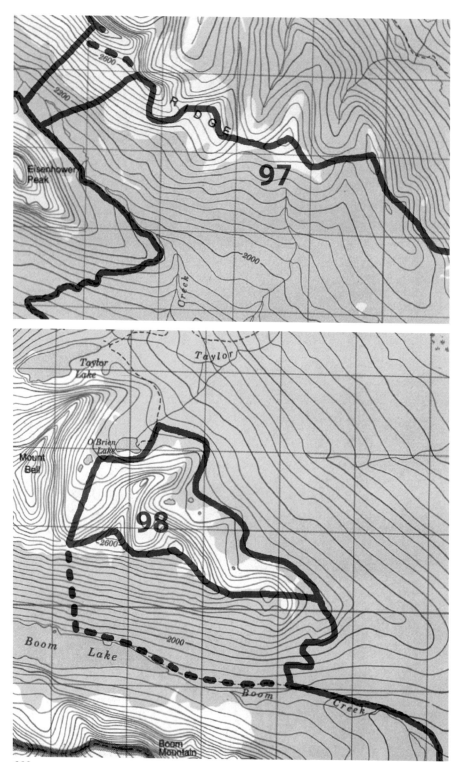

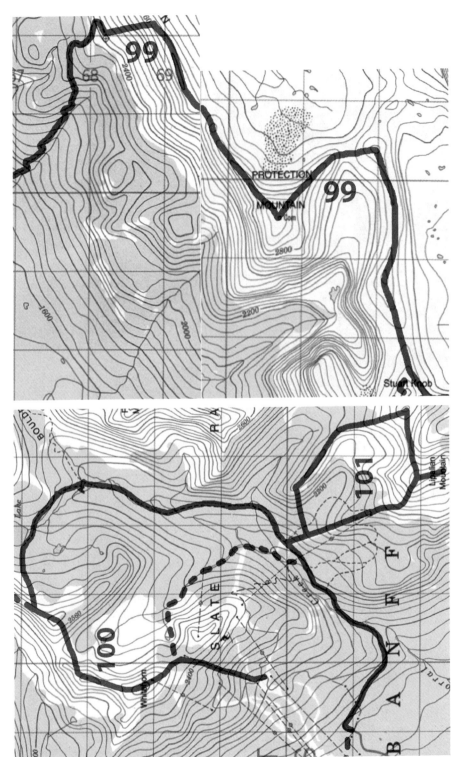

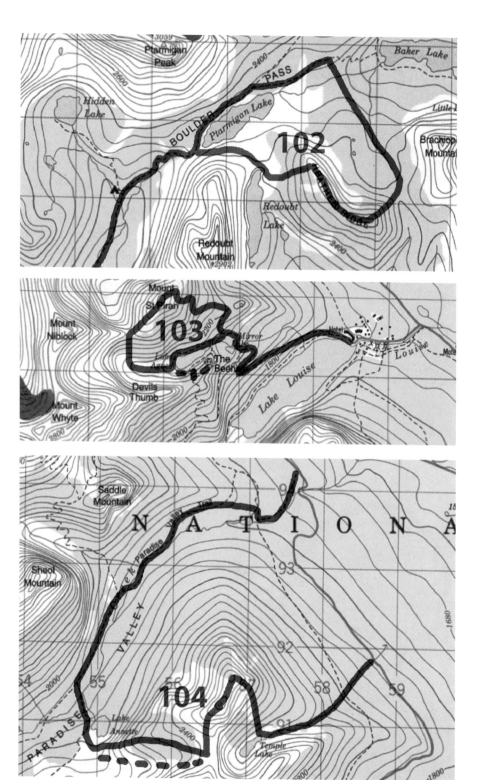

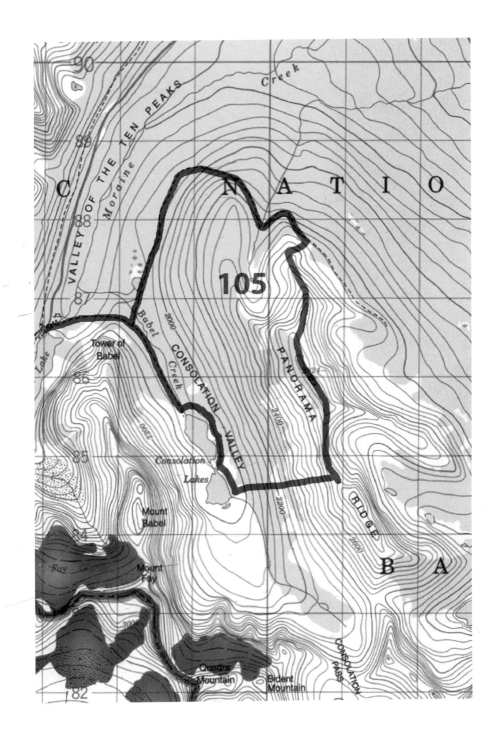

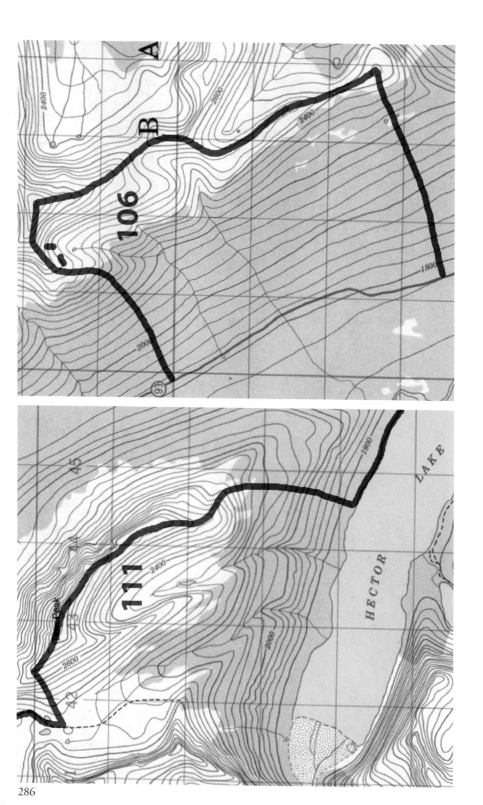

286

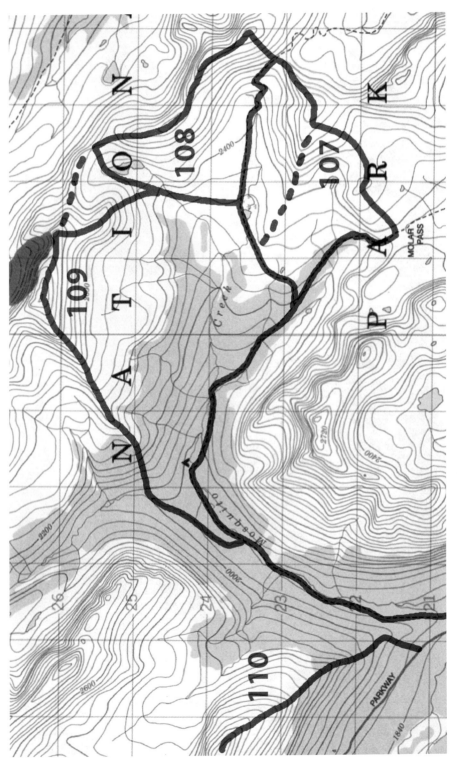

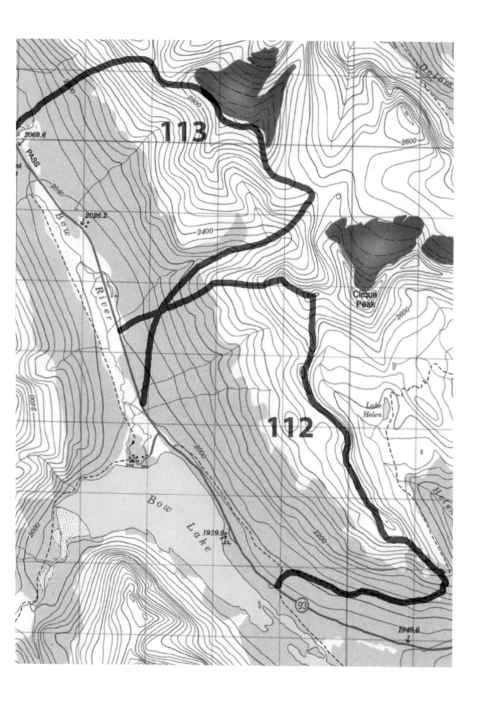

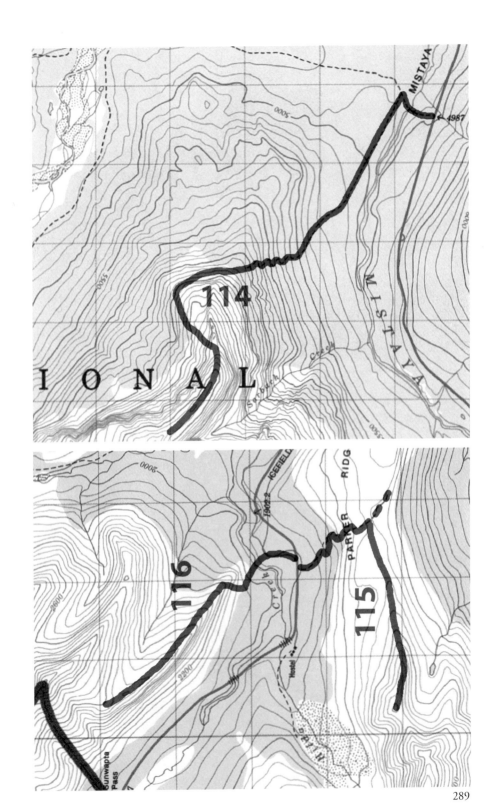

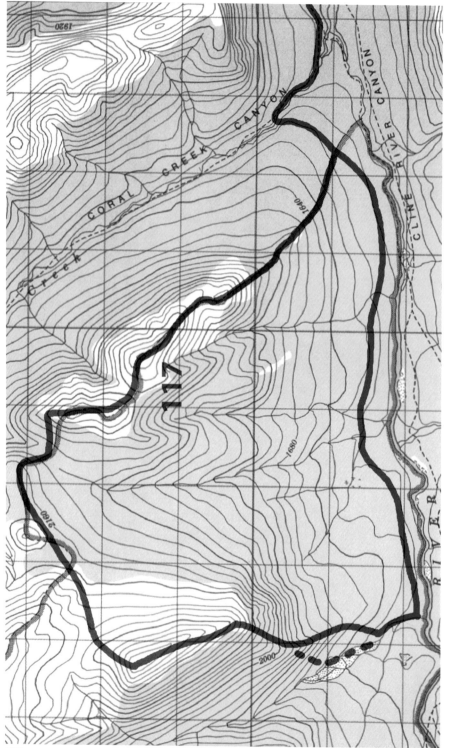

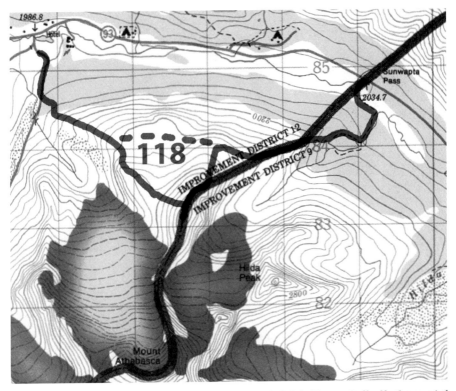

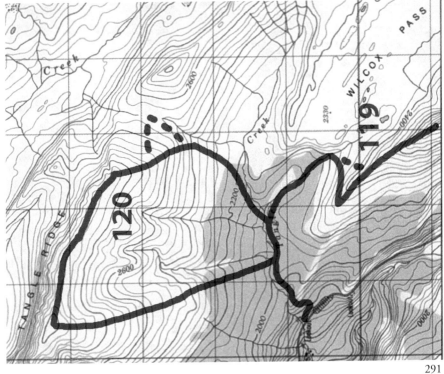

291

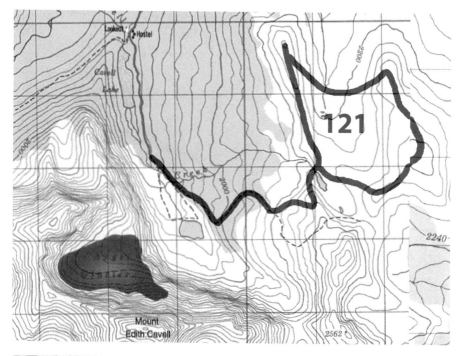

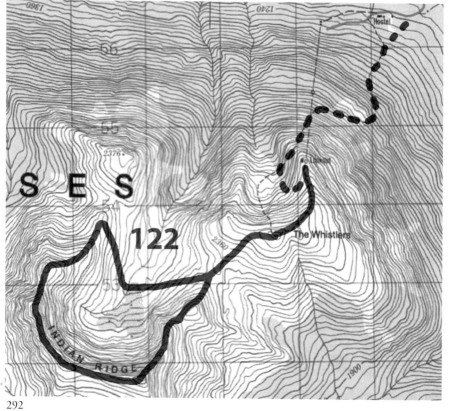

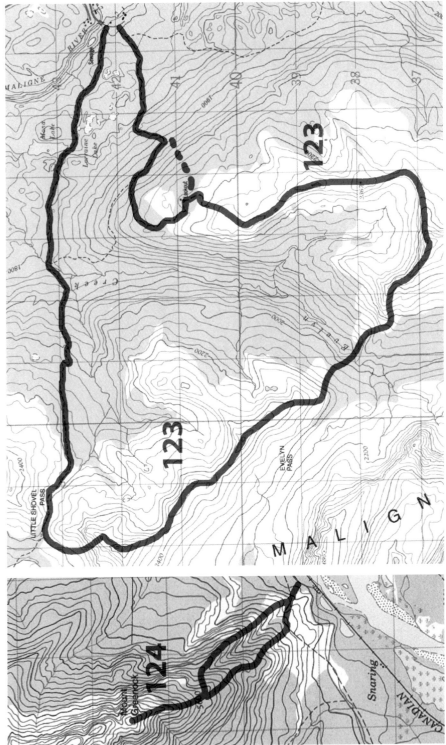

293

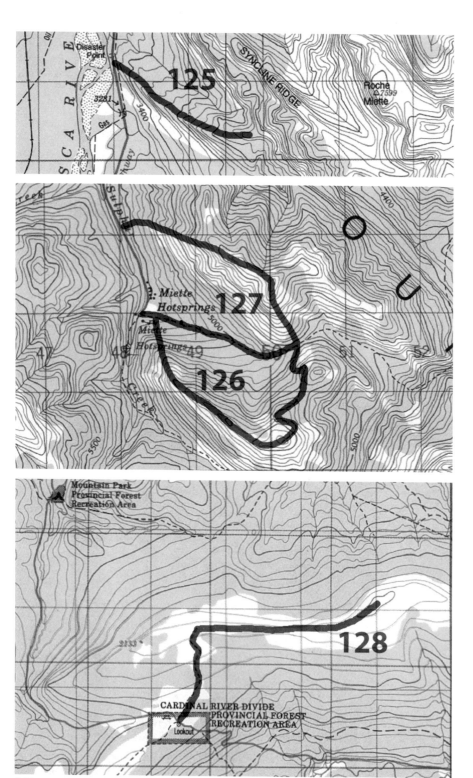

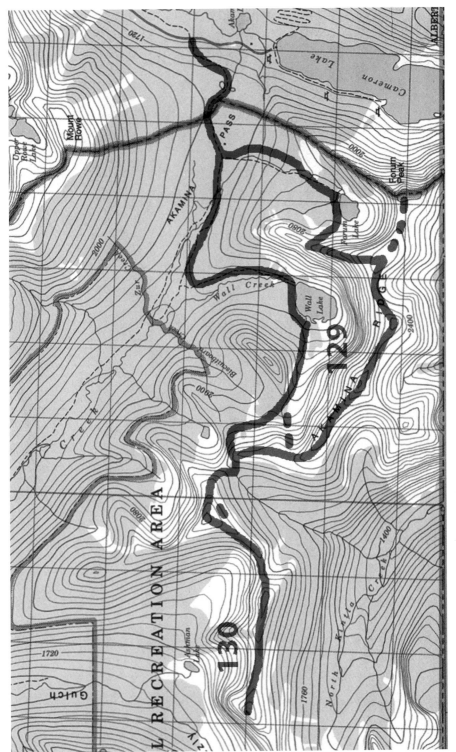

295

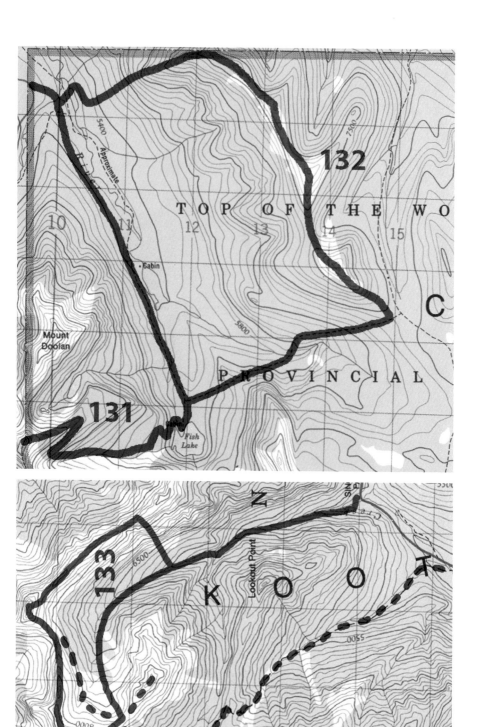

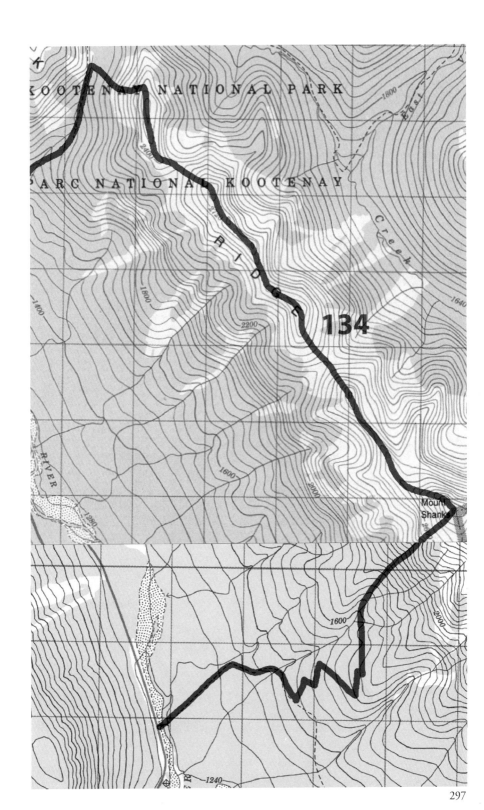

KOOTENAY NATIONAL PARK

PARC NATIONAL KOOTENAY

R I D G E

Creek

134

Mount
Shanks

RIVER

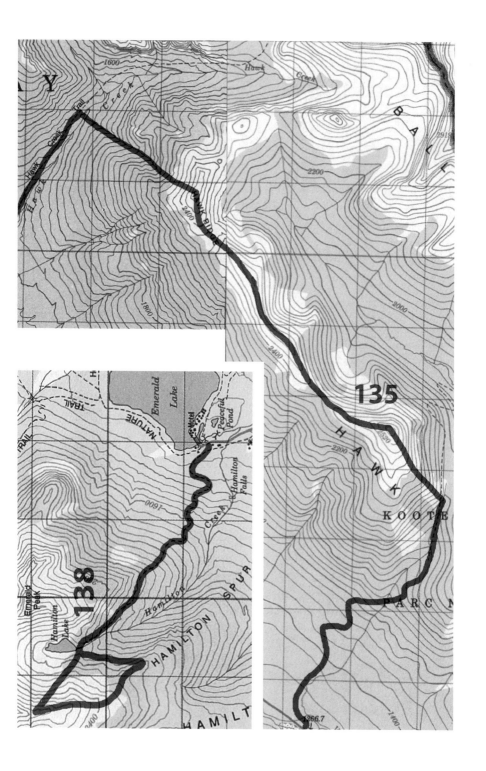

298

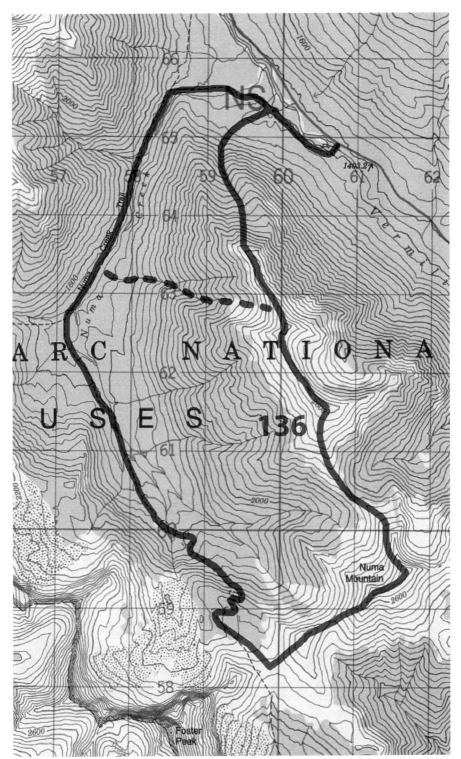

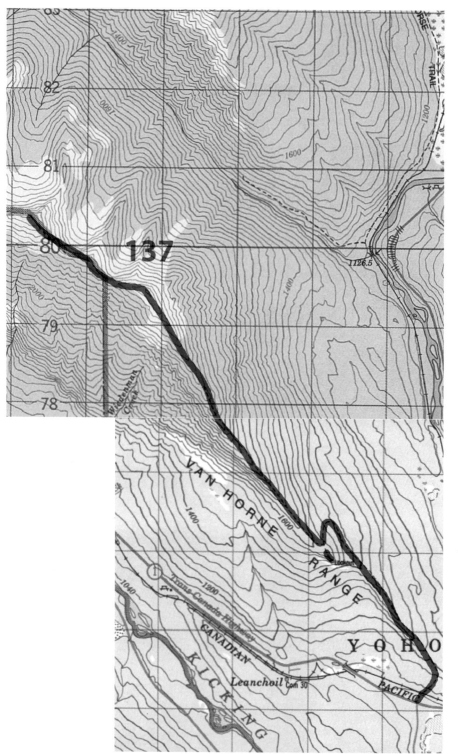

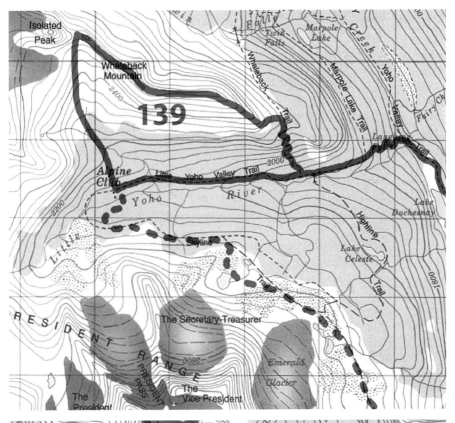

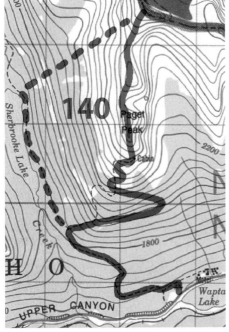

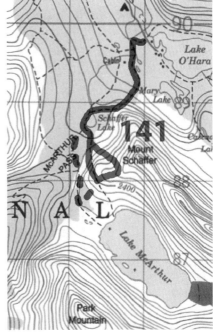

Further Reading

Blaxley, Bob, **The Whaleback: A Walking Guide**, Rocky Mountain Books, Calgary, Alberta, 1997.

Daffern, Gillean, **Kananaskis Country Trail Guide, Third Edition, Volumes 1 and 2**, Rocky Mountain Books, Calgary, Alberta, 1996 and 1997.

Gadd, Ben, **Handbook of the Canadian Rockies, Second Edition**, Corax Press, Jasper, Alberta, 1995.

Karamitsanis, Aphrodite, **Place Names of Alberta, Volume 1: Mountains, Mountain Parks and Foothills**, University of Calgary Press, Calgary, Alberta, 1991.

Marriott, John, **Central Rockies Mammals**, Luminous Compositions, Turner Valley, Alberta, 1997.

Patterson, R.M., **The Buffalo Head, Reprint of 1961 First Edition**, Horsdal & Schubart, Victoria, British Columbia, 1994.

Potter, Mike, **Backcountry Banff, Reprint with Revisions of 1992 First Edition**, Luminous Compositions, Turner Valley, Alberta, 1997. New edition scheduled 2001

Potter, Mike, **Central Rockies Placenames**, Luminous Compositions, Turner Valley, Alberta, 1997.

Potter, Mike, **Central Rockies Wildflowers**, Luminous Compositions, Turner Valley, Alberta, 1996.

Potter, Mike, **Fire Lookout Hikes in the Canadian Rockies**, Luminous Compositions, Turner Valley, Alberta, 1998.

Potter, Mike, **Hiking Lake Louise, Third Edition**, Luminous Compositions, Turner Valley, Alberta, 1999.

The Author

Mike Potter on Mt. Rundle Southeast Ridge (Ridgewalk 84).

INDEX

Sections

Alphabetical